"'If there is a God, and if God is good, then how can God allow suffering and injustice?' Perhaps no other question so urgently occupies young people struggling with religious commitment. But it cannot be avoided if one is to lay claim to honest and mature Christian faith. In her superb book *If God Is for Us*, Gloria Schaab probes various options and offers a way forward that takes both Christian belief and the reality of suffering seriously. She does not seek to offer final 'answers,' which would ultimately prove inadequate, but rather to offer approaches to the question that will yield deeper insights."

—Dave Gentry-Akin
Saint Mary's College of California

"In *If God Is for Us*, Gloria Schaab leads readers through a panoply of contexts, classical and contemporary, out of which theologians have engaged the existential questions that suffering evokes. Schaab's careful definition of terms, attention to social analysis, and deft representation of theologians from antiquity to the present combine with her own theological contribution to make this an invaluable resource. Comprehensive and compact, *If God Is For Us* will be treasured in theology courses concerned with how to 'speak rightly of God' in the midst of suffering."

—Kathleen McManus, OP
University of Portland

"Gloria Schaab's well-researched and insightful book, *If God Is for Us: Christian Perspectives on God and Suffering*, analyzes a wide range of experiences of suffering in the world, interspersing personal testimonies from people who have struggled to find meaning in those experiences. She expounds a rich diversity of classical and contextual theological approaches to the mystery of suffering and leads her readers through an examination of these approaches in a way that enables them to grasp their meaning and relevance. Schaab's book is a valuable resource on the ever-present reality of suffering in the world."

—Robin Ryan
Catholic Theological Union

Author Acknowledgments

It has long been a desire of mine to write this book on God and suffering. My desire stemmed not only from the experience of wrestling with the question of God and suffering in my own life but also from the challenge this question poses for so many people I have encountered in my life and ministry. I eagerly look forward to its publication and gratefully acknowledge the following people who have helped me bring it to completion:

Margie Thompson, SSJ. As always, her questions, comments, and challenges moved me forward, even as her encouragement and good humor kept me balanced.

Jerry Ruff, Maura Hagarty, Penny Koehler, and all at Anselm Academic, whose support, vision, and respect for the Catholic intellectual tradition gave this book the opportunity to reach fulfillment. Their persistence in researching permissions for the literary materials used in this book enabled it to maintain the depth and quality I desired. I am especially grateful to Kathleen Walsh, my editor, whose literary skills, theological sensibilities, and thought-provoking questions were vital to the outcome.

Karen Callaghan, Dean of the College of Arts and Sciences; Mark Wedig, OP, Department Chair; and my colleagues in theology and philosophy at Barry University, who supported and preserved my sabbatical time and space. I am especially grateful to James Nickoloff, Dave Fletcher, and Elsie Miranda who provided essential materials at critical points in the process.

The undergraduate and graduate students at Barry University, whose willingness to delve into the mystery of God and suffering enriched my thinking and bolstered my enthusiasm. I especially thank the students in my Spring 2014 course, THE 308: God and Suffering—often affectionately referred to as "Suffering with Sister Gloria"—for their input and feedback on new ideas and chapter drafts.

Finally, my religious congregation of the Sisters of Saint Joseph of Philadelphia, especially Anne Myers, our President, and our Councilors—Mary Dacey, Regina Bell, Carol Zinn, Constance Gilder, Eileen Marnien, Maureen Erdlen, and Theresa Shaw. Their unwavering support enables me to be faithful to my calling as theologian.

Ad majorem Dei gloriam!

Publisher Acknowledgments

Thank you to the following individuals who reviewed this work in progress:

Scott Geis, *Christian Brothers University, Memphis, Tennessee*

Gregory Jones, *Valparaiso University, Valparaiso, Indiana*

William Reiser, *College of the Holy Cross, Worcester, Massachusetts*

If God Is for Us

Christian Perspectives on God and Suffering

Gloria L. Schaab

ANSELM
ACADEMIC

Created by the publishing team of Anselm Academic.

The scriptural quotations contained herein unless otherwise indicated are from the New Revised Standard Version of the Bible, Catholic Edition. Copyright © 1993 and 1989 by the Division of Christian Education of the National Council of the Churches of Christ in the United States of America. All rights reserved.

Cover image: ©Jacob Clausnitzer / shutterstock.com

Printed in the United States of America

7072

ISBN 978-1-59982-563-2

To
Margie Thompson, SSJ

dearest friend, confidante, and Sister

■

artist, teacher, spiritual director

■

whose own experience of God in suffering
has brought insight and consolation to many others

Contents

Introduction

A gunman walks into an elementary school on a crisp December morning; within eleven minutes, he shoots and kills twenty first-graders and six adults. A "superstorm" named Sandy marches its way from Kingston, Jamaica, up the eastern coast of the United States, leaving $68 billion of destruction in its wake. A megalomaniac in Germany orchestrates the persecution and murder of more than six million Jews and other persons deemed "racially inferior" while most of the world's peoples and leaders turn a blind eye. An undersea megathrust earthquake with a magnitude of more than 9.1 sets off tsunamis causing more than 230,000 deaths in fourteen countries and shaking most of the planet. An outbreak of the Ebola virus in West Africa infects more than 17,000 people and results in more than 6,400 deaths, prompting the World Health Organization to call it the most "severe public health emergency of modern times."[1]

These represent but a few of the instances of suffering and death that garnered national and international attention in the last hundred years. These examples barely scratch the surface of the history of human tragedy. Moreover, these large-scale events mirror the billions of individual instances of suffering and death that occur on a daily basis. In addition to the personal and social cost of such experiences, the pervasiveness of pain, suffering, and death provokes profound existential questions, especially for those who profess belief in God. How does one speak rightly about God in the midst of such suffering and death? Moreover, *if* God is for us and *if* God is all-powerful, all-knowing, and all-loving—as most believers deem God to be—how can God cause or allow such egregious misery?

The answer to such questions is profound mystery—the mystery of God, the mystery of suffering, and the mystery of the relationship between the two. Although each of these is essentially mystery, none fully eludes understanding. Indeed, those willing to enter into the depths of God and human experience through study and prayer find inexhaustible insights into these mysteries. This book offers a means by which to venture into those depths by exploring the depth, breadth, and diversity of ways in which theologians have responded to the question of God and suffering throughout the centuries. No one theology has all

---

1. World Health Organization, "Experimental Therapies: Growing Interest in the Use of Whole Blood or Plasma from Recovered Ebola Patients (Convalescent Therapies)," World Health Organization, Media Centre, September 26, 2014, *http://www.who.int/mediacentre/news /ebola/26-september-2014/en/*.

the answers; each bears possibilities and problems, has strengths and limitations, for those who seek to speak rightly about God in the midst of suffering.

As this text shows, Christian theologians have tried to plumb the mystery of God and suffering using two broad theological approaches: the classical and the contextual. Theologians using the first approach respond to the question of God and suffering through the lens of classical theism. Conceived within the worldview of Platonic and Aristotelian philosophy, the God of classical theism is all-powerful, all-knowing, and all-loving, as well as unchangeable and unaffected by the experiences and events of history.[2] Holding such attributes of God inviolable, classical theologians interpret the relation between God and suffering in ways consistent with those divine attributes.

In recent years, however, many Christian theologians have shifted from this classical approach to use a contextual approach to the question of God and suffering.[3] They focus on God within the context of specific historical events or contexts that have caused or perpetrated suffering. Holding the suffering in history paramount, contextual theologians interpret the relation between God and suffering in ways that respond to the miseries associated with a particular historical context.

Recognizing the validity of each approach, this book engages both classical and contextual Christian interpretations of the relationship between God and suffering. Part I engages classical interpretations of this mystery, while Part II investigates contextual interpretations. In so doing, the text seeks to preserve the integrity of particular theological interpretations by presenting each in its own context, in its own voice, and on its own merits without critique. Nonetheless, each chapter poses questions for reflection and discussion through which to discern and analyze the possibilities and problems each theology holds. To facilitate this analysis, each chapter concludes with a "Case in Point," drawn from literary sources or from the life experiences of notable individuals, in order to "flesh out" the concepts and consequences of the theologies of suffering examined in that chapter. In addition, each chapter includes suggestions for further reading as well as audio and video resources to promote deeper engagement.

The first chapter begins the journey into the mystery of God and suffering by clarifying the terms of the investigation and outlining the key questions to be explored in later chapters. It distinguishes the phenomenon of suffering from that of evil and explores the various sources of each. The chapter then examines

---

2. In classical terms, God is omnipotent, omniscient, and omnibenevolent, as well as immutable and impassible.

3. It is important to note that even "classical" theologies are in fact "contextual." They arose at a particular moment of history and derive from a specific worldview. Nonetheless, they envision their outcomes as universal in scope, rather than as identifiable with a distinct historical event or period. Chapters 6–10 exemplify and expand on this distinction.

the traditional defense of the God of classical theism, a defense which is called theodicy, and surveys the challenges to this defense that atheism proposes.

Because questions about God and suffering often begin with presumptions about the nature of God, chapter 2 investigates the language used to describe God. It begins with a review of Thomas Aquinas's description of how names and attributes are applied to God. Aquinas's descriptions are important to note when discussing the mystery of God and suffering. They remind the reader that human words can never encompass the totality of God. This understanding provides an important precaution for all the language used about God in this text, including some of the most time-honored classical attributes that Christianity has applied to God.

Chapters 3 sifts and weighs the variety of ways the Christian Scriptures have interpreted the relation between God and suffering. Recognizing that the life, ministry, and paschal mystery of Jesus Christ have shaped the way Christians think about the presence of God in the midst of suffering and death, chapter 3 investigates the words and actions of Jesus in response to suffering in dialogue with the writings of Paul in the epistles. It does so in three contexts: suffering and the reign of God, the suffering and death of Jesus, and suffering and discipleship.

Having examined the Christian biblical responses to the question of God and suffering, the focus of the text turns to insights from Christian theological traditions. Chapter 4 attends to the proposals of three of the most significant theologians from the classical tradition: Augustine, Aquinas, and Irenaeus. Their writings bring philosophical reason to bear on biblical faith and their claims have influenced the way many theologians and people of faith have understood the relation between God and suffering for centuries. Representing Christian theology from a Western philosophical worldview, these theologians accept and defend classical theism's understanding of God, which greatly influences their conclusions about the relationship of God, evil, and suffering. Two main themes emerge from the writings of these theologians: evil as privation of good and evil as alienation.

In the last hundred years or so, however, theologians have increasingly criticized the approach of classical theism. Their critiques have focused primarily on the presumption of the universality of theological claims. Many scholars point out that few theological interpretations—even those of classical theology—have universal applicability. All are influenced by their historical and cultural *context*, a term that refers to the personal, social, and religious influences and worldviews a theologian brings to interpretation. As a result of their historical or cultural context, specific theologies have inherent limitations. While this does not limit God's self-revelation *to* a particular experience or event, it does recognize that the living God reveals Godself *through* particular experiences and events. Therefore, it is incumbent upon those who seek God in the midst of suffering to attend to the unique historical and cultural contexts in which suffering has emerged. It is this kind of attention to context that the theologians noted in the second part of this text have undertaken. Each chapter in this section includes a description of the context of suffering and death in which each theologian reflects on the revelation of God. The diverse images of God and of Christ that derive from these contexts demonstrate the breadth and depth of God's response to those afflicted by so many forms of suffering.

In chapter 5, theologians directly confront the mystery of God in the context of horrific suffering during the twentieth century—namely, the Holocaust, the bombings of Hiroshima and Nagasaki, the civil war in El Salvador, and the ecological crisis facing the planet and its inhabitants. In ways unique to the context in which they write, each affirms that "only the suffering God can help," the God who is "pushed out of the world on to the cross."[4] Feminist theologians in chapter 6 point to the absence of women's voices and experiences in speaking about God as part of the silencing and suffering experienced by women as a result of sexism. This suffering is manifest not only in theology but also in economic, educational, and political life, resulting in hostility and violence against women, from which they frequently have little or no legal or religious recourse. In response, feminist, womanist, and *mujerista* theologians describe how God sustains and energizes the lives of marginalized women from basic survival through full flourishing.

From the world stage, chapter 7 moves to the suffering and fear experienced by oppressed people in the United States. It explores the phenomenon of xenophobia—the fear and hatred of anything perceived as foreign or different—not only as ethnic prejudice and discrimination but also as racist and heterosexist oppression. These institutionalized forms of prejudice spread beyond an individual's fears or biases and infect national policies and practices. In response, black, Hispanic, and gay theologians offer transformative theologies based on the God of the Exodus and the crucified and Risen Christ in order to inspire people who were once voiceless and powerless to confront injustice and marginalization and to proclaim dignity and liberation.

Focusing on a pervasive yet often misinterpreted locus of human suffering, chapter 8 explores theologies written from the context of disabilities. It underscores that most theology assumes an able-bodied human experience. The near absence of persons with disabilities in theology has marginalized and misrepresented their lives not only in theological discourse but also in church and society. Theologies of disabilities point out that the suffering experienced by those with disabilities is not so much caused by their physical or mental impairments as by social, cultural, and religious assumptions that prevent people with impairments from meaningful participation in society. As a result, these theologians see new

---

4. Dietrich Bonhoeffer, *Letters and Papers from Prison*, ed. John W. de Gruchy (Minneapolis: Augsburg Fortress, 2009), 479.

theological perspectives as necessary to alleviate the suffering of those with disabilities as well as to effect a transformation in society and in the church.

The final chapter broadens the scope of suffering beyond the personal and societal to the question of suffering in an evolving cosmos. In dialogue with the sciences, it engages the problem of suffering stemming from evolution and nature, which seems to involve too much suffering and death to be the intent of a loving and provident God. With two other theologians, I present my own theological response to the mystery of God and suffering in this chapter, a response that I develop more fully in two of my previous books, *The Creative Suffering of the Triune God* (Oxford, 2007) and *Trinity in Relation: Creation, Incarnation and Grace in an Evolving Cosmos* (Anselm, 2012). Because my contribution is one of three responses in that chapter, I refer to myself in the third person to lend the same objectivity to my proposal as is given to those preceding mine. While doing so felt a bit strange, it enabled me to remain objective, to clarify my thinking at several points along the way, and to see my own theological proposals with new eyes.

Traversing the terrain of so many different Christian perspectives and respecting the differences among them, this book does not argue for one theological perspective on God and suffering over another. Rather, it leads readers through a variety of approaches grounded in scripture, tradition, and human experience, which readers can then study and evaluate within their own experience. As stated earlier, no one theology has all the answers; each bears possibilities and problems. Nonetheless, my hope is that those who venture into the mystery of God and suffering through the words of this book, who dare the subjunctive "If God is for us," will discover a way forward.

Part I

Classical Theologies of Suffering

The problem of evil does not attach itself as a threat to any and every concept of deity. It arises only for a religion which insists that the object of its worship is at once perfectly good and unlimitedly powerful.

—JOHN HICK, *EVIL AND THE GOD OF LOVE*

CHAPTER 1

Setting the Stage, Raising the Questions

> At the basis of the whole world of suffering, there inevitably arises the question: why? It is a question about the cause, the reason, and equally, about the purpose of suffering, and, in brief, a question about its meaning. Not only does it accompany human suffering, but it seems even to determine its human content, what makes suffering precisely human suffering.
>
> JOHN PAUL II, *SALVIFICI DOLORIS*[1]

Introduction

The reality of suffering has persistently provoked theological debate. How may one speak of God in the midst of suffering? To prepare for theological responses to such debate, this opening chapter pursues tasks critical to formulating theologies of suffering. Chapter 1 clarifies key terms and introduces crucial questions explored in later chapters. It demonstrates that the existence of suffering in this world provokes not only theistic responses but also non-theistic and a-theistic explanations that eschew any possibility that suffering and evil could coexist with the one whom believers call God. Finally, this chapter contends that the question of suffering cannot and must not be ignored by those who believe in God.

Terms of the Investigation

Throughout this text, two terms appear many times in isolation and in combination: *suffering* and *evil*. While few would contest associating the two concepts, the nature of this association is often tainted by an inadequate understanding of the difference and the relationship between suffering and evil. For example,

---

1. John Paul II, *Salvifici Doloris* (*On the Christian Meaning of Human Suffering*, 1984), no. 9; available at *http://w2.vatican.va/content/john-paul-ii/en/apost_letters/1984/documents/hf_jp-ii_apl _11021984_salvifici-doloris.html*.

some actions or events are deemed evil because they cause suffering. However, this view is problematic, since some well-intended human actions, such as treatments for disease, also cause suffering, and few would call them "evil." In addition, certain weather events like hurricanes or tornadoes are often considered natural evils because of their harmful effects on life and property. Nonetheless, such events are expected occurrences in the natural world. Hence it is critical at the outset to clarify what suffering and evil mean and how the two both differ and relate.

Suffering

Suffering is a complex experience. Sometimes it involves a conscious choice to endure pain or distress; at other times, it consists of a disruption of inner harmony caused by a physical, mental, emotional, or spiritual force. Unlike pain, which is primarily a *physical* sensation caused by damaging stimuli and "associated with actual or potential tissue damage,"[2] *suffering* in this text refers to a constellation of mental, emotional, or spiritual sensations experienced in response to internal and external conditions. Moreover, according to philosopher Ulrich Diehl, "When people suffer they always suffer as a whole human being. The emotional, cognitive and spiritual suffering of human beings cannot be completely separated from all other kinds of suffering, such as from harmful natural, ecological, political, economic and social conditions."[3]

Consider, for example, those burdened by unemployment, especially in uncertain economic times. Their suffering is not only financial but also emotional, psychological, spiritual, and physical. As one person described it, "Unemployment is terrifying. It feels like the world is caving in on you slowly and quickly at the same time. The financial pressure mounts and mounts and you stare God in the face, realizing that apart from faith, there is no real security in life. Faith is great, but security is equally great—and faith won't pay the bills."[4] People living in parts of the world plagued by natural disasters or domestic terrorism, economic depression or inadequate health care experience higher levels of emotional and even spiritual distress. As these levels of distress increase, the capacity to confront and overcome such conditions decreases.[5] This dynamic results in a vicious and self-perpetuating cycle of suffering. Furthermore, not every person within a particular condition of suffering reacts in the same way:

---

2. "Pain," International Association for the Study of Pain, *http://www.iasp-pain.org/Taxonomy ?navItemNumber=576#Pain*.

3. Ulrich Diehl, "Human Suffering as a Challenge for the Meaning of Life," *Existenz: An International Journal in Philosophy, Religion, Politics, and the Arts* 4 (Fall 2009), available at *www.bu.edu /paideia/existenz/volumes/Vol.4-2Diehl.pdf*.

4. "Learning the Hard Way What Matters Most," *About.com*, available at *http://jobsearch.about .com/u/sty/unemployment/unemployedstory/Learning-the-Hard-Way-What-Matters-Most.htm*.

5. Diehl, "Human Suffering," 38.

Individual people can cope, react and act in different, various and individual ways when confronted with the same harmful conditions. . . . For example, some may react . . . with frustration, passivity, and depression; others may react with vigilance, activity, and responsibility. For this reason there is a certain individuality and subjectivity . . . of emotional, cognitive, and spiritual suffering with respect to . . . outer sources or harmful conditions.[6]

In his essay "Human Suffering as a Challenge for the Meaning of Life," Diehl discusses two conditions of suffering. The first he terms "external conditions of human suffering" and the second "personal conditions of human suffering."[7] While clearly affirming the capacity for suffering in other living beings, Diehl argues for a "special quality of human suffering" that stems from the human capacity to experience, reflect upon, make judgments, and evaluate the suffering of self and of others.[8]

External Conditions of Human Suffering

Diehl highlights eight external conditions of human suffering: (1) natural, (2) ecological, (3) political, (4) economic, (5) social, (6) emotional, (7) cognitive/spiritual, and (8) meaninglessness. *Natural conditions* include earthquakes, volcanic eruptions, tsunamis, hurricanes, tornadoes, mudslides, and other extreme situations, which Diehl distinguishes from *ecological conditions*, such as chemical contamination of food or water supplies or biological contaminations causing epidemics. Under *political conditions*, Diehl lists dictatorship, anarchy, war, or terrorism, while *economic conditions* encompass such situations as unemployment, inflation, and globalization. *Social conditions* refer to the inadequate fulfillment of human needs for food, shelter, clothing, and personal security. As *emotional conditions*, Diehl includes the inability to satisfy the human need for belonging, acceptance, meaningful work, self-respect, and self-determination, and *cognitive/spiritual conditions* focus on the incapacity to negotiate the natural and social world or to understand the unique position of humans in the world created by language, communication, community, cooperation, and self-transcendence. Finally, inspired by the work of psychiatrist and Holocaust survivor Viktor Frankl,[9] Diehl includes the condition of *meaninglessness*, an inability to find fulfillment and worth under the concrete and contingent circumstances of one's

---

6. Ibid.

7. Ibid., 37–40.

8. Ibid., 41–42.

9. Cf. Viktor Frankl, *Man's Search for Meaning* (Boston: Beacon Press, 2006), first published in German in 1946 under the title *Ein Psycholog Erlebt das Konzentrationslager*. Based on Frankl's life in Nazi death camps between 1942 and 1945, the memoir argues that one cannot avoid suffering but can choose how to cope with it, find meaning in it, and move forward with renewed purpose.

life. These conditions influence each other as well as the theological responses explored in later chapters of this text.

> ### Reflect and Discuss
>
> Are there types of suffering in your experience that do not reflect one or more of these conditions? What are they? What is their source?

Personal Conditions of Human Suffering

Personal conditions of suffering explored by Diehl include those originating within a given human being. This category includes (1) physical, (2) emotional, (3) cognitive, (4) spiritual, and (5) reflective sources. *Physical conditions* affect the body through aches, pains, and wounds. *Emotional conditions* stem from positive and negative stress, mourning or grief, guilt or shame, fear or depression, whereas *cognitive conditions* derive from loss of memory, concentration, flexibility, or judgment. Suffering may also result from *spiritual conditions*. These originate from anxiety concerning questions about identity, values, principles, goals, norms, and beliefs. Finally, Diehl identifies suffering that arises from an awareness of the suffering experienced by others. As he describes it,

> This is not only a quantitative difference or additional factor among the various ways of human suffering (especially when compared with higher mammals). The human capacity to be aware of, to focus on and to reflect on (thinking, understanding and explaining) their own human suffering and the suffering of other human beings is changing the very quality of human suffering in many different ways.[10]

It is this reflective awareness of suffering that leads to Diehl's proposal that the capacity to focus and reflect on one's own suffering and that of others "is an essential element . . . of being human within the world."[11] In other words, the very capacity that humans have to reflect upon their own and others' suffering distinguishes them and makes them unique among all creatures "as far as we know and understand them." In comparison to human beings, there are physical entities (e.g., matter and energy) that are unable to suffer, and living entities (e.g., plants) that cannot feel pain. Furthermore, some creatures do feel pain but, unlike humans, do not have reflective awareness of their own suffering and cannot reflectively explain their own suffering during or after its occurrence. Ultimately, human beings possess the unique capacity to reflect upon and

---

10. Diehl, "Human Suffering," 40.

11. Ibid., 41.

change their attitudes toward the suffering of others, as well as to choose how they approach and evaluate their own and others' suffering. Diehl admits that the uniqueness of the human response to suffering seems a dubious advantage at best. However, even in this, humanity has the capacity to reflect, choose, and evaluate whether to embrace or reject this uniqueness. [12]

Reflect and Discuss

Do you agree with Diehl's description of the uniqueness of human suffering? Why or why not? What examples can you give to support your position?

A story of one such choice—and the difference that choice made—is that of former New Orleans Saints safety Steve Gleason. In 2011, Gleason revealed his battle with amyotrophic lateral sclerosis (ALS), also known as Lou Gehrig's disease. ALS is a debilitating disease characterized by progressive weakness and muscle atrophy. In the face of suffering, Gleason made a decision concerning his human condition.

I have been diagnosed with Amyotrophic Lateral Sclerosis (ALS). It's a terminal disease with an average lifespan of two to five years post-diagnosis. . . . So, how does a person react when he or she learns there are two to five years left with which to live? Denial. Frustration. Anger. Despair. But at some point, I understood that acceptance of this diagnosis was not admitting defeat. That was critical for me personally . . . because it makes you focus on the things and people you truly love. After that realization, I started to dig in, to look forward to what might be in my future. . . . Still, I can't deny that it's a struggle. . . . As humans, we are able to conjure and attach meaning to almost any circumstance or development. When handed what feels like a terminal diagnosis, it's human nature to ask, Why did this happen to me?! or What does this mean?! . . . We cannot measure, verify or confirm meaning. We, as humans, create and apply meaning. When something happens to us, we become the author of meaning. The best philosophy I have adopted is to apply a useful and productive meaning . . . regardless of the circumstances in my life.[13]

---

12. Ibid., 42.

13. To read the story of Steve Gleason's decision in his own words, see, inter alia, "Guest MMQB: Steve Gleason on His Life with ALS, Mission for a Cure," *SI.Com*, available at *www.si.com/nfl/2013/06/17/steve-gleason-monday-morning-quarterback*.

Evil

Like suffering, evil is a complicated and multifaceted phenomenon that has been defined by scholars in a variety of ways throughout history. Some define it in terms of what they consider good. Augustine and Aquinas thought of evil as the privation or negation of the good; the Manichaeans viewed evil as a force in a continuous struggle with the power of good. "By *good*," philosopher Benedict (Baruch) de Spinoza proposed, "I understand that which we certainly know is useful to us. By *evil*, on the contrary, I understand that which we certainly know hinders us from possessing anything that is good."[14]

Other sources define evil in terms of the suffering it causes. The *Catholic Encyclopedia*, for example, proposes that "Evil, in a large sense, may be described as the sum of the opposition, which experience shows to exist in the universe, to the desires and needs of individuals; whence arises, among human beings at least, the sufferings in which life abounds."[15] In his three-part series of articles, "An Analysis of the Problem of Evil," Episcopal priest and professor R. Franklin Terry offered the following definition:

> Evil may be defined as any object, event, influence, occurrence, act, experience, or combination of these, be the source human or extra-human, which thwarts, disrupts, threatens, frustrates, or destroys the life of a human being or group of human beings, or jeopardizes what is valued or cherished by human beings.[16]

Philosopher of religion John Hick succinctly defines evil according to its manifestations. Hick writes,

> Rather than attempt to define "evil" in terms of some . . . theory, it seems better to define it ostensively, by indicating that to which the word refers. It refers to physical pain, mental suffering, and moral wickedness. The last is one of the causes of the first two, for an enormous amount of human pain arises from people's inhumanity.[17]

Reflect and Discuss

How would you define evil?

---

14. Benedict de Spinoza, *Ethics*, part IV, "Of Human Bondage or the Strength of the Emotions," definitions 1 and 2, available at *http://capone.mtsu.edu/rbombard/RB/Spinoza/ethica4.html.*

15. "Evil," *The Catholic Encyclopedia*, available at *www.newadvent.org/cathen/05649a.htm.*

16. R. Franklin Terry, "An Analysis of the Problem of Evil: Part Two: Theoretical Dimensions," *Iliff Review* 23 (1966): 15–25, at 15. Terry acknowledges that his definition is "intentionally man-centered" and explicitly excludes other animate and inanimate beings.

17. John H. Hick, *Philosophy of Religion* (Upper Saddle River, NJ: Prentice-Hall, 1990), 39.

Despite commonalities among various definitions, understanding evil either in terms of the good it prevents or the suffering it causes proves problematic. First, to judge evil in terms of "good" presumes a clear and even universal conception of what constitutes "good" per se. Thus, "good" becomes no less relative a concept than "evil." Second, to designate as "evil" that which causes suffering runs the risk of indicting something as *necessarily* evil rather than *contingently* so because of its deleterious effects on life and property. If a hurricane spins east off the coast of Africa and twists northward into the mid-Atlantic without impact on life or land, one can hardly consider that an evil event. Particular medical treatments, especially those for cancer, damage cells in the human organs and nervous system, yet most would not judge chemotherapy as evil. Therefore, differentiating between what is necessarily evil in and of itself, regardless of circumstances, and what is contingently evil because of its circumstances or results proves crucial. To do so is to differentiate between intrinsic and extrinsic evil.

Intrinsic versus Extrinsic Evils

Christian moral theology recognizes "that there are objects of the human act which are by their nature 'incapable of being ordered' to God, because they radically contradict the good of the person made in his image." Such acts are termed *intrinsic evil* because "on account of their very object, and quite apart from the ulterior intentions of the one acting and the circumstances," they are contrary to reason, to nature, and to God.[18] The "intrinsically evil" action is judged neither by its intention nor its effects. Rather, the act is considered evil "in itself" or "for its own sake" or "as such" or "in its own right." Such acts include homicide or genocide; mutilation, physical and mental torture; subhuman living conditions, arbitrary imprisonment, deportation, slavery, prostitution, and human trafficking—"all these and the like are a disgrace, and . . . a negation of the honor due to the Creator."[19] In contrast to these intrinsic evils, an act is considered an *extrinsic evil* when the intention or circumstances surrounding it result in outcomes harmful to life and well-being. Hence the *nature* of the act or event is not evil in itself, but only its circumstances or results.

Why is the discussion about intrinsic and extrinsic evil important? First, it highlights that what is truly evil is often moral in character. This means that calling something "evil" is most appropriate when it stems from an action that is voluntary and when it impedes the ability of a creature to develop and flourish. Second, it cautions against ascribing evil to the involuntary or organic processes of the cosmos. While these processes can wreak havoc on creation and inflict

---

18. John Paul II, *Veritatis Splendor* (*The Splendor of Truth*, 1993), no. 80, available at *http://w2.vatican.va/content/john-paul-ii/en/encyclicals/documents/hf_jp-ii_enc_06081993_veritatis-splendor.html.*

19. Vatican Council II, *Gaudium et spes* (*Pastoral Constitution on the Church in the Modern World*, 1965), no. 27, available at *www.vatican.va/archive/hist_councils/ii_vatican_council/documents/vat-ii_const_19651207_gaudium-et-spes_en.html.*

suffering and even death on its creatures, they are not necessarily contrary to reason, to nature, or to God. Finally, the difference between intrinsic and extrinsic evil impacts thought and speech about God, evil, and suffering. Is God, as Creator of heaven and earth, the maker of evil as well? Is the source of evil in the intention of God or in the voluntary exercise of human freedom? If aspects of God's creation are evil in and of themselves, what does that say about the omnipotence, omniscience, and omnibenevolence of God? Theologians propose different answers to such questions. However, one thing remains certain:

> The problem of evil is one of our oldest intellectual conundrums. Volumes have been written attempting to define evil, to catalog its horrors, to account for its persistence, to explain its appeal, to confront its consequences. The moment we begin to ask questions about the nature of evil, however, we begin to understand how difficult it is to answer them. One way to start the discussion is to narrow the focus.[20]

This chapter now narrows the focus, moving from attempts to define the *nature* of evil to the task of identifying the conditions and sources of evil that call for human and divine response.

Conditions and Sources of Evil

Like suffering, evil has been described in relation to external conditions of nature and society, as well as to internal conditions of human freedom and finitude. Most scholars recognize two broad classifications of evil that subsume these internal and external conditions—natural evil and moral evil. Moral evil generally refers to evils perpetrated through the free and deliberate choices of human beings, while natural evil is associated with the activities of nonhuman creation and its creatures. Nonetheless, the complexity of evil calls for a more careful distinction of its various sources. R. Franklin Terry delineates five forms of evil that plague human and nonhuman beings—natural evil, physical evil, moral evil, social and cultural evil, and the evils of finitude.[21]

Natural Sources of Evil. While the grandeur of the natural world has inspired art, poetry, and praise of God, it also demonstrates indiscriminate savagery and force, leading to instances of *natural evil*. As John Stuart Mill so aptly describes this propensity of nature,

> Nature impales [creatures] . . . starves them with hunger, freezes them with cold, poisons them by the quick or slow venom of [its]

---

20. Alan Wolfe, "Evildoers and Us," *Chronicle of Higher* Education, September 11, 2011, available at *http://chronicle.com/article/EvildoersUs/128910/*.

21. R. Franklin Terry, "An Analysis of the Problem of Evil, Part One: The Reality of Evil," *Iliff Review* 21 (1964): 11.

exhalations . . . with the most supercilious disregard both of mercy and of justice . . . upon the best and noblest indifferently with the meanest and worst; upon those who are engaged in the highest and worthiest enterprise, and often as a direct consequence of the noble acts . . . [and] with as little compunction as those whose death is a relief to themselves, or a blessings to those under their noxious influence.[22]

Some theologians and philosophers, especially those in dialogue with the sciences, question the attribution of "evil" to events like earthquakes, floods, hurricanes, and the like, which involve seemingly pointless suffering and tragedy, as well as loss of human health and life. These scholars point out that the evolutionary emergence of life often takes place through these very kinds of occurrences. Because of this, they argue that such events of nature must be regarded as aspects of the free processes of evolution rather than as manifestations of evil.

A final category related to natural sources of evil is that of *evils of finitude*. The concept of finitude usually refers to the state of creatures as dependent and contingent beings, physically and temporally limited. However, in Terry's schema, it refers not to physical or temporal limitations, but to the psychological dimensions experienced by humans that derive from these limitations. Dependence and contingency, for example, often arouse anxiety and fear in human beings; physical limitations sometimes bring about feelings of loneliness, isolation, or despair. Although "some would deny the anxious moment, or would be unable or unwilling to recall moments of sudden or irrational fear,"[23] most view the psychological effects of finitude as universal.

Moral Sources of Evil. *Moral evil* results from the exercise of human freedom. The conundrum concerning natural sources of evil does not surface when considering moral sources of evil because "nature can hardly assume the attributes of freedom in [its] wrongdoing. We do not impugn nature for murder, nor does [nature] suffer remorse for [its] cruelties."[24] While the consequences of human moral freedom stem from both conscious and unconscious wrongdoing,[25] the harmful outcome remains, regardless of the volition or intention involved. The list of moral evils is extensive; it includes murder, lying, stealing, cheating, adultery, slander, blasphemy, pollution, and abuse. Whether willful or unintentional, conscious or unconscious, moral evil is perpetrated by humans acting in ways harmful to creation or failing to prevent such harm.

---

22. John Stuart Mill, "Nature," in James Eli Adams, "Philosophical Forgetfulness: John Stuart Mill's 'Nature,'" *Journal of the History of Ideas* 53 (July–September, 1992): 437.

23. Terry, "The Reality of Evil," 14.

24. Ibid., 12.

25. The issue dealt with here is not one of moral culpability but rather the source of or condition that results from human moral choice.

Issues of moral freedom and wrongdoing permeate religious traditions. The Jewish and Christian traditions refer to moral wrongdoing as "sin." Religious traditions identify various kinds of sin, some of which refer to individual acts and others to more pervasive realities. Examples of the first are termed personal sins, while the second refer to original, social, or systemic sins. Terry categorizes these latter sins as *social and cultural evil*.

Social and cultural evil is "an extension of moral evil into the larger nexus of human groups."[26] It results from attitudes, values, or beliefs in society that diminish human dignity by perpetuating oppression, marginalization, or exploitation. Such attitudes include racism, sexism, heterosexism, xenophobia, consumerism, materialism, environmental despoliation, or combinations of these. When these attitudes become institutionalized in legal, economic, or political policies, they may be termed systemic or structural evil. In the United States alone, violence and blight afflict urban areas, sexist discrimination impacts hiring practices and fair wages, and ethnic and racial profiling oppress and marginalize citizen and immigrants. Moreover, because so many persons are unwittingly complicit in social and cultural evil, it is notoriously difficult to address. Nonetheless, "encounter with evil on this level is imperative for those . . . who are sensitive to these conditions." This rings especially true for people of faith who realize that religious traditions cannot shrink from their "mission isolated from the world"[27] when the encounter with evil creates the problem of reconciling the suffering it causes with the existence of God.

The Problem of God, Suffering, and Evil

While the demand for a reasonable theological response to the question of how to speak about God amidst suffering is a centuries-old endeavor, it was not until 1710 that the term *theodicy* came into currency to describe it. The term was coined by German philosopher Gottfried Leibniz in his work, *Essais de Théodicée sur la Bonte de Dieu, la Liberté de l'Homme et l'Origine du Mal* (*Essays of Theodicy on the Goodness of God, the Freedom of Man and the Origin of Evil*) and derived from the Greek words *theos* ("God") and *dike* ("judgment"). A theodicy attempts to justify or defend God in the face of suffering and evil. "For," as R. Franklin Terry explains, "to the extent that *God is believed to be absolutely powerful and benevolent*, to that same extent the burden of vindicating God is felt."[28]

So, although the term *theodicy* is frequently used in a generic sense to refer to the attempt to interpret suffering and evil in dialogue with *any* conception

---

26. Terry, "The Reality of Evil," 13.

27. Ibid., 14.

28. R. Franklin Terry, "An Analysis of the Problem of Evil, Part Two: Theoretical Dimensions," *Iliff Review* 23 (1966): 21, emphasis added.

of God, it technically refers to the effort to "reinterpret the nature of evil *leaving intact the other major presuppositions concerning the nature of God* and his creation."[29] Theodicy in this sense presupposes divine omnipotence, omniscience, and omnibenevolence, as well as the existence of evil in creation. Thus, the classical form of the problem can be summarized in three propositions that appear logically incompatible: (1) God is omnipotent, (2) God is totally good, and (3) evil exists.[30] The following expanded form of the argument reveals both its assumptions and inferences:

1. God is omnipotent, omniscient, and omnibenevolent.

    a. Because God is omnipotent, God has the power to do any and all things.

    b. Because God is omniscient, God knows any and all things.

    c. Because God is omnibenevolent, God is all-loving and infinitely good.

2. The universe exists in an ongoing relationship to God.

    a. The universe was created by God.

    b. The universe is sustained by God.

    c. God acts in/interacts with the universe.

3. Nonetheless, evil exists in the universe.

The burden of theodicy, therefore, consists of defending this specific understanding of God in light of the reality of evil and suffering. The conundrum of doing so was aptly stated by the philosopher Epicurus in the fourth century BCE:

> God either wishes to take away evils, and is unable; or He is able, and is unwilling; or He is neither willing nor able, or He is both willing and able. If he is willing and is unable, He is feeble, which is not in accordance with the character of God; if He is able and unwilling, He is envious, which is equally at variance with God; if He is neither willing nor able, He is both envious and feeble, and therefore is not God; if He is both willing and able, which alone is suitable to God, from what source then are evils? Or why does He not remove them?[31]

Philosopher David Hume expresses the issue in more contemporary form: "Is [God] willing to prevent evil, but not able? Then he is impotent. Is he able, but not willing? Then he is malevolent. Is he both able and willing? Then where

---

29. Ibid.

30. This formulation is attributed to J. L. Mackie in his essay "Evil and Omnipotence," *Mind* 64 (1955): 200–212.

31. Epicurus, in Lactantius, "On the Anger of God," chap. 13, in *The Writings of the Ante-Nicene Fathers*, trans. William Fletcher, available at *www.ecmarsh.com/fathers/anf/ANF-07/anf07-13 .htm#P3322_1348266.*

does evil come from ?"[32] Hence, to the extent that one understands God solely in terms of omnipotence, omniscience, and omnibenevolence, to that extent the problem of God and suffering looms large.

Leibniz and the Problem of Evil

In the essay "Leibniz on the Problem of Evil," philosophers Michael Murray and Sean Greenberg point out that, during the period in which Leibniz worked, philosophers as a whole accepted the arguments for the existence of God based on reason and experience alone.[33] Hence, the philosopher Leibniz wrestled with the problem of the *coexistence* of God and evil. He did so by addressing two arguments: the blot on divine holiness and the flaw in divine creativity.

Since God is the Creator of the world, the existence of evil seems to be a blot on divine holiness. In divine holiness, and as the primary cause of all that exists, God is worthy of worship, awe, and reverence. However, some would argue that, as the cause of existence, God is also the cause of evil and thus unworthy of devotion and love. In response to this, some theologians had contended that evil is a privation of the good, a "no-thing" instead of a something. In this view,

> evil has no more reality than the hole in the center of a donut. Making a donut does not require putting together two components, the cake and the hole: the cake is all that there is to the donut, and the hole is just the "privation of cake." It therefore would be silly to say that making the donut requires causing both the cake and the hole to exist. Causing the cake to exist causes the hole as a "by-product" of causing a particular kind of cake to exist. Thus, we need not assume any additional cause for the hole beyond that assumed for the causing of the cake.[34]

Leibniz rejected both this "donut and hole" reasoning and the definition of evil as the privation of good. In his essay "The Author of Sin," he contends that if God is responsible for creating the positive forms in the universe, then God must be the creator of its negative manifestations as well. Leibniz asks, "What if a painter created two works of art, the second simply a smaller version of the first?" It would be ludicrous, Leibniz states,

---

32. David Hume, *Dialogues Concerning Natural Religion*, 44, available at *www.earlymoderntexts .com/assets/pdfs/hume1779.pdf*.

33. Michael Murray and Sean Greenberg, "Leibniz on the Problem of Evil," *Stanford Encyclopedia of Philosophy* (Spring 2013 edition), available at *http://plato.stanford.edu/archives/spr2013 /entries/leibniz-evil/*. Arguments from natural theology for the existence of God rest principally on reason rather than revelation. Two classic examples are the *ontological argument* of eleventh-century Archbishop Anselm of Canterbury (see Paul Halsall, "Medieval Sourcebook: Anselm [1033–1109]: *Proslogium*," chap. 2, available at *https://legacy.fordham.edu/halsall/basis/anselm-proslogium.asp*) and the *Quinque viae* (*Five Ways*) of theologian Thomas Aquinas (see Halsall, "Medieval Sourcebook: *Thomas Aquinas: Reasons in Proof of the Existence of God, 1270*," available at *http://legacy.fordham .edu/halsall/source/aquinas3.asp*).

34. Murray and Greenberg, "Leibniz on the Problem of Evil.

to say that the painter is the author of all that is real in the two paintings, without however being the author of what is lacking or the disproportion between the larger and the smaller painting. . . . In effect, what is lacking is nothing more than a simple result of an infallible consequence of that which is positive, without any need for a distinct author.[35]

In response to the problem of divine holiness, Leibniz proposes that while God wills the good as *decretory*—that is, fixed by decree or decision—God's will is only *permissive* of evil. In other words, God explicitly intends and produces the good; however, God only allows evil to exist if it furthers God's intention to create the best of all possible worlds.

Reflect and Discuss

What is your response to Leibniz's contention that God is the author of evil as well as good? Does his conclusion that God wills evil only permissively influence your thinking on this matter?

This notion of "the best of all possible worlds" informs Leibniz's response to the second charge of flawed divine creativity. Leibniz asserts that because of divine omnipotence and omniscience, nothing can impede God from creating the best of all possible worlds. Moreover, because of divine omnibenevolence, God desires to create nothing other than the best of all possible worlds as a consequence of divine nature itself. However, while Leibniz argued that this is the best of all possible worlds, one could ask whether this really is best in view of the reality of evil. In light of the shootings at Columbine, Aurora, and Sandy Hook Elementary; the bombings in Oklahoma City and the Boston Marathon; the terrorist attacks on the World Trade Center, the Pentagon, and aboard Flight 93; and other recent examples of evil in the United States, one could argue, "Surely a world without that event would be better than the actual world. And there is no reason why God couldn't have created the world without that event. Thus, this is not the best possible world."[36]

In disputing this conclusion, Leibniz first challenges the capacity of human beings to determine that this is not the best of all possible worlds because of certain events. As finite beings, humans have neither the knowledge of any world other than this nor the awareness of how one event connects to another. While particular occurrences may strike individuals as world-shattering, they are but

---

35. Leibniz, *Sämtliche Schriften und Briefe*, 6.3.151, in Murray and Greenberg, "Leibniz on the Problem of Evil."

36. Murray and Greenberg, "Leibniz on the Problem of Evil."

temporal, isolated episodes in an infinite sequence, and there is no way to know whether altering a specific situation would result in a better or worse world on the whole. As Leibniz explains,

> it might be said that the whole sequence of things to infinity may be the best possible, although what exists all through the universe in each portion of time be not the best. It might be therefore that the universe became even better and better, if the nature of things were such that it was not permitted to attain to the best all at once. But these are problems of which it is hard for us to judge.[37]

Moreover, Leibniz asserts, it is not only imprudent to assess the whole on the merits of one part but also ill-advised to presume that God employs the same standards as human beings in judging what constitutes the best possible world. This led Leibniz to the following conclusion:

> With God, it is plain that his understanding contains the ideas of all possible things, and that is how everything is in him in a transcendent manner. These ideas represent to him the good and evil, the perfection and imperfection, the order and disorder, the congruity and incongruity of possibles; and his superabundant goodness makes him choose the most advantageous. God therefore determines himself by himself; his will acts by virtue of his goodness, but it is particularized and directed in action by understanding filled with wisdom. And since his understanding is perfect, since his thoughts are always clear, his inclinations always good, he never fails to do the best; whereas we may be deceived by the mere semblances of truth and goodness. . . . There was therefore in him a reason anterior to the resolution; and, as I have said so many times, it was neither by chance nor without cause, nor even by necessity, that God created this world, but rather as a result of his inclination, which always prompts him to the best.[38]

Reflect and Discuss

What do you think of the idea that this is "the best of all possible worlds" according to Leibniz? Is his argument compelling? Would you dispute it? If so, how?

---

37. Gottfried Leibniz, *Theodicy: Essays on the Goodness of God, the Freedom of Man and the Origin of Evil*, no. 202, p. 254, Project Gutenberg eBook, available at *www.gutenberg.org/files /17147/17147-h/17147-h.htm*.

38. Ibid., 429.

Engaging the Problem of Theodicy

In view of its complexity, addressing the problem of theodicy in philosophy and theology has taken several forms. One deals with the problem of God and suffering as a *logical problem* as it proceeds "to *think through* the contradiction that stands between the goodness, omniscience, and omnipotence of God, on the one hand, and the massive misery and undeserved suffering that characterize God's world, on the other."[39] Thus it questions whether coupling the existence of evil with the proposition of the Divine as omnipotent, omniscient, and omnibenevolent leads to the rational conclusion that God exists. Using deduction, a thinker would follow this logical sequence that generally arrives at the nonexistence of God: (1) God exists and is omnipotent, omniscient, and omnibenevolent. (2) As omnipotent, no limits exist to God's abilities. (3) As omnibenevolent, God will always eliminate evil. (4) However, evil exists. (5) Therefore, God must not exist. In response, theists sometimes attempt to resolve the incongruity between God's attributes and the existence of evil by abandoning or rejecting certain postulates in order to preserve others. So a theist might dispute the deduction that an omnibenevolent being always eliminates evil and amend it by asserting that God will always eliminate evil *unless* God in divine omniscience and wisdom has a good reason for allowing that evil to exist. The logician, however, would contend that nothing justifies God's permitting evil and therefore would once again conclude that God does not exist.

A second way theodicy addresses suffering and evil is as an *evidential problem*. While the existence of God and of evil may not be logically reconcilable, some would argue that the scope and kinds of evil in history provide evidence that militates against the nature of God that theodicy defends.

Approaching the problem in this way raises questions like the following: Could God have eliminated evil and still have accomplished the divine purpose? Is all suffering and evil truly connected to divine purposes? How can God's purposes be served when some suffer so much more often and greatly than others? Can any divine goal justify horrors like the Holocaust, the Black Death plague, or the nuclear bombing of Hiroshima and Nagasaki? And even if one could answer yes to all these questions, the core issue lingers still: Is a God who accomplishes divine purposes in this way worthy of love and worship? The theodicist may justify God by pointing out that "God's foolishness is wiser than human wisdom"(1 Cor. 1:25), or may proclaim, "How unsearchable are his judgments and how inscrutable his ways" (Rom. 11:33), or hear the divine declaration, "For my thoughts are not your thoughts, nor are your ways my ways" (Isa. 55:8). Nonetheless, the ultimate concern persists: can such a God lay claim to human love and praise?

---

39. Ralph C. Wood, "Ivan Karamazov's Mistake," *First Things* (December 2002), available at *www.firstthings.com/article/2002/12/ivan-karamazovs-mistake*, emphasis in the original.

A third approach considers suffering and evil as an *existential problem*. Rather than focusing on the theological questions of why God allows the existence of evil or of what kind of God would do so, considering suffering and evil as an existential problem focuses on a religious or pastoral response to specific experiences of suffering.

Although theologians and ministers using this approach may explore the social, systemic, and structural causes of evil, they emphasize pastorally effective responses to eliminate, alleviate, or at least cope with the experience of suffering. In addition, they are concerned with how people of faith might respond and relate to God in the midst of tragedy and suffering.

Reflect and Discuss

Which approach to the problem of God and evil seems most efficacious to you? Why? Which presents the greatest challenge to resolve? Why?

Nonetheless, the entire enterprise of theodicy at times elicits protests from some religious thinkers who claim that efforts to vindicate God's ways are impious, irreligious, and pretentious.[40] Rather than judging or defending God, such critics counsel that, like Job, people ought to abandon the search for "things too wonderful for [them]" and simply "despise [themselves] . . . and repent in dust and ashes" (Job 42:3, 6). Nonetheless, most scholars contend that the theological investigation of the problem of God and suffering can be approached "with the utmost humility and sincerity of spirit and from a standpoint of firm Christian commitment."[41] Rather than presuming to justify God in response to the problem of evil, theologians delve into these realities to understand the mystery of God and suffering in terms of how it relates to humanity, which is the goal of all theological investigation. As John Hick explains, for those who suffer, "Evil is not a problem to be solved, but a mystery to be encountered and lived through." However, it also presents "an intellectual problem, which invites rational reflection . . . distinct from the experienced mystery." Thus the "obligation to grapple with" the reality of God and suffering—whether conceived as problem or mystery—is not "in any degree lessened."[42]

---

40. See, for example, Anders Nygren, *Commentary on Romans*, trans. Carl C. Rasmussen (London: SCM Press, 1952), 365, and Henry L. Mansel, *The Limits of Religious Thought* (London: John Murray, 1859), 13.

41. Hick, *Evil and the God of Love*, 7.

42. Ibid., 10.

> ### Reflect and Discuss
>
> In your opinion, is it impious, irreligious, or pretentious to question God about the existence of and reason for evil? Why or why not?

The theologians discussed in the upcoming chapters offer theologies of suffering based in biblical, religious, and theological traditions as well as in the social and biological sciences. Some who affirm the coexistence of God, evil, and suffering offer theistic responses to the reality of suffering and evil. These responses assert the agency of human free will, the effect of suffering on character development, the promise of eschatological hope, the theology of the cross, and the suffering of God along with the afflicted in order to reconcile a particular image of God with the existence of evil. However, some who look upon the travail of the world and its creatures conclude that there is no God or at least no God who can lay claim to being all-powerful, all-loving, all-knowing, and all-just. This conclusion frequently provides a philosophical starting point for the argument of atheism.

The Challenge of Atheism

From a philosophical viewpoint, there are more arguments for atheism than those rooted in the existence of suffering and evil,[43] and there are more non-theistic than atheistic responses to the existence of suffering and evil.[44] In either case, suffering and evil remain enigmatic because the question of why they exist and how they impact the order and meaningfulness of the world remains. This is because "the problem of evil is a *human* problem, not exclusively a *religious* one."

---

43. The case for atheism has been made on a variety of bases. Arguments include the incompatibility of free will and omniscience, the conflicting revelations of different religious traditions, the imperfect design of created life-forms, the incongruity between the notion of hell and the omnibenevolence of God, and the principle of parsimony, related to Occam's razor, which maintains that, among competing hypotheses, the hypothesis with the fewest assumptions should be selected. Consistent with the principle of parsimony are also those atheistic responses deriving from the rejection of God or the "supernatural hypothesis" on the basis of science and its "natural hypotheses." Recent works on such topics include Richard Dawkins, *The God Delusion* (New York: Houghton Mifflin, 2006); Daniel Dennett, *Breaking the Spell: Religion as a Natural Phenomenon* (New York: Viking, 2006); Sam Harris, *The End of Faith: Religion, Terror, and the Future of Reason* (New York: W. W. Norton & Co., 2004); Christopher Hitchens, *God Is Not Great: How Religion Poisons Everything* (New York: Twelve, Hachette Book Group, 2007); Victor Stenger, *God: The Failed Hypothesis* (Amherst, NY: Prometheus, 2007); and Lewis Wolpert, *Six Impossible Things before Breakfast: The Evolutionary Origins of Belief* (New York: W. W. Norton & Co., 2007).

44. R. Franklin Terry lists the following nontheistic responses to the problem of evil: agnosticism, existentialism, nihilism, and positivism. His discussion appears in "An Analysis of the Problem of Evil, Part Two: Theoretical Dimensions," 15–25.

All people, regardless of their religious convictions or lack thereof, require conceptual categories to deal with evil, whether this is human authored or "natural" evil such as hurricanes or earthquakes. It is not only the theist who must give an account of her God in the face of evil; the atheist must give an account of his moral outrage at the evil in the world as well.[45]

Because of its focus on suffering, this text centers only on the form of atheism that responds to the existence of suffering and evil, commonly referred to as protest atheism. It does so by examining the argument for atheism constructed by philosopher William L. Rowe. Rowe approaches the problem of God and suffering as both a logical and an evidential problem.

In his classic essay, "The Problem of Evil and Some Varieties of Atheism," Rowe restates the premises of the atheistic argument concerning God and evil in this way:

1. There exist instances of intense suffering which an omnipotent, omniscient being could have prevented without thereby losing some greater good or permitting some evil equally bad or worse.

2. An omniscient, wholly good being would prevent the occurrence of any intense suffering it could, unless it could not do so without thereby losing some greater good or permitting some evil equally bad or worse.

3. There does not exist an omnipotent, omniscient, wholly good being.[46]

In his statement of the problem, Rowe concedes the possibility that an omnipotent, omniscient, wholly good being *could* permit suffering if *not doing so* resulted in the loss of a greater good or in the occurrence of an equally bad or worse evil. In so doing, Rowe acknowledges that

if the intense suffering leads to some greater good, a good we could not have obtained without undergoing the suffering in question, we might conclude that the suffering is justified, but it remains an evil nevertheless. . . . In such a case, while remaining an evil in itself, the intense human or animal suffering is, nevertheless, an evil which someone might be morally justified in permitting.[47]

---

45. Ryan Dueck, "Angry at the God Who Isn't There: The New Atheism as Theodicy," *Direction: A Mennonite Brethren Forum* 40, no. 1 (Spring 2011): 3–16, available at *www.directionjournal .org/40/1/angry-at-god-who-isnt-there-new-atheism.html*, emphasis added.

46. William L. Rowe, "The Problem of Evil and Some Varieties of Atheism," *American Philosophical Quarterly* 16 (October 1979): 336.

47. Ibid., 335.

This acknowledgment adds a critical element to most arguments for atheism that ordinarily offer no such concessions. Conceding the possibility of gaining a greater good or avoiding a worse evil to legitimize suffering suggests that the existence of intense suffering does not necessarily negate the existence of an omnipotent, omniscient, and wholly good God.

Rowe offers the hypothetical situation of a fawn trapped in a forest fire ignited by a lightning strike, detailing how the fawn is "horribly burned, and lies in terrible agony for several days before death relieves its suffering." In so doing, he exemplifies the classic argument of protest atheism: in view of the scope and the intensity of suffering in creation and its creatures, belief in the existence of an omnipotent, omniscient, and omnibenevolent God is logically and evidentially indefensible.

> So far as we can see, the fawn's intense suffering is pointless. For there does not appear to be any greater good such that the prevention of the fawn's suffering would require either the loss of that good or the occurrence of an evil equally bad or worse. . . . Could an omnipotent, omniscient being have prevented the fawn's apparently pointless suffering? The answer is obvious. . . . Since the fawn's intense suffering was preventable and, so far as we can see, pointless, doesn't it appear that . . . there do exist instances of intense suffering which an omnipotent, omniscient being could have prevented without thereby losing some greater good or permitting some evil equally bad or worse.[48]

This conclusion serves as the crux of the protest atheist's challenge. Even if one were to acknowledge that some experiences of suffering may be justifiable to obtain a greater good or to prevent a worse evil, the protest atheist points to the innumerable instances of pointless or innocent suffering that have afflicted all manner of creatures throughout history. Holding that it is unlikely that such pointless and innocent suffering is "intimately related" to greater good or worse evil, the protest atheist avers that even if it was so related, a truly omnipotent, omniscient being could have achieved those goods or avoided those evils without the need for such intense suffering. Therefore,

> In light of our experience and knowledge of the variety and scale of human and animal suffering in our world, the idea that none of this could have been prevented by an omnipotent being without thereby losing a greater good or permitting an evil at least as bad seems an extraordinarily absurd idea, quite beyond our belief. . . . Returning now to our argument for atheism . . . it does seem that we have *rational support* for atheism, that it is reasonable for us to believe that the theistic God does not exist.[49]

---

48. Ibid., 337.

49. Ibid., emphasis in the original.

Rowe himself offers a variety of approaches for the theist to respond to protest atheism. In one approach, the theist could delineate the goods an all-powerful and all-knowing God could achieve only by leading to suffering; in another approach, the theist may point out the spiritual and moral character development occasioned by the experience of suffering. A third way consists of the assertion that much suffering results from the free exercise of human choice; in a final tack, the theist may invoke the mystery of both God's purposes and the randomness of suffering.

Case in Point: *The Brothers Karamazov*

The Brothers Karamazov by Fyodor Dostoyevsky is a deeply philosophical novel set in nineteenth-century Russia that debates ethical questions of God, free will, and morality. In a section entitled "Rebellion," the book offers a famous criticism of any defense that derives from theological or philosophical approaches to evil. Moved by the realization that "the earth is sodden from its crust down to the center with tears,"[50] the antagonist Ivan Karamazov, who identifies himself as a believer in God, laments the scandal of suffering borne by innocent children. Ivan acknowledges that the suffering of adults may be deserved because of their depravity and complicity in the sins of history, after all,

> they've eaten the apple and know good and evil, and they have become "like gods." They go on eating it still. But the children haven't eaten anything, and are so far innocent. . . . If they, too, suffer horribly on earth, they must suffer for their fathers' sins . . . . The innocent must not suffer for another's sins, and especially such innocents![51]

---

50. Luigi Pareyson, "Pointless Suffering in the Brothers Karamazov," *Cross Currents* 37 (Summer/Fall 1987): 274.

51. Fyodor Dostoyevsky, *The Brothers Karamazov* (1980), 260, available as a Project Gutenberg eBook at *www.gutenberg.org/files/28054/28054-h/28054-h.html#toc83*.

Case in Point: *The Brothers Karamazov* (continued)

However, Ivan finds the suffering of children unconscionable. In a poignant conversation with his younger brother Alyosha, a novice in an Orthodox monastery, Ivan recounts numerous examples of abuses inflicted upon children and agonizes over two in particular. The first is a child of five abused by her mother. As Ivan tells it,

> This poor child of five was subjected to every possible torture by those cultivated parents. They beat her, thrashed her, kicked her for no reason till her body was one bruise. . . . Can you understand why a little creature, who can't even understand what's done to her, should beat her little aching heart with her tiny fist in the dark and the cold, and weep her meek unresentful tears to dear, kind God to protect her? . . . Do you understand why this infamy must be and is permitted?[52]

This narrative reflects one of the ways theodicists defend divine permission of evil: God allows evil so that humans can better understand and recognize good. This argument defends the existence of evil as part of the harmonious perfection of creation, a premise Ivan flatly rejects: "Why should he know that diabolical good and evil when it costs so much? Why, the whole world of knowledge is not worth that child's prayer to 'dear, kind God'!"[53]

The next story Ivan tells is about "a serf-boy, a little child of eight, [who] threw a stone in play and hurt the paw of the general's favorite hound." When the general saw the injured hound and found out that the eight-year-old child was inadvertently responsible,

> He was taken—taken from his mother and kept shut up all night. Early [the next] morning the general comes out on horseback . . . the child is brought from the lock-up. . . . The child is stripped naked. . . ." Make him run," commands the general. . . . And he sets the whole pack of hounds on the child. The hounds catch him, and tear him to pieces before his mother's eyes![54]

---

52. Ibid., 265.

53. Ibid.

54. Ibid., 266.

There can be for Ivan no morally acceptable reason for allowing such cruelty and suffering, especially one that would leave the understanding of God as omnibenevolent unchallenged. Ivan then asks his brother to put himself in God's place:

> Imagine that you are creating a fabric of human destiny with the object of making men happy in the end, giving them peace and rest at last, but that it was essential and inevitable to torture to death only one tiny creature . . . would you consent to be the architect on those conditions? Tell me, and tell the truth.[55]

At this point, even the pious Alyosha demurs and admits he would not consent. Throughout Ivan's diatribe, like theodicists who assert the sublimity of divine wisdom, Alyosha argues that Ivan may not know and understand all things as God does. "I don't want to understand anything now," Ivan retorts, "I want to stick to the fact. . . . If I try to understand anything, I shall be false to the fact, and I have determined to stick to the fact." Moreover, Ivan rejects any pious or pastoral response to the evil and suffering inflicted on the child by the general:

> If the sufferings of children go to swell the sum of sufferings which was necessary to pay for truth, then I protest that the truth is not worth such a price. I don't want the mother to embrace the oppressor who threw her son to the dogs! She dare not forgive him! And . . . if they dare not forgive, what becomes of harmony?[56]

For even if such suffering were the price to be paid for cosmic harmony, Ivan protests,

> I don't want harmony. From love for humanity I don't want it. . . . Too high a price is asked for harmony; it's beyond our means to pay so much to enter on it. And so I hasten to give back my entrance ticket . . . And that I am doing. It's not God that I don't accept . . . only I most respectfully return him the ticket.[57]

---

55. Ibid., 269.
56. Ibid., 268–69.
57. Ibid., 269.

For Further Reading

Dostoyevsky, Fyodor. *The Brothers Karamazov*. Translated by Andrew R. MacAndrew. New York: Bantam Classics, 1982.

Frankl, Viktor. *Man's Search for Meaning*. Boston: Beacon Press, 2006.

Hick, John. *Evil and the God of Love*. New York: Palgrave Macmillan, 2010.

Rowe, William L. "The Problem of Evil and Some Varieties of Atheism." *American Philosophical Quarterly* 16 (October 1979): 335–41.

Stewart, Matthew, *The Courtier and the Heretic: Leibniz, Spinoza, and the Fate of God in the Modern World*. New York: Norton, 2006.

Terry, R. Franklin. "An Analysis of the Problem of Evil, Part One: The Reality of Evil." *Iliff Review* 21 (1964): 9–15.

Terry, R. Franklin. "An Analysis of the Problem of Evil, Part Two: Theoretical Dimensions." *Iliff Review* 23 (1966): 15–25.

Internet Resources

Center for Christian Studies, Gordon College. "Theodicy, God and Suffering— A Debate between Dinesh D'Souza and Bart Ehrman." Available from *www.youtube.com/watch?v=Isg6Kx-3xdI* (time: 1:42:27).

Center for Christian Thought, Biola University. "The Existential Problem of Evil and *The Brothers Karamazov*." Available from *www.youtube.com /watch?v=bj-sxNNDuNU* (time: 0:12:39).

CHAPTER 2

The Claims of Classical Theism

Human attempts to encompass and "capture" the divine constitute an ever-present temptation, against which one must be constantly on one's guard. Indeed, such temptation begins to exercise its allure as soon as one begins the very process of speaking about God.

—GAVIN HYMAN, *A SHORT HISTORY OF ATHEISM*

Introduction

Of all the assertions religious traditions have made about God, the most fundamental is that God is an incomprehensible mystery. This means God so utterly transcends the world of experience that the finite minds of human beings are unable to grasp or express the fullness of God. Unlike the created world, God is Spirit (John 4:24) and as Spirit, cannot be seen, touched, or heard in the same ways in which the physical elements of the natural world can. In view of divine mystery, therefore, one must question how persons come to truly know and speak of God.

God as Self-Communicating

The Christian tradition teaches that persons of faith can come to know the Divine because God has chosen to reveal Godself in freedom and in love. In creation, in the sacred scriptures that contain human experiences of God, and preeminently in Jesus Christ, Christianity professes that God has revealed Godself out of love for creation. Twentieth-century Jesuit theologian Karl Rahner taught that God's very nature is one of free and self-communicating love and that God communicates to human beings through all God has created. Therefore, those seeking to explore and express the mystery of the living God must begin in those places through which God reveals Godself.

The Christian understanding of God begins in the book of Genesis, which proclaims in its opening lines, "In the beginning when God created the heavens and the earth, . . . God said, 'Let there be light'; and there was light. And God saw that the light was good" (Gen. 1:1–4a). "*God said.*" God spoke—God communicated Godself—at the advent of creation. While most theologians regard this creation story in Genesis as a form of sacred allegory or myth, it nonetheless expresses an important Christian understanding of truth in any attempt to speak of the divine mystery. In addition to revealing that God is the source of all creation, it also reveals that all of creation is the self-expression of God. Therefore, one can come to know God by attending carefully to God's self-communication through creation and its creatures. As God's own self-expression, everything is full of sacred presence; everything has the capacity to reveal the living God.

Thomas Aquinas formalized this understanding of how God as Creator can be known through what God creates. In his *Summa Contra Gentiles*, Aquinas summarized his idea thus: "There is some manner of likeness of creatures to God. . . . [Thus] from the attributes found in creatures we are led to a knowledge of the attributes of God."[1] Theologians term this likeness *the analogy of being*. This analogy between created and divine being makes it possible to draw inferences about the attributes and purposes of God based on the natural order because, in creating the world, God, who is the source of all being, shares "being" in the form of life with creation. Thus, everything that *has* being participates in God, who *is* Being itself. Moreover, because God *as* Being causes a creature

---

1. Thomas Aquinas, *Summa Contra Gentiles*, 1.33, *Dominican House of Studies*, trans. Anton C. Pegis, available at *http://dhspriory.org/thomas/ContraGentiles.htm*.

to come *into* being, not only do creatures exist in God, but God exists in all creatures: "As the giver of all existence, God exists in everything, not just at the beginning of something's coming to be but as long as it exists."[2] This understanding influences the way many theologians think about who God is and how God acts in the midst of creaturely suffering.

Reflect and Discuss

What is your response to Aquinas's claim that you exist in God and God exists in you? If you agree with Aquinas that God exists in you, what attributes of God are embodied in you?

Speaking Rightly of God

In the words of T. S. Eliot, words often "strain, crack, and sometimes break under the burden" of speaking rightly about such mystery.[3] Nonetheless, throughout history, many have found relationship with God so significant to their existence that they literally feel compelled to speak about God. However, no matter how fitting human speech is, it inevitably falls short of the infinite Being of God. As Aquinas explained in *Summa Theologica*, "No name belongs to God in the same sense that it belongs to creatures. . . . Hence, no name is predicated *univocally* of God and creatures."[4] To state this more plainly, the qualities attributed to God do not apply *in the same exact way* to creatures; words applied to God and to creatures are not *univocal*.

Nonetheless, while words applied to God and to creatures do not have exactly the same meaning, neither do they mean something entirely different. To use Aquinas's terms, words are not *equivocal*, "Because if that were so, it follows that from creatures nothing at all could be known or demonstrated about God. . . . Such a view is against . . . what the Apostle says: *The invisible things of God are clearly seen being understood by the things that are made*" (Rom. 1:20).[5] If such words were equivocal, nothing humans think or say could express anything about God or their relationship with God. According to Aquinas, then, "it must be said that these names are said of God and creatures in an analogous sense, that is, according to proportion."[6]

---

2. Robin Ryan, *God and the Mystery of Human Suffering* (Mahwah, NJ: Paulist Press, 2011), 121.

3. T. S. Eliot, "Burnt Norton V," from *Four Quartets: Art of Europe*, available at *www.artofeurope .com/eliot/eli5.htm*.

4. Thomas Aquinas, *Summa Theologica* (*ST*), I. 13, a. 5, 64, online ed. Kevin Knight, trans. Fathers of the English Dominican Province, available at *www.newadvent.org/summa/*.

5. Ibid., emphasis in the original.

6. *ST* 1.13a.5.64.

This statement asserts that attributes applied to God and to creation differ less in kind than in degree or proportion. To reinforce the proportional nature of analogy, Aquinas taught that all attributions about God must go through a threefold process or "way" of purification: the way of affirmation (*via affirmativa*), the way of negation (*via negativa*), and the way of eminence (*via eminentia*). Theologian Elizabeth Johnson explains this three-way process using the attribute of "goodness" in God. Johnson notes that humans "derive a concept of goodness" from experiences of goodness in the world.

> We then *affirm* [the goodness] of God who created all these good things [*via affirmativa*]. But God is infinite, so we need to remove anything that smacks of restriction. Thus, we *negate* the finite way goodness exists in the world [*via negativa*]. . . . But we still think God is good, so we *negate that particular negation* and judge that God is good in a supremely excellent way that surpasses all understanding [*via eminentia*]. According to analogy . . . the theological meaning is this: God is good; but God is not good the way creatures are good; but God is good in a supereminent way as Source of all that is good.[7]

Reflect and Discuss

What names, images, or descriptions of God do you clearly understand as being analogical, that is, not to be understood as literal in meaning? What names or images of God do you take as intended in a more literal sense?

How does this relate to the attributes humans ascribe to God? Simply this: while speech about God is truly appropriate, it remains always contingent and partial. Nonetheless, in the face of human experience of God, it is far more misleading to say nothing about God than to humbly say something, however conditional and inadequate. This proves an important precaution when considering some of the most time-honored attributes that Christianity has applied to God. These too are included in the cautions that apply to all speech about God: "No name belongs to God in the same sense that it belongs to creatures."[8]

---

7. Elizabeth A. Johnson, *Quest for the Living God: Mapping Frontiers in the Theology of God* (New York: Continuum, 2007), 18.

8. *ST* 1.13a.5.64.

Attributes of God

Against the backdrop of this Thomistic understanding of religious language, this chapter examines the classical attributes of God that stem from both revelation and reason. As previously discussed, Christianity derives its understanding of divine attributes based on the revelation of God in the Hebrew and Christian scriptures. However, classical theism also affirms certain divine attributes on the basis of rational and philosophic inquiry into the nature of God. Aquinas, who was both theologian and philosopher, explicitly differentiates these two sources as a "twofold mode of truth."

> There is a twofold mode of truth in what we profess about God. Some truths about God exceed all the ability of human reason. Such is the truth that God is triune. But there are some truths which the natural reason . . . is able to reach. Such are the truth that God exists, that he is one, and the like. In fact, such truths about God have been proved demonstratively by the philosophers, guided by the light of natural reason.[9]

While most theologians would readily acknowledge the relationship between revelation and reason, some disagree about whether the dialogue between them has had positive or negative effects on the Christian message. In their attempt to parse out what have often been termed the "God of Revelation" and "God of the Philosophers,"[10] some have contended that the message of the scriptures was co-opted by Hellenistic philosophy. However, others suggest a far more mutual and complex relationship than this contention implies. In his book *God and the Mystery of Human Suffering*, Robin Ryan notes the multifaceted influence of philosophy on theology:

> In the early Church, Christian theologians attempted to forge a synthesis between the biblical message of revelation and the great philosophical currents of the day. . . . They included Stoicism, various forms of dualist philosophy, and a development of Platonism that, in its Neoplatonist expression, incorporated elements of Aristotelian thought. . . . Moreover, while Christian thinkers appealed to and employed Greek philosophical categories, they did so critically, in the light of the revelation of God in Christ.[11]

---

9. *Summa Contra Gentiles*, 1.3.2.

10. This distinction was used in the 1909 version of the *Catholic Encyclopedia* to distinguish natural theology from revealed theology. See Patrick Toner, "The Nature and Attributes of God," *The Catholic Encyclopedia*, vol. 6 (New York: Robert Appleton Company, 1909), available at *www.new advent.org/cathen/06612a.htm*.

11. Ryan, *God and the Mystery of Human Suffering*, 84.

The Stoics, for example, used the term *Logos* to refer to the divine principle and cause of the world, which permeates all creation. Through the work of first-century Jewish philosopher Philo, however, *Logos* came to represent the Word (*Logos*) of God-made-flesh proclaimed in the Gospel of John.[12] The Platonic notion of Forms or Ideas also influenced Christian theology, especially in the thought of Augustine of Hippo. For Plato, Forms exhibit certain attributes; they are *transcendent, unchanging,* and *unbounded by space or time.* They are *pure,* exemplifying only one property. Forms *cause* all things; they "provide the explanation of why anything is the way it is, and . . . they are the source or origin of the being of all things."[13] Because of the understanding of Forms as the origin of the physical world, some interpreted them as the thoughts of God.[14] However, in Christianity, Plato's theory of Forms eventually transcended that interpretation and affected the way Christian theologians described the attributes of God.

Whereas Plato's focus on the "more real and perfect realm" of Forms provided one path to knowledge of God through reason, Aristotle provided an alternative. According to Aristotle, one acquires knowledge by proceeding inductively through sense experience. This means that one must proceed "from the appearances to their causes,"[15] or from "the things of sense to that which does not fall under sensory perception, the immaterial world."[16] Influenced by Aristotle, Thomas Aquinas used this approach to craft his famous *Quinque Viae,* or "five ways," to demonstrate the existence of God. Often termed "proofs," they are rather five arguments that lead from human experience to the entity "to which everyone gives the name God."[17] Aquinas began each argument with various forms of the phrase "it is certain and evident to our senses" or "we find in nature." He then moved by way of regress or induction to affirm the source of these phenomena in what "everyone understands to be God."[18] In this way, Aquinas not only argued that God exists "from those of His effects which are known to us"[19] but also identified God as first Cause and Intelligent Being "by whom all natural things are directed to their end"—"and this being we call God."[20]

---

12. Marian Hillar, "Philo of Alexandria (c. 20 BCE–40 CE)," *Internet Encyclopedia of Philosophy,* available at *www.iep.utm.edu/philo/.*

13. David Banach, "Plato's Theory of Forms," *St. Anselm College,* available at *www.anselm.edu /homepage/dbanach/platform.htm.*

14. Werner Jaeger, *Early Christianity and Greek Paideia* (Cambridge, MA: Belknap, 1961), 45.

15. Terence Irwin, *Aristotle's First Principles* (New York: Oxford University Press, 1989), 32.

16. Mary Michael Spangler, *Aristotle on Teaching* (Lanham, MD: University Press of America, 1998), 108.

17. *ST* 1.2.3.13.

18. *ST* 1.2.3.13–14.

19. *ST* 1.2.2.12.

20. *ST* 1.2.3.13–14.

Attributes of God in Classical Theism

Christian claims about the nature and attributes of God stretch from the earliest years after Christ. The First Vatican Council, held in 1870, expounded on these attributes at length. While articulated by Catholicism, they nonetheless represent the fundamental beliefs about the attributes of God shared by the majority of Christian denominations.

> The holy Catholic Apostolic Roman Church believes and confesses that there is one true and living God, Creator and Lord of heaven and earth, almighty, eternal, immense, incomprehensible, infinite in intelligence, in will, and in all perfection, who, as being one, sole, absolutely simple and immutable spiritual substance, is to be declared as really and essentially distinct from the world, of supreme beatitude in and from himself, and ineffably exalted above all things which exist, or are conceivable, except himself.[21]

Of these attributes, certain ones prove particularly relevant to the problem of God and suffering, notably the triad of omnipotence, omniscience, and omnibenevolence defended by theodicy, as well as immutability and impassibility, which are seen as logical extensions of those three.[22] The section that follows defines these significant attributes, raises questions about them from revelation and reason, and points out their interdependence in classical theism.

Omnipotence

In its most basic definition, omnipotence refers to the quality of being unlimited or universal in power, authority, or force. Revelation makes a variety of

---

21. Pius IX, "Dogmatic Decrees of the Vatican Council Concerning the Catholic Faith and the Church of Christ," III, cap. I, *De Deo*, available at *www.ccel.org/ccel/schaff/creeds2.v.ii.i.html*.

22. It is interesting to note that only two of these five attributes are mentioned in the Vatican I decree—namely, "almighty" or omnipotent, and "immutable." Other core attributes predicated of God include infinity (God is unlimited in perfection), simplicity (God is a unity, not an assembly of parts, degrees, or distinctions), incorporeality (God is nonphysical), eternity (God exists forever without beginning or end), and omnipresence (God is present to, yet transcends the limits of actual and possible space). See, inter alia, Patrick Toner "The Nature and Attributes of God," *The Catholic Encyclopedia*, available at *www.newadvent.org/cathen/06612a.htm*, and Brian Morley, "Western Concepts of God," *Internet Encyclopedia of Philosophy*, available at *www.iep.utm.edu/god-west/*.

assertions about the omnipotence of God. The book of Job asserts God's infinite power when it acknowledges God can do whatever God wills (Job 42:2). The Gospels testify that "for God all things are possible" (Mark 10:27) and, conversely, that "nothing will be impossible with God" (Luke 1:37). Moreover, this type of power is possessed by God alone (Tob. 13:4), for "there is but one who is wise, greatly to be feared, seated upon his throne" (Sir. 1:8). Even God asks Jeremiah, "Is anything too difficult for me?" (Jer. 32:27).

From the approach of reason, many scholars assert that omnipotence implies the power to bring about *any state of affairs whatsoever, including necessary and impossible states of affairs.* However, it seems that as soon as one defines this quality, one is obligated to qualify it. For example, "Could an omnipotent agent create a stone so massive that that agent could not move it? . . . Could such an agent have the power to create or overturn necessary truths of logic and mathematics? Could an agent of this kind bring about or alter the past?[23] In view of such philosophical questions, some modify the notion of omnipotence to mean "the power to *perform certain tasks*" or "the power to *bring about certain possible states of affairs*"[24] or "the power . . . to effect whatever is not *intrinsically impossible.*"[25]

Reflect and Discuss

How might you answer these philosophical questions regarding the omnipotent nature of God? Are there others you would raise about divine omnipotence?

Two characteristics make an action "intrinsically impossible" according to standards of reason. The first is an action that is out of harmony with the agent's nature or attributes, like a flying elephant or a singing horse; the second is an action that connotes mutually exclusive elements, like a square circle or a round cube. Hence, Aquinas would say that it is intrinsically impossible for God to sin, for "to be able to sin is to be able to fall short in action" and, since God for Aquinas is pure act, to fall short in action is contrary to God's nature."[26] Likewise, it is intrinsically impossible for God to undo a past event, for this implies a contradiction, like saying "that Socrates . . . has sat, and did not sit."[27] To say

---

23. Joshua Hoffman and Gary Rosenkrantz, "Omnipotence," *Stanford Encyclopedia of Philosophy*, ed. Edward N. Zalta, available at *http://plato.stanford.edu/entries/omnipotence/*.

24. Ibid.

25. John McHugh, "Omnipotence," *The Catholic Encyclopedia*, vol. 11 (New York: Robert Appleton Company, 1911), available at *www.newadvent.org/cathen/11251c.htm*, emphasis added.

26. *ST* 1.25.3.138.

27. *ST* 1.25.4.139.

that Socrates sat is to affirm an event that happened; to subsequently say that he did not sit contradicts what actually happened.

Omniscience

Divine omniscience is defined as having "the most perfect knowledge of all things." It includes God's knowledge and comprehension of Godself, as well as of all creation—"Everything, in a word, which to our finite minds signifies perfections and completeness of knowledge."[28] Revelation in the Hebrew Scriptures testifies that divine "understanding is beyond measure" (Ps. 147:5) and that God "searches every mind, and understands every plan and thought" (1 Chron. 28:9). God is "the one whose knowledge is perfect" (Job 37:16), who knows every person before he or she was formed in the womb (Jer. 1:5). The Christian epistles proclaim that "God is greater than our hearts, and . . . knows everything" (1 John 3:20). God knows the hearts of all (Acts 1:24) and searches all things (1 Cor. 2:10); no creature is hidden from God's sight (Heb. 4:13). In the Gospels, Jesus counsels his disciples against undue worry about "what you are to eat and what you are to drink . . . [for] your Father knows that you need [these things]" (Luke 12:29–30, cf. Matt. 6:31–32). Furthermore, Jesus revealed how intimate God's knowledge of each person is, to the extent that "Even the hairs of your head are all counted" (Matt. 10:30; Luke 12:7).

As with omnipotence, reason brings its own insights and provisos to bear on omniscience. One such proviso involves the distinction between knowledge and foreknowledge. Knowledge involves awareness, comprehension, and understanding of events that have already been actualized and belong to present or past existence. Foreknowledge, however, involves awareness, comprehension, and understanding of events that have not yet been actualized and thus belong to an unformed and undisclosed future. For many Christians, belief in divine foreknowledge brings consolation. As one pastor told the members of his church community,

> Therefore, be encouraged today that things are not out of control. . . . The Lord knows your situation, circumstances, and struggles. He is intimately acquainted with your life, moment by moment. He has a purpose and a plan for you. . . . Your ways are fully known to the Lord, and He knows your tomorrow. . . . His plans will unfold at just the right time.[29]

However, two things are at stake in claiming divine foreknowledge: first, the reality of human freedom; and second, the presence of randomness in the cosmos.

In the first case, many theorists accept divine knowledge, but dispute divine *fore*knowledge because "it would be logically incoherent if God did know this

---

28. Toner, "The Nature and Attributes of God: Divine Knowledge," *The Catholic Encyclopedia*, available at *www.newadvent.org/cathen/06612a.htm*. See II.D.1.

29. Mark Hiehle, "God Knows the Future," *At the Center* (Summer 2008), available at *www .atcmag.com/Issues/ID/299/God-Knows-The-Future*.

and human beings were genuinely free."[30] The argument that divine foreknowledge precludes human freedom runs like this: "For any future act you will perform, if some being infallibly believed in the past that the act would occur [i.e., before it happens] . . . you cannot do otherwise than what he believed you would do. And if you cannot do otherwise, you will not perform the act freely."[31] Nonetheless, others defend the compatibility of divine omniscience and human freedom by distinguishing between divine knowledge and foreknowledge based on the classical understanding of the relation of God to time. In this understanding, time is defined as "the numbering of movements by *before* and *after*."[32] In the classical view, God transcends time and has no before or after, no beginning or end. As a result, instead of knowing events successively within time, God knows events within eternity. Rather than knowing human activity in a series of befores and afters, God knows these activities as a simultaneous whole.

Imagine, for example, that all events of history take place within a huge arena or stadium. These events occur one after another with beginning and end because they happen within time. Moreover, these events and actions occur as a result of free human choices and have real human consequences. Now further imagine that God, who transcends time, also transcends this huge arena. Because God is outside the confines of the arena, God can observe all events and actions in an eternal present time, so to speak. God's knowledge of history's events and actions, therefore, is not *fore*knowledge of future things, which would preclude free will, but is *knowledge* of what is eternally present to divine awareness. This preserves cosmic freedom because the acts of created beings are not *fore*known and predetermined in advance, but remain truly free.

Reflect and Discuss

Is this argument concerning knowledge and foreknowledge compelling to you? Does it safeguard human freedom while preserving divine omniscience?

In the second case, certain conditions in the cosmos would seem to limit divine omniscience. These involve the operation of chance in evolutionary creativity as well as the unpredictability of outcomes at the quantum level. In cosmic evolution, life-forms display continuity from one to another because of the

---

30. Arthur Peacocke, *Theology for a Scientific Age* (Minneapolis: Augsburg Fortress, 1993), 122, emphasis in the original.

31. Linda Zabzedski, "Foreknowledge and Free Will," *Stanford Encyclopedia of Philosophy* (Fall 2011 edition), ed. Edward N. Zalta, available at *http://plato.stanford.edu/archives/fall2011/entries/free-will-foreknowledge/*.

32. *ST* 1.10.2.41, emphasis in the original.

natural laws that guide the possibilities of cosmic change. However, life-forms also display discontinuity as unique and unexpected forms continuously emerge. The emergence of these novel and unexpected forms convinced scientists that the cosmos not only responded to lawfulness but also to randomness and chance. Furthermore, research in quantum physics suggests that contingency and unpredictability are ontological features of the cosmos and not simply deficiencies in human knowledge.[33] Therefore, if God is the Creator of the cosmos, it follows that "God has so made the natural order that it is, in principle, impossible even for God . . . to predict the precise, future values of certain variables."[34]

In the light of these arguments, some theorists have sought to redefine omniscience. Scientist-theologian Arthur Peacocke, for example, defined omniscience as "the ability to know all that it is logically possible to know."[35] This definition of divine omniscience excludes knowledge of those things that are not logically coherent as well as foreknowledge of future or quantum events. Oxford professor Keith Ward proposed that omniscience is "the capacity to know everything that becomes actual, whenever it does so."[36] In a somewhat novel manner, physicist-theologian John Polkinghorne suggests that, because of the free creativity that God has bestowed on the cosmos, even God "does not know the unformed future . . . for the future is not yet there to be known." In so doing, Polkinghorne does not rest his proposal on a distinction between knowledge and foreknowledge or on God's relation to time, but on "the logic of love, which requires the freedom of the beloved." As a result, Polkinghorne maintains that the limitation of God's omniscience "is no imperfection in the divine nature" but the natural consequence of the freedom God bestows on creation out of the fullness of divine love.[37]

Reflect and Discuss

Is there an argument concerning God's omniscience that is particularly convincing to you?

---

33. Physicist Werner Heisenberg discovered an "uncertainty relation" between the position and the momentum of a subatomic particle. His experiments demonstrated that one may measure the *position* of a particular subatomic particle *or* the *momentum* of that same subatomic particle, but one cannot *simultaneously* determine both. This led to the conclusion that events at the quantum level are intrinsically unpredictable. See John Jefferson Davis, "Quantum Indeterminacy and the Omniscience of God," *Science and Christian Belief* 9, no. 2 (1997): 129–44.

34. Arthur R. Peacocke, "God's Interaction with the World: The Implications of Deterministic 'Chaos' and of Interconnected and Interdependent Complexity," in *Chaos and Complexity*, ed. Robert J. Russell, Nancey Murphy, and Arthur R. Peacocke (Vatican City State: Vatican Observatory, 1995), 280.

35. Arthur Peacocke, *Paths from Science towards God* (Oxford: Oneworld, 2001), 59.

36. Keith Ward, *Religion and Creation* (Oxford: Clarendon, 1996), 188.

37. John Polkinghorne, *Science and Christian Belief: Reflections of a Bottom-Up Thinker* (London: SPCK, 1994), 81.

Omnibenevolence

Omnibenevolence refers to the state or capacity of being all-loving, infinitely good, and perfectly moral. However, benevolence is not simply synonymous with goodness, but refers to the specific aspect of goodness that "wills the benefit of another."[38] The Scriptures contain specific references to the omnibenevolence of God. Hebrew Scriptures capture this quality in the term *hesed* or steadfast love associated with God's covenant and saving action on behalf of the chosen people. The book of Genesis speaks of the *hesed* shown by God to Abraham (24:11–28) and Joseph (39:21), and Exodus proclaims the *hesed* of God in freeing the Israelites from slavery in Egypt (15:13). The unconditional nature of divine *hesed* is demonstrated clearly in the Davidic covenant when God promises that "when he [the king] commits iniquity, I will punish him . . . but I will not take my steadfast love from him" (2 Sam. 7:14–15). Many psalms acknowledge and praise this steadfast love of God (cf. Ps. 62:12, 63:3, 118:1–4) as better than life and enduring forever. Moreover, God's self-proclaimed identity makes *hesed* explicit: "The Lord, the Lord, a God merciful and gracious, slow to anger, and abounding in steadfast love" (Exod. 34:6). Israel could depend upon the *hesed* of God, therefore, not as their due but as a function of God's free choice to be true to Godself and to the covenant relationship.

In the Christian testament, divine omnibenevolence centers in the person of Jesus Christ as the incarnate love of God and as the way of salvation. In his ministry of teaching, healing, forgiveness, and fellowship, Jesus proclaimed the steadfast love of God and embodied its reality in his actions. Jesus emphasized the unconditional nature of this perfect love: "Love your enemies and pray for those who persecute you, so that you may be children of your Father in heaven; for he makes his sun rise on the evil and on the good, and sends rain on the righteous and on the unrighteous. . . . Be perfect, therefore, as your heavenly Father is perfect" (Matt. 5:43–48). The love of God that Jesus lived and preached reached its apex in the paschal mystery of the cross and resurrection: "God's love was revealed among us in this way: God sent his only Son into the world so that we might live through him. In this is love, not that we loved God but that he loved us and sent his Son to be the atoning sacrifice for our sins" (1 John 4:9–10). Moreover, the Christian Scriptures claim that love is not only what God does but also who God is: "*God is love*, and those who abide in love abide in God, and God abides in them" (1 John 4:16, emphasis added).

The philosophical foundation of divine omnibenevolence is associated with the infinity and perfection of God. Divine infinity refers to the belief that God is "the self-existing, uncreated Being" who "cannot be limited." This line of thought suggests that the "omni-attributes" of God, including omnibenevolence, are essentially an aspect of that infinity: "His omnipotence is but the infinity

---

38. Morley, "Western Concepts of God."

of His power; His omniscience, the infinity of His knowledge. Whatever is known to be a pure . . . perfection must be an attribute of God on account of His infinity."[39] Such a definition has led to the practical conclusion that "God is perfectly good: in all circumstances he acts for the best, intending the best possible outcome."[40]

Despite the apparent logic behind this conclusion, reason also questions the attribute of omnibenevolence when the problem of God and suffering arises. One philosopher frames the problem this way: "Since the very fact of evil implies that God did not prevent it and since his omnipotence and omniscience rule out the usual excuses for allowing it, evil is a direct challenge to God's benevolence."[41] Therefore, while one may be able to reconcile evil with divine benevolence itself, it is clearly more difficult to do so in combination with the attributes of omnipotence and omniscience also ascribed to the Christian God. Christian theism, nonetheless, maintains all three, which often leads to familiar arguments for the coexistence of evil, suffering, and omnibenevolence. Suffering is said to occur "for a greater good" or "as a consequence of free will" or "for a reason God alone knows." These possibilities notwithstanding, some scholars have reconceived the meaning of omnibenevolence, as done with omnipotence and omniscience.

Nonetheless, philosopher Joel Thomas Tierno discusses three alternative views of omnibenevolence. The first suggests that "an omnibenevolent being *never causes any harm*." However, this does not necessarily mean that such a being does any *good*. The second view proposes that "an omnibenevolent being does good *whenever it can*." This represents a higher degree of benevolence since it affirms that, when it acts, an omnibenevolent being actually *does good*, rather than simply *avoiding harm*. Moreover, the phrase "whenever it can" implies that such a being "never passes up an opportunity to do good." Finally, Tierno's third view holds that "an omnibenevolent being *always does* what is best." The highest degree on Tierno's scale claims that an omnibenevolent being not only does *good*, but does the very *best*, and does so at *every opportunity*.[42] God, according to Tierno, is omnibenevolent in this third way and, thus, "is more perfect than a being that only meets either of the other two senses."[43] However, each of these three views sidesteps the issue of omnipotence. Each of Tierno's degrees of benevolence has the proviso of "whenever it can" or "whenever it acts." Hence

---

39. Otto Zimmerman, "Infinity," *The Catholic Encyclopedia*, vol. 8 (New York: Robert Appleton Company, 1910), available at *www.newadvent.org/cathen/08004a.htm*.

40. Hugh J. McCann, "Divine Providence," *Stanford Encyclopedia of Philosophy*, ed. Edward N. Zalta (Winter 2012 edition), available at *http://plato.stanford.edu/archives/win2012/entries/providence -divine*.

41. Arthur Flemming, "Omnibenevolence and Evil," *Ethics* 96 (January 1986): 265.

42. Joel Thomas Tierno, "Omnibenevolence, Omnipotence, and God's Ability to Do Evil," *Sophia* 36 (September-October 1997): 5, emphasis added.

43. Ibid., 6.

none intimates that God *necessarily* acts in any situation; all simply imply that *when* God acts, God does so for the good.

Another approach to understanding divine omnibenevolence focuses on the more literal definition of the word. Many dictionary definitions describe benevolence as a desire, inclination, disposition, or intention to do good, to show kindness, to be generous, or to act charitably. As omnibenevolent in this way, God may desire the good even if God does not bring about the good. This approach has been used as a type of theodicy since it makes no claim that God is able or obligated to do what is good, only that God desires it. Moreover, this definition supports the coexistence of omnipotence, omniscience, and omnibenevolence, since it only requires that God desire what is good, generous, kind, or charitable, without insisting that God actually put that desire into action. Most theists, however, would find such a description of God unsatisfying: why would an omnipotent God who desires the good not actualize it?

Reflect and Discuss

What do you think of these alternative proposals concerning omnibenevolence? Do you see any problems with them? If so, how would you respond critically to them?

Immutability

To attribute immutability to God is to assert "that it is impossible for God to be in any way changeable."[44] The Scriptures often proclaim the unchangeableness of God in comparison with humans. The book of Numbers in the Hebrew Scriptures declares, "God is not a human being, that he should lie, or a mortal, that he should change his mind" (23:19-20). In a similar fashion, the first book of Samuel affirms that "the Glory of Israel [God] will not recant or change his mind; for he is not a mortal" (15:29). Furthermore, in the context of the covenant with Israel, God asserts the immutability of the divine nature in promising, "I the Lord do not change; therefore you, O children of Jacob, have not perished" (Mal. 3:6). The Christian Scriptures maintain this belief in the immutability of God. The second letter to Timothy assures the early Christian that even "if we are faithless, [God] remains faithful—for he cannot deny himself" (2:13). So that "we who have taken refuge [in God] might be strongly encouraged to seize the hope set before us," the letter to the Hebrews points out, "In the same way, when God desired to show even more clearly to the heirs of the promise the unchangeable character of his purpose, he guaranteed it by an

---

44. *ST* 1.9.1.

oath . . . in which it is impossible that God would prove false" (6:17–18). The letter of James reinforces this assurance when it declares, "Every generous act of giving, with every perfect gift, is from above, coming down from the Father of lights, with whom there is no variation or shadow due to change" (1:17).

Nonetheless, other biblical passages seem to indicate that God is truly capable of change. In response to the pleas of Moses on behalf of his people, who had turned to idolatry, "the Lord changed his mind about the disaster that he planned to bring on his people" (Exod. 32:14). Moreover, God did so because Moses appealed to the essential nature of God's relationship with the chosen people:

> Turn from your fierce wrath; change your mind and do not bring disaster on your people. Remember Abraham, Isaac, and Israel, your servants, how you swore to them by your own self, saying to them, "I will multiply your descendants like the stars of heaven, and all this land that I have promised I will give to your descendants, and they shall inherit it forever." (Exod. 32:12–13)

This exchange is reminiscent of the one between Abraham and God over the fate of Sodom and Gomorrah. Seeing their iniquity, God determined to destroy the cities. God's servant Abraham intervened, making his argument on the basis of God's own character.

> Abraham came near and said, "Will you indeed sweep away the righteous with the wicked? Suppose there are fifty righteous within the city; will you then sweep away the place and not forgive it for the fifty righteous who are in it? . . . . Far be that from you! Shall not the Judge of all the earth do what is just?" And the Lord said, "If I find at Sodom fifty righteous in the city, I will forgive the whole place for their sake." (Gen. 18:23–26)

Abraham continued to plead, "Suppose forty. . . . Suppose thirty. . . . Suppose twenty. . . . Suppose ten are found there?" [The Lord] answered, "For the sake of ten I will not destroy it" (Gen. 18:27–32). The Lord was willing to relent because of the divine nature and in response to the pleadings of Abraham.

The appeal of God's favored ones is not the only thing that could inspire a change in God. The prophet Jeremiah contends that a change in the errant behavior of the Israelites might do the same: "Now therefore amend your ways and your doings, and obey the voice of the Lord your God, and the Lord will change his mind about the disaster that he has pronounced against you" (26:13). Similarly, in his prophecy against the people of Nineveh, Jonah asks, "Who knows? God may relent and change his mind; he may turn from his fierce anger, so that we do not perish" (3:9). Moreover, this is just what came to pass: "When God saw what they did, how they turned from their evil ways, God changed his mind about the calamity that he had said he would bring upon them; and he did not do it" (3:10). Some have used scriptural analysis to suggest that words like "change" or "relent" or "repent" do not mean the same when applied to God as to humans. Nonetheless, it is difficult to reconcile the question either way, so the claim of divine immutability on the basis of Scripture remains more than a bit ambiguous.

From the perspective of reason, God's immutability connects to a variety of other divine attributes. Classical theism cites the attribute of divine simplicity to support immutability. As wholly simple, God's being excludes any component parts that could change, evolve, or devolve. Unlike human creatures, for example, God has no changing characteristics or "accidents" in the divine "substance," to use the philosophical terms. Rather, God *is* "the self-existent or infinite being in whom essence and existence are completely identified." God's being is thus essentially simple and, as a result, immutable.[45]

Aquinas links divine immutability to the concept of God as "pure act" (*actus purus*). This description of God derives from God's infinite perfection, which, by definition, is an absolute, devoid of the possibility for increase or decrease. If God is infinitely perfect, then God is fully actualized with no unfulfilled potentiality. This makes it inconceivable to suggest that God would change for the better or the worse.[46] Aquinas also relates immutability to the Aristotelian concept of the Unmoved Mover. In this explanation, Aquinas uses the word "moved" as a synonym for "changed" and thus "mutable." According to Aquinas, "everything which is moved acquires something by its movement, and attains to what it had not attained previously. But since God is *infinite*, comprehending in Himself all the plenitude of *perfection* of all being, He cannot acquire anything new. . . . Hence movement in no way belongs to Him."[47]

In this explanation, Aquinas demonstrates the inextricability of the classical attributes of God, as he entwines immutability with infinity, simplicity, and perfection. Because Aquinas and other classical theists relate these attributes logically to many others, each attribute depends upon the others for legitimacy and support. Hence, a challenge to any one of these attributes in God looms as a potential liability to every theological statement that considers these philosophical and theological attributes unquestionable.

Reflect and Discuss

Having considered the biblical and philosophical evidence concerning God's immutability, where do you stand on the question?

---

45. Toner, "The Nature and Attributes of God."

46. *ST* 1.3.7.

47. *ST* 1.9.1

Impassibility

In its general sense, *impassibility* refers to God's inability to suffer, to experience pain, or to feel creaturely emotion. In a more technical sense, it asserts that God is incapable of being acted upon by an external force. If this is the case, then God cannot feel anger or serenity, sadness or happiness, jealousy or pleasure, grief or consolation, vengeance or compassion. As a result, these emotions cannot motivate God's actions either. This may make sense from the philosophical viewpoint of immutability, but the Bible seems to present a vastly different picture of God.

From the very outset of the Hebrew Scriptures, the book of Genesis speaks of God's distress over the wickedness of humankind: "The Lord saw that the wickedness of humankind was great in the earth. . . . And the Lord was sorry that he had made humankind on the earth, and it grieved him to his heart" (6:5–7). In response to Israel's rebellion after the exodus from Egypt, Moses tells the people that "When the Lord heard your words, he was wrathful and swore: 'Not one of these . . . shall see the good land that I swore to give to your ancestors. . . .' Even with me the Lord was angry on your account, saying, 'You also shall not enter there'" (Deut. 1:34–37). In the laws given by God at the time of the Exodus, God gave the people a prohibition and a consequence: "You shall not wrong or oppress a resident alien. . . . You shall not abuse any widow or orphan. If you do abuse them . . . my wrath will burn, and I will kill you with the sword" (Exod. 22:21–24).

Lest it seem that God experiences only negative feelings, the Scriptures also proclaim tender and loving emotions of God. The Psalms recount the impact that Israel's action had on God: "They sinned still more against him. . . . Therefore, when the Lord heard, he was full of rage. . . . Yet he, being compassionate, forgave their iniquity . . . restrained his anger, and did not stir up all his wrath" (78:17, 21, 38). When Solomon made his prayer for wisdom, "It pleased the Lord that Solomon had asked this" (1 Kings 3:10). When Israel was oppressed and persecuted at the hands of their enemies, the Lord was "moved to pity by their groaning" (Judg. 2:18). Through the prophet Isaiah, God promises, "'With everlasting love I will have compassion on you,' says the Lord, your Redeemer" (Isa. 54:8). Recognizing God's commitment to redeem the chosen people, Isaiah proclaims, "You shall no more be termed Forsaken, and your land shall no more be termed Desolate; . . . for the Lord delights in you. . . . and as the bridegroom rejoices over the bride, so shall your God rejoice over you" (62:4–5). God's words to this effect are echoed by the prophet Jeremiah, who writes, "I will rejoice in doing good to them and I will plant them in this land in faithfulness, with all my heart and with all my soul" (32:41), as well as by the prophet Zephaniah: "The Lord, your God, is in your midst . . . he will rejoice over you with gladness, he will renew you in his love; he will exult over you with loud singing" (3:17). Such passages clearly do not suggest an impassible God!

The New Testament more often associates the emotions of God with those of Jesus. Expressions of emotion by Jesus, however, often do not impact the question of divine impassibility since they are usually associated with his human nature, rather than his divine nature. Nonetheless, if Christ "is the image of the invisible God, the firstborn of all creation" (Col. 1:15), then perhaps Jesus' emotional responses are relevant to this question of impassibility in God. Thus Matthew writes, "When he saw the crowds, [Jesus] had compassion for them, because they were harassed and helpless, like sheep without a shepherd" (9:36). In Jesus' encounter with the man with the withered hand, Mark recounts that Jesus looked at his critics with anger and "was grieved at their hardness of heart" (Mark 3:5). On at least three occasions, Jesus is said to have wept: at the loss of his friend Lazarus (John 11:32–35), over the city of Jerusalem (Luke 19:41), and in prayer and supplication (Heb. 5:7). Jesus also suffered agony in Gethsemane (Luke 22:44) and was greatly disturbed in spirit, groaning at the tomb of Lazarus (John 11:38). Quite clearly on the cross, Jesus suffered not only emotional torment and abandonment but also physical pain, crying out "with a loud voice, 'Eli, Eli, lema sabachthani?'—that is, 'My God, my God, why have you forsaken me?'" (Matt. 27:46).

Do these incidents in the life of Jesus shed any light on the capacity of God to suffer, to weep, or to groan, to experience torment, agony, or grief? One approach to answering this question consists of pondering the belief that Jesus is truly the visible image of the invisible God, the self-revelation and self-expression of God made flesh. If this is so, then his emotions—both positive and negative—may be seen as the visible expression of the emotions of the invisible God. Another approach to this question asks whether these experiences of Jesus can be attributed solely to his *human nature*—which most of classical theism contends—or to his *full personhood*. If ascribed to his *human nature* only, these emotional responses can be set aside in the discussion of the passibility of God. If, on the other hand, they are ascribed to his *personhood* in its fullness as the union of his human and divine natures, then these incidents in the life of Jesus may well shed some light on the passibility of God.

When philosophical reason is brought to bear on the question of divine impassibility, the attribute is understood to logically extend from divine immutability, infinity, and perfection, as demonstrated in this definition:

> Impassibility is that divine attribute whereby God is said not to experience inner emotional changes of state whether enacted freely from within or effected by his relationship to and interaction with human beings and the created order. More specifically, impassibility means that God does not experience suffering and pain, and thus does not have feelings that are analogous to human feelings. Divine impassibility follows upon His immutability, in that, since God is changeless and

unchangeable, his inner emotional state cannot change from joy to sorrow or from delight to suffering.[48]

According to this definition, impassibility is self-evident because of the attribute of immutability.[49] However, others trace impassibility to specific philosophical influences, such as the Greek conception of perfection. Aristotle, for example, understood God as "Self-Thinking Thought, since for Aristotle thinking is the highest expression of being."[50] This led Aristotle to conclude that God "is a substance which is eternal and immovable and separate from sensible things . . . [and thus] is impassive and unalterable."[51] Adding to Aristotle's influence, the Stoic value of *apatheia* ruled out the possibility that a perfect being such as God could be affected by or responsive to external influences. So when this notion of Stoic perfection combined with Aristotle's concept of God as the Self-Thinking Thought or the Unmoved Mover, it resulted in a deity seen as untouched by, unmoved by, and incapable of emotional affect. Rather than being aroused by compassion and covenant, this God was prized for self-sufficiency and invulnerability, for rationality rather than relatedness. Gradually, the dynamic and impassioned God of Israel and of Jesus Christ seems to have transmuted through interaction with Greek philosophy into "the quintessential fulfillment of the Greek ideal of perfection."[52]

Nonetheless, commentators on patristic thought defend the emphasis on divine impassibility as critical to maintaining God's fidelity and constancy. George L. Prestige, a scholar whose work focused on the early Church Fathers, advanced this alternative perspective:

> It is clear that impassibility means not that God is inactive or uninterested . . . from the shelter of metaphysical isolation, but that his will is determined from within instead of being swayed from without. Impassibility . . . [involves] the larger question of self-consistency. God is, in the fullest sense, the same yesterday, today, and forever.[53]

Dutch theologian Franz Jozef van Beeck supports this point of view in his comments on the meaning of *apatheia* in God. Van Beeck holds that "*apatheia* safeguards God's transcendent freedom . . . to communicate the divine Self to the

---

48. Thomas Weinandy, "Impassibility of God," *Encyclopedia.com*, available at *www.encyclopedia.com/article-1G2-3407705591/impassibility-god.html*.

49. Thomas Weinandy, "Does God Suffer?," *First Things* (November 2001), available at *www.firstthings.com/article/2001/11/does-god-suffer*.

50. Ryan, *God and the Mystery of Human Suffering*, 88.

51. Aristotle, *Metaphysics*, 1073a, in Ryan, *God and the Mystery of Human Suffering*, 88.

52. Ryan, *God and the Mystery of Human Suffering*, 88.

53. George L. Prestige, *God in Patristic Thought* (London: SPCK, 1952), 7 and 11.

world in wholly self-initiated love, irrespective of human or cosmic readiness of response."[54] From this variety of views, one can conclude that divine impassibility remains an open question, one explored in later chapters that investigate more contemporary proposals concerning the suffering of God.

Reflect and Discuss

What is at stake if God truly cannot be moved by external influences—by the woes of humans or the travail of nature? If God cannot be moved, why pray?

Case in Point: *Faith and Doubt at Ground Zero*

Many classical theists put considerable thought into maintaining the coexistence of these divine attributes and reconciling any perceived contradictions stemming from evil and suffering in the world. In the end, such efforts frequently lead to the following conclusion: if God is omnipotent, omniscient, omnibenevolent, immutable, and impassible, then there must be a valid reason that such a God would permit or require suffering.

This "Case in Point" draws on transcripts from the documentary *Faith and Doubt at Ground Zero*,[55] which records painfully honest interviews with those who lost loved ones in the September 11, 2001, attack on the World Trade Center in New York, as well as those who experienced the impact of the event. It does this for two purposes: first, to demonstrate the conclusions people come to when trying to reconcile particular beliefs about God in the midst of their suffering; and second, to consider these conclusions and ask, "What does this say about God?" Both purposes are reflected in the following words of an Episcopal priest:

> The face of God for me was one that was strong, secure, consistent, a face that while at times seemed distant, could

---

54. Franz J. van Beeck, "'This Weakness of God's Is Stronger' (1 Cor. 1:25): An Inquiry beyond the Power of Being," *Toronto Journal of Theology* 9, no.1 (1993): 20, 22.

55. Helen Whitney and Ron Rosenbaum, "Faith and Doubt at Ground Zero," *Frontline PBS.org*, available at *www.pbs.org/wgbh/pages/frontline/shows/faith/etc/script.html*. Unless otherwise indicated, all the narratives in this section are drawn from the transcripts of this documentary.

more or less be counted on to be there, who kept things in order—the sun would come up, the sun would go down— who'd provide, could be counted on. After September 11th, the face of God was a blank slate for me. God couldn't be counted on in the way I thought God could be counted on. That's what I felt as I stood on Ground Zero. God seemed absent. And it was frightening because the attributes that I had depended upon had all been stripped away. And I was left with nothing but that thing we call faith. But faith in what? I wasn't so sure.

As this excerpt demonstrates, believers attempt to reconcile their belief in God with the suffering they endure. One way is by ascribing certain reasons for which God would permit or require suffering. In his book *When Bad Things Happen to Good People*, Rabbi Harold Kushner explores several of the reasons most commonly voiced by people of faith in the midst of suffering. The first, according to Kushner, sees misfortunes as a punishment for sins. Based on the assumption that "God is a righteous judge who gives them what they deserve," such reasoning enables people to "maintain an image of God as all-loving, all-powerful and totally in control."[56] Using this rationale, Augustine of Hippo could assert that there is no such thing as innocent suffering because "everything that is called evil is either sin or punishment for sin."[57] It is interesting to note that none of those interviewed after the World Trade Center attack connected the tragedy to punishment for sin.

A second means to reconcile God and suffering according to Kushner embraces "the idea that God has His reasons for making this happen to them, reasons that they are in no position to judge."[58] This response, which works to preserve divine omnipotence, omniscience, and omnibenevolence, appeared in different forms by those affected on 9-11. Some suggested that God had a greater purpose known to

---

56. Harold Kushner, *When Bad Things Happen to Good People* (New York: Avon, 1981), 9.

57. Augustine of Hippo, *De Genesi ad litteram imperfectus liber* 1.3, in *Augustine's Confessions*, ed. William E. Mann (Lanham, MD: Rowman and Littlefield, 2006), 79.

58. Kushner, *When Bad Things Happen*, 14.

God alone or that God allowed this loss to stave off greater suffering for the victim in the future. In the end, it came down to asserting that the suffering was part of the plan or will of a sovereign God. A retired NYC police officer who lost her daughter on 9-11 articulated it with great poignancy:

> I never question why God didn't intervene. . . . I have come to the conclusion that I felt God knew something I didn't know. And maybe he felt that—maybe she was—even though she was here 23 years, that she was suffering a lot more than I knew about. And I felt that God knew best. I always felt that way when he takes someone, that he knows better than we do.

Some who survived the calamity of 9-11 also saw the hand of God in their survival, but it was not always a source of consolation. In one case, two businessmen escaped the building together before its collapse. Each, however, had very a different response to the outcome. In the words of one survivor, God's omnipotence and omniscience are foremost.

> Just like he intervenes in everybody's life, God intervened in my life that day. It—I couldn't predict what he was going to do. I didn't feel like he was intervening at any second, particular second. It just unfolded, and here I am. Clearly, everybody had different experiences. My experience was . . . to get ourselves out of the building. Other people didn't have that same experience. Whatever God's plan is or was and shall be—is, was, and shall be. I can't question it.

The other survivor, however, had a significantly different reaction to the experience. The plan and power of God were not a source of consolation for him.

> So here I am, running, screaming, like everybody else. My Lord upheld this building. Then we were in perfect safety. The building collapsed. And here I am, God-delivered, and I'm angry, angry because all these good people who were there—the firefighters, the cops, the EMS workers—all of

these good people who were left in this building, which I'm
sure they were, that couldn't come down from the 81st or
82nd floor, coming down because of all of this debris, they
perished. So I'm angry.

For some who sought reasons and found no satisfactory ones in the
midst of this tragedy, the impact was shattering to the image of God
they held. One security guard stated,

I really can't see the purpose why all these people had to
die. I can't accept this. Right now, God's not giving me that
comfort. . . . I knew close to 30 people who died at the
World Trade. . . . I miss them dearly. I don't know if I'm
ever going to get over a couple of them. . . . And I had
to come down here to the beachfront to just let loose, and
it was brutal. I let loose at God. I fired all my barrels at him.
It might sound crazy, but I cursed him. I damned him. I think
God could have just ended this all. . . . I didn't have any
love for God the weeks that followed September 11th. It was
really hatred. I can't accept this unless I can have an answer
as to why it all occurred. . . . It was too barbaric, the way
the lives were taken. . . . So I look at him now as a barbar-
ian, and I probably will. And it's a sad situation. . . . I have
a different view and image of him now, and I can't replace it
with the old image.

Reflect and Discuss

How would you assess the possibilities and problems of believing that God has a reason or purpose for suffering and evil,
one often beyond human knowledge or comprehension? What
image of God does this approach inspire?

A third approach understands the experience of suffering as
educative. In this light, events of suffering give clarity, develop character, or foster understanding about the human condition or about
God. They may even be seen as a test of one's faith or fortitude

rather than as a challenge to God's power, knowledge, or love. And the learning that came from 9-11 could be both consoling and disturbing:

> Right after September 11th, a good many individuals that I talked to were reexamining their relationships and taking concrete steps to reconcile relationships that were not reconciled. Some have said to me, "I was so materialistic. I'm trying to be more spiritual," whatever that means. Those are the positive changes, people wanting to mend relationships, become more spiritual. There are other changes that I'm not pleased to see, and some of those changes are in myself—a deepened sense of cynicism, a sense of being more alone than before September 11th.

For some, the educational experience of September came in the form of a test—a test of faith, a test of stamina, a test of spirit. One survivor recognized that 9-11 tested his understanding of faith and religion:

> There is a sense in me, and in many others that I've spoken with, that we're surviving. . . . We don't know what's coming . . . but we know we have to survive, and some have numbed ourselves, hardened ourselves. To be vulnerable is very difficult right now. And to be open to faith takes vulnerability, and some people aren't willing to do that because we've been burned—some literally—by religion.

More often, the test of faith directly concerned one's relationship with God:

> My conversations with God that I used to have, I don't have anymore. I just can't bring myself to—I used to talk quietly to myself or to God and say, "Thank you. . . . for my life. God bless everyone. God bless the children." You know, "Please heal the sick." You know, the usual blessings. And now I can't bring myself to speak to him anymore because I feel so abandoned. But I guess deep down inside, I know he still exists and that I have to forgive and move on. But I'm not ready to do that yet.

Case in Point: *Faith and Doubt at Ground Zero* (continued)

Reflect and Discuss

How would you assess the possibilities and problems of understanding suffering and evil as a means by which God teaches us or tests one's faith? What image of God does this approach inspire?

Rabbi Kushner points out that all of these approaches have one thing in common: "They all assume that God is the cause of our suffering, and they try to understand why God would want us to suffer." He then proposes another approach, one held by others in the chapters that follow: "Maybe God does not cause our suffering."[59] This perspective was reflected by two of those interviewed in *Faith and Doubt at Ground Zero*: one a former firefighter who lost a son who was also a firefighter and the other an Orthodox rabbi. Despite his personal loss and his hope for a different outcome, the firefighter expressed a clear understanding of where he believed God was on September 11 and how God's power and love were manifested:

> At this stage, I haven't questioned him saying—you know, I asked him in the beginning, you know, "If you can give me this one, I'd appreciate it." But it—he had nothing to do with this. There were a lot more people that could have been killed. He was fighting the evil that day, like he does every day. . . . You know, firemen call fire "The Devil." And that day we fought the devil, and we saved a lot of people, you know? But the devil's the devil. You got to—you know, you got to fight the devil. And just—God's always around.

The rabbi's comments, however, focused on an understanding of God as mystery. People sought him out for answers to the 9-11 tragedy. Rather than having the answers or attempting to defend certain attributes of God, the rabbi believes that his "job as a rabbi is to help them live with those questions." The rabbi explains,

---

59. Ibid., 29.

Case in Point: *Faith and Doubt at Ground Zero* (continued)

If God's ways are mysterious, live with the mystery. It's upsetting. It's scary. It's painful. It's deep. And it's interesting. No plan. That's what mystery is. It's all of those things. You want plan? Then tell me about plan. But if you're going to tell me about how the plan saved you, you better also be able to explain how the plan killed them. And the test of that has nothing to do with saying it in your synagogue or your church. The test of that has to do with going and saying it to the person who just buried someone and look in their eyes and tell them God's plan was to blow your loved one apart. Look at them and tell them that God's plan was that their children should go to bed every night for the rest of their lives without a parent. And if you can say that, well, at least you're honest. I don't worship the same God, but that at least has integrity. It's just, it's too easy. That's my problem with the answer. Not that I think they're being inauthentic when people say it or being dishonest, it's just too damn easy. It's easy because it gets God off the hook. And it's easy because it gets their religious beliefs off the hook. And right now, everything is on the hook.

Reflect and Discuss

How would you assess the possibilities and problems of the proposal that God is not the cause of suffering and evil? What image of God does this approach inspire?

For Further Reading

Kushner, Harold. *When Bad Things Happen to Good People.* New York: Avon, 1981.

Tierno, Joel Thomas. "Omnibenevolence, Omnipotence, and God's Ability to Do Evil." *Sophia* 36 (September-October 1997): 1–11.

Weinandy, Thomas. "Does God Suffer?" *First Things* (November 2001). Available at *www.firstthings.com/article/2001/11/does-god-suffer.*

Internet Resources

Evil and Suffering: A Religious Perspective. Films on Demand. Films Media Group, 2011. Available at *http://digital.films.com/PortalPlaylists.aspx?aid =12097&xtid=49822.* (Note: This site requires logging in.)

Whitney, Helen, and Ron Rosenbaum. *Faith and Doubt at Ground Zero. Front-line.* Public Broadcasting Service, 2002. Available at *www.pbs.org/wgbh /pages/frontline/shows/faith/view/* (time: 1:54:03).

CHAPTER 3

God and Suffering in the Christian Scriptures

> Christians make the scandalous claim that one who entered into the uttermost depths of human suffering, who was brutally executed as a criminal, is the savior of humanity. They even confess him to be the Son of God.
>
> —ROBIN RYAN, *GOD AND THE MYSTERY OF HUMAN SUFFERING*

Introduction

The Christian tradition asserts that the life and ministry, death and resurrection of Jesus Christ have irrevocably altered the human relationship with and perception of God. In the words of Robin Ryan, Christianity believes that the "ministry and the destiny of Jesus shine new light on the relationship of God to the human family." Moreover, "This revelation illumines the way Christians think about the presence of God in the midst of suffering and death."[1] As a result, scholars who ponder the theme of God and suffering in the Christian Scriptures seek out how Jesus understood the suffering of people he encountered, his own suffering, and his disciples' suffering for the sake of the gospel.

Nonetheless, because the scripture of most early Christians was the Hebrew Bible, the first believers interpreted the meaning of suffering in the light of that revelation. Therefore, one cannot grasp the meaning of God and suffering in the Christian Scriptures without recognizing that, along with his followers, Jesus was a devout Jew, steeped in the Hebrew Scriptures and schooled in the language, beliefs, and traditions of Jewish culture and religion. He believed in one God, studied the Torah, recited the *Shema*, celebrated the Sabbath and the Passover, sang the psalms, heeded the prophets, preached like a rabbi, and taught his disciples the Great Commandments of the law: "Love the Lord your God with all your heart, and with all your soul, and with all your might" (Deut. 6:5) and

---

1. Robin Ryan, *God and the Mystery of Human Suffering* (Mahwah, NJ: Paulist Press, 2011), 51.

"Love your neighbor as yourself" (Lev. 19:18). The Servant Songs of the prophet Isaiah resonated through his life and teaching:

> Here is my servant, whom I uphold, my chosen, in whom my soul
>   delights;
> I have put my spirit upon him; he will bring forth justice to the nations.
> He will not cry or lift up his voice, or make it heard in the street;
> a bruised reed he will not break, and a dimly burning wick he will not
>   quench . . . .
> I have given you as a covenant to the people, a light to the nations,
> to open the eyes that are blind,
> to bring out the prisoners from the dungeon,
> from the prison those who sit in darkness.
>
> (Isa. 42:1–3, 6–7)

As Isaiah proclaims, the servant's mission is to alleviate the suffering of the people by promoting justice in the nations. As a sign of God's covenantal love for the people (v. 6), the servant is a compassionate presence (v. 3) who liberates people from all that confines them physically and spiritually (v. 7).

This teaching nonetheless contrasts with a key interpretation of God and suffering that permeates the Hebrew Scriptures: the law of retribution. Intimately connected to the covenant between God and the chosen people of Israel, this law is best articulated as the belief that God rewards the righteous for fidelity and punishes the wicked for infidelity. Because of this, any form of suffering signaled the disfavor of God. While it is only one among a number of approaches to the mystery of God and suffering in the Hebrew Scriptures,[2] the law of retribution was prominent and powerful in the minds of many people of Jesus' time. It shaped their understanding of God as well as the meaning of their own and others' suffering.

While God was often seen as the source of Israel's suffering, prophet after prophet also bore witness to the pain and anguish of God in response to the sufferings that befall the chosen people as a result of injustice and infidelity. This divine anguish "is never the wailing sympathy of an uninvolved onlooker, but the genuine pain of one who is directly affected, the suffering of a comrade, who takes upon himself a part of the burden."[3] As Terence Fretheim points out in his book, *The Suffering of God*, the God of Israel suffers *because* of the people's rejection, *with* the people who are suffering, and *for* the people themselves.[4]

---

2. See Daniel J. Harrington, *Why Do We Suffer? A Scriptural Approach to the Human Condition* (Franklin, WI: Sheed and Ward, 2000), 1–86.

3. Erhard Gerstenberger and Wolfgang Schrage, *Suffering*, trans. John E. Steely (Nashville: Abingdon, 1980), 99.

4. Terence Fretheim, *The Suffering of God: An Old Testament Perspective* (Philadelphia: Fortress, 1984), 108, emphasis added.

"By bearing the sins of the people over a period of time, God suffers in some sense on their behalf."[5] Moreover, such divine participation in the suffering of Israel was deemed salvific for them—"he became their savior in all their distress. . . . It was . . . his presence that saved them; in his love and in his pity he redeemed them" (Isa. 63:9).

As a result of belief in both divine retribution and divine suffering, interpreting the God of Israel within the Hebrew Scriptures sometimes produced conflicting perceptions of God that provoked many questions in relation to suffering. One scholar suggests the question that looms largest "is that of God's own character, of who God is, especially in light of who we, in pain, think we want God to be."[6] This question is the backdrop against which the Christian Scriptures engage the mystery of God and suffering. To find the earliest perspectives on God and suffering in Christianity, this chapter plumbs these Scriptures to see how Jesus' life and ministry, death and resurrection illuminate the mystery of God and suffering. It does so in three contexts: suffering and the reign of God, the suffering and death of Jesus, and suffering and discipleship.

Suffering and the Reign of God

The kingdom or the reign of God was the primary focus of Jesus' life and ministry. He proclaimed it in word and deed—in his teachings, his healings and exorcisms, and his table fellowship with those who were sinners, outcast, and marginalized. The term does not refer to a particular territory or community. Rather, it points to "the sovereignty of God . . . in the most concrete possible manner, i.e., to his *activity* in ruling."[7] The notion of the kingdom or reign of God was familiar to Jesus' listeners because it reflected a well-known Hebrew concept: the *malkuth* of heaven. To the Jewish people, it connoted those activities or situations in which God "is revealed as King or sovereign Lord of His people, or of the universe which He created."[8]

The earliest reference in the Scriptures to the *malkuth* of heaven is found in Exodus 15:11–13, in which God's reign is demonstrated in the deliverance of the people of Israel from Egypt: "Who is like you, O Lord, among the gods? Who is like you, majestic in holiness, awesome in splendor, doing wonders? You stretched out your right hand, the earth swallowed them. In your steadfast love you led the people whom you redeemed." God's sovereign activity is later

---

5. Ibid., 140.

6. Jason A. Mahn, "Between Presence and Explanation: Thinking through Suffering with Thomas Long," *Theology Today* 69 (July 2012): 229.

7. Norman Perrin, "The Kingdom of God," in *Rediscovering the Teaching of Jesus* (New York: Harper & Row, 1967), available at *www.religion-online.org/showchapter.asp?title=1564&C=1445*, emphasis in the original.

8. C. H. Dodd, *The Parables of the Kingdom* (New York: Scribner, 1961), 21.

extolled in the psalms (45, 93, 96, 97–99), which speak of both a present reality and a future hope. They reveal that, for the Jewish people, the kingdom of God involved two dimensions.

> First, God is King of His people Israel, and His kingly rule is effective in so far as Israel is obedient to the divine will as revealed in the Torah. . . . In this sense "The Kingdom of God" is a present fact. But in another sense "The Kingdom of God" is something yet to be revealed. God is more than King of Israel; He is King of all the world. But the world does not recognize Him as King. . . . In this sense, "The Kingdom of God" is a hope for the future. . . . When it pleases God to "reveal" or "set up" His kingly rule, then there will be judgment on all the wrong that is in the world, victory over all powers of evil and, for those who have accepted His sovereignty, deliverance and a blessed life in communion with Him.[9]

Whether present or future, Hebrew writings on the reign of God reveal the common underlying idea of divine power becoming effective in human experience. Christians believe that God's power was made effective in a preeminent way through Jesus of Nazareth as he announced the coming of the kingdom of God in his life and ministry.

As Jesus' ministry demonstrated, "What is unmistakable about . . . the coming of the kingdom of God is that it . . . encompasses the fullness of human existence to bring healing and restoration where there is disorder, disease, brokenness, and despair."[10] In other words, the coming of the kingdom represents the reversal of the suffering and evil that afflicts creation and its creatures and signals a drastic change in human status and interaction. For this reason, the inbreaking of the kingdom is often "unexpected, shocking, and topsy-turvy to human sensibilities,"[11] and Jesus spent a good deal of time and effort in explaining and demonstrating it.

Reflect and Discuss

What do you think of when you hear the phrase "the kingdom of God" or "the reign of God"? What might this look like in human history?

---

9. Ibid., 22, 23, 24.

10. J. Mark Beach, "The Kingdom of God: A Brief Exposition of Its Meaning and Implications," *Mid-America Journal of Theology* 23 (2012): 53, 54.

11. Jonathan T. Pennington, "The Kingdom of Heaven in the Gospel of Matthew," *Southern Baptist Journal of Theology* 12 (2008): 47.

Jesus' Self-Understanding in Terms of the Kingdom of God

Jesus first points toward the kingdom of God through his description of his own ministry. In the Gospel of Matthew, when John the Baptist sends his disciples to see if Jesus is "the one to is to come," that is, the awaited Messiah, Jesus answers in words that describe the healing nature of the reign of God: "Go and tell John what you hear and see: the blind receive their sight, the lame walk, the lepers are cleansed, the deaf hear, the dead are raised, and the poor have good news brought to them " (Matt. 11:4–5). Luke's Gospel expands the healing impact of the reign of God by announcing its liberating aspects as well: "The Spirit of the Lord is upon me, because he has anointed me to bring good news to the poor. He has sent me to proclaim release to the captives and recovery of sight to the blind, to let the oppressed go free, to proclaim the year of the Lord's favor" (Luke 4:18–19). In these descriptions, Jesus clearly implies that the coming of the reign of God represents a triumph over suffering, disease, disability, and injustice of every kind. In Jesus' proclamation of the kingdom, God is not the source of suffering, death, and oppression but the source of healing and liberation.

> ### Reflect and Discuss
>
> What do you notice about the way Jesus describes his messianic mission? Is this what we usually associate with those whom we see as liberators in human history?

Jesus' Actions as Signs of the Kingdom of God

Jesus reinforces his self-description through actions that make the reign of God tangible in the lives of those he encountered. The Gospels are full of stories of healings, which became the hallmark of Jesus' reputation. On one occasion, the Gospel of Mark states that "people at once recognized him, and rushed about that whole region and began to bring the sick on mats to wherever they heard he was. And wherever he went, into villages or cities or farms, they laid the sick in the marketplaces, and begged him that they might touch even the fringe of his cloak; and all who touched it were healed" (Mark 6:54–56). The Gospel of Luke points out that "a great crowd of his disciples and a great multitude of people . . . had come to hear him and to be healed of their diseases; and those who were troubled with unclean spirits were cured. And all in the crowd were trying to touch him, for power came out from him and healed all of them" (Luke 6:17–19).

In the Gospel of John, Jesus directly challenges the claim sin was the source of diseases and afflictions. It records an encounter between Jesus and a man born blind: "His disciples asked him, 'Rabbi, who sinned, this man or his parents, that he was born blind?' Jesus answered, 'Neither this man nor his parents sinned; he was born blind so that God's works might be revealed in him'" (John 9:2–3). Not only did Jesus demonstrate God's reign over sickness and demonic possession but also over death itself. The Gospel of Mark tells the following remarkable story about a man named Jairus who came to Jesus, "fell at his feet and begged him repeatedly, 'My little daughter is at the point of death. Come and lay your hands on her, so that she may be made well, and live.' So he went with him." While he was on the way,

> some people came from the leader's house to say, "Your daughter is dead. Why trouble the teacher any further?" But overhearing what they said, Jesus said to the leader of the synagogue, "Do not fear, only believe." . . . When they came to the house of the leader of the synagogue, he saw a commotion, people weeping and wailing loudly. When he had entered, he said to them, "Why do you make a commotion and weep? The child is not dead but sleeping. . . ." He took her by the hand and said to her, "*Talitha cum*," which means, "Little girl, get up!" And immediately the girl got up and began to walk about (she was twelve years of age). At this they were overcome with amazement. (5:22–24, 35–42)

A similar event occurred in the Gospel of John in the raising of Jesus' own friend Lazarus.

> When Jesus arrived, he found that Lazarus had already been in the tomb four days. . . . Then Jesus, again greatly disturbed, came to the tomb. It was a cave, and a stone was lying against it. Jesus said, "Take away the stone." . . . When he had said this, he cried with a loud voice, "Lazarus, come out!" The dead man came out, his hands and feet bound with strips of cloth, and his face wrapped in a cloth. Jesus said to them, "Unbind him, and let him go." (11:17, 38–44, passim)

Remarkable as they are, stories such as these raise a perturbing question. If the reign of God with its healing and liberating power had truly come in the life and ministry of Jesus of Nazareth, why is it that suffering and death continues to afflict the people in his time, in the centuries since that time, and even to this very day? Biblical scholars address this question by pointing out that Jesus spoke of the reign of God as both a present and a future reality, *already* present in the life and ministry of Jesus, but *not yet* established in its fullness.

Reflect and Discuss

If, as Christians believe, Jesus initiated the reign of God with its heal-ing and liberating power, why is it that suffering and death continued to afflict the people in his time, in the centuries since that time, and even to this very day?

The Kingdom of God: Present or Future

The Gospels record a number of sayings that suggest Jesus considered the reign of God already present in his life and ministry. At the beginning of his Galilean ministry in Mark's Gospel, for example, "Jesus came to Galilee, proclaiming the good news of God, and saying, 'The time is fulfilled, and the kingdom of God has come near; repent, and believe in the good news'" (1:15). A similar per-spective surfaces when Jesus is accused of casting out demons by the power of Satan, the prince of demons. Jesus replies to this accusation by speaking of two kingdoms—that of Satan and that of God: "Every kingdom divided against itself is laid waste. . . . If Satan casts out Satan, he is divided against himself; how then will his kingdom stand? . . . But if it is by the Spirit of God that I cast out demons, then the kingdom of God has come to you" (Matt. 12:25–28). Moreover, when asked directly by a group of Pharisees when the kingdom of God was coming, Jesus answered, "The kingdom of God is not coming with things that can be observed; nor will they say, 'Look, here it is!' or 'There it is!' For, in fact, the kingdom of God is among you" (Luke 17:20–21). Thus Jesus declares his healings and exorcisms "to be both manifestations and at least par-tial realizations of God's coming in power to rule his people in the end time."[12] These sayings signal that "the Kingdom of God is a fact of present experi-ence . . . the sovereign power of God has come into effective operation."[13]

On the other hand, Jesus' proclamation of the reign of God also implies a future coming of God. Perhaps the clearest indication of this future com-ing is found in the prayer Jesus himself taught his disciples: "Our Father in heaven, hallowed be your name. *Your kingdom come*" (Matt. 6:9–10; Luke 11:2, emphasis added). In several other places, Jesus indicates that the kingdom comes to its fullness only at "the end of the age" (Matt. 13:49), and in "the age to come" (Mark 10:30). Jesus also speaks in the future tense of those who will enter the kingdom at some time to come. He states that "many will come from east and west and will eat with Abraham and Isaac and Jacob in the kingdom of heaven" (Matt. 8:11; Luke 13:28–29). He also warns of a day of judgment when the

---

12. John Meier, *A Marginal Jew: Rethinking the Historical Jesus*, vol. 2: *Mentor, Message and Mira-cles* (New York: Doubleday, 1994), 450.

13. Dodd, *The Parables of the Kingdom*, 29.

righteous will be ushered in and the wicked will be banished from the kingdom of God. As part of his discourse in Matthew's Gospel, Jesus advises his listeners, "Not everyone who says to me, 'Lord, Lord,' will enter the kingdom of heaven, but only the one who does the will of my Father in heaven" (Matt. 7:21). Finally, at the Last Supper, Jesus tells his disciples, "You are those who have stood by me in my trials; and I confer on you, just as my Father has conferred on me, a kingdom, so that you may eat and drink at my table in my kingdom, and you will sit on thrones judging the twelve tribes of Israel" (Luke 22:28–30). Furthermore, he declares, "I will never again drink of this fruit of the vine from now on until that day when I drink it new with you in my Father's kingdom" (Matt. 26:29).

So what conclusions may be drawn concerning the presence of the kingdom of God as it relates to evil and suffering? From the perspective of those Jews who witnessed Jesus' healings and exorcisms, Jesus' acts of power represented "the restoration of creation that Israel expected with the advent of God's rule."[14] The reign of God was present and active in his words and works, which "Jesus used to reclaim people and the world from the domination of evil. When Jesus healed the sick or resuscitated the dead, he was breaking the satanic power that manifested itself in illness and death."[15]

Nonetheless, while the reign of God with its healing and liberating effects is already present in the life and ministry of Jesus, human experience from the time of Jesus to this very day testifies that the reign of God has not yet come in its fullness. This is clearly evident in Jesus' own speech about the coming of the kingdom of God. In the Gospel of John, Jesus refers to both the "already" and the "not yet" of the kingdom in the same discourse: "Very truly, I tell you, the hour is coming [not yet], and is now here [already], when the dead will hear the voice of the Son of God, and those who hear will live. . . . The hour is coming [not yet] when all who are in their graves [already] will hear his voice and will come out" (John 5:25, 28–29).

Hence, while Jesus' "healings were signs pointing toward the fullness of God's kingdom, where there will be no more suffering. . . . For now, suffering remains part of human existence."[16] Clearly, the Gospels testify that Jesus engaged in a daily struggle against the afflictions, conditions, and authorities that rob human beings of physical, emotional, and psychological well-being. In so doing, Jesus demonstrated God's unequivocal desire that all creation and its creatures flourish into fullness of life. In his life and ministry centered on the reign of God, Jesus "not only pointed . . . to God's future, but in a comprehensive way stood up to the affliction and misery of this world and . . . brought . . . holistic help and salvation."[17]

---

14. Ryan, *God and the Mystery of Human Suffering*, 55.

15. Raymond Brown, *Introduction to New Testament Christology* (New York: Paulist Press, 1994), 64–65.

16. Harrington, *Why Do We Suffer?*, 103.

17. Gerstenberger and Schrage, *Suffering*, 243.

> ### Reflect and Discuss
>
> The ministry of Jesus gives the distinct impression that God's kingdom can come at least partially in human history. How might people of faith advance the coming of God's kingdom in this world?

Suffering and the Death of Jesus

In his discussion of the death of Jesus in relation to the mystery of suffering, author Robin Ryan points out the following: "When believers search for the meaning of human suffering and the presence of God in the midst of the experience of suffering, they inevitably turn to the destiny of this one they call the Christ."[18] However, doing so raises a myriad of questions. Thousands of texts from the greatest thinkers in the Christian tradition have wrestled with these questions. What led to the way of the cross? Was it Jesus' radical life and preaching or was it willed by God as the ultimate price to be paid for salvation? Can the meaning of the cross be understood without the resurrection? Interpretations of Jesus' suffering and death have shaped Christian understandings of the mystery of God and suffering for centuries. In the Christian tradition, particular responses have gained traction while others have slipped into the background. Nonetheless, each interpretation of the suffering and death of Jesus has implications for the way in which believers understand the relationship between God and suffering.

> ### Reflect and Discuss
>
> From your own understanding, answer any one of the questions posed in the paragraph above. What influences your answer?

The Cross as a Result of Jesus' Radical Life and Ministry

The Synoptic Gospels set Jesus' suffering and death in the context of the religious and political rejection of his teaching and actions. In these three Gospels, opposition to Jesus arises quite early in his life. At Jesus' presentation in the Temple in the Gospel of Luke, Simeon warns his mother Mary, "This child is destined for the falling and the rising of many in Israel, and to be a sign that will

---

18. Ryan, *God and the Mystery of Human Suffering*, 57.

be opposed" (Luke 2:34). Jesus fared no better in the early chapters of the Gospel of Matthew. Shortly after Jesus was born,

> wise men from the East came to Jerusalem, asking, "Where is the child who has been born king of the Jews? For we observed his star at its rising, and have come to pay him homage." When King Herod heard this, he was frightened, and all Jerusalem with him. . . . Now after they had left, an angel of the Lord appeared to Joseph in a dream and said, "Get up, take the child and his mother, and flee to Egypt . . . for Herod is about to search for the child, to destroy him." (Matt. 2:1–3, 13)

Of all the Gospel narratives, however, the Gospel of Mark presents the most compressed account of the conspiracies that brewed around Jesus from the outset of his ministry and ultimately resulted in his crucifixion. On one occasion, after pointed exchanges with the Pharisees over the custom of fasting and of work on the Sabbath, Jesus "entered the synagogue, and a man was there who had a withered hand."

> [The Pharisees] watched him to see whether he would cure him on the sabbath, so that they might accuse him. And he said to the man who had the withered hand, "Come forward." Then he said to [the Pharisees], "Is it lawful to do good or to do harm on the sabbath, to save life or to kill?" But they were silent. He looked around at them with anger; he was grieved at their hardness of heart and said to the man, "Stretch out your hand." He stretched it out, and his hand was restored. The Pharisees went out and immediately conspired with the Herodians against him, how to destroy him. (Mark 3:1–6)[19]

This early encounter reveals how Jesus had antagonized both the religious authorities, represented by the Pharisees, and the political authorities, represented by the Herodians. Moreover, that "Jesus suffered . . . throughout his public ministry is clear from Mark's Gospel, which is aptly called 'the Gospel of Suffering.'"[20] After healing the man with the withered hand, Jesus continued to teach, to heal, and to exorcise demons (3:7–12). While this swelled the crowds that followed him, it made his relatives think "He has gone out of his mind" (3:21) and caused the scribes from Jerusalem to state, "He has Beelzebul, and by

---

19. The Pharisees were "a group of influential Jews active in Palestine from 2nd century BCE through 1st century CE; they advocated and adhered to strict observance of the Sabbath rest, purity rituals, tithing, and food restrictions based on the Hebrew Scriptures and on later traditions." The Herodians were "probably a faction that supported the policies and government of the Herodian family, especially during the time of Herod Antipas, ruler over Galilee and Perea during the lifetimes of John the Baptist and of Jesus." See Felix Just, SJ, "Jewish Groups at the Time of Jesus," *Catholic -Resources.org, available at http://catholic-resources.org/Bible/Jewish_Groups.htm.*

20. Harrington, *Why Do We Suffer?*, 115–16.

the ruler of the demons he casts out demons" (3:22).[21] When Jesus returns to his home in Nazareth, he is met with questions that challenge his teachings and his "deeds of power" (6:2): "They said, 'Where did this man get all this? . . . What deeds of power are being done by his hands! Is not this the carpenter, the son of Mary and brother of James and Joses and Judas and Simon, and are not his sisters here with us?' And they took offense at him" (6:2–3).

As the Gospel of Mark unfolds, the opposition toward Jesus from the scribes and Pharisees intensifies and Jesus responds to their opposition with equal intensity: "Isaiah prophesied rightly about you hypocrites, as it is written, 'This people honors me with their lips, but their hearts are far from me . . .' You abandon the commandment of God and hold to human tradition" (7:6–8). Even as astonishment grew among his followers, confrontations with religious authorities dogged him as he made his way toward Jerusalem. On the way, Jesus forewarned his disciples of the fate that awaited him on three separate occasions: "The Son of Man must undergo great suffering, and be rejected by the elders, the chief priests, and the scribes, and be killed, and after three days rise again." (8:31; cf. 9:31, 10:33–34)

His actions in Jerusalem did little to quell the hostility toward him. After Jesus rid the temple of the money changers and sellers who were doing business there, the chief priests and scribes "kept looking for a way to kill him; for they were afraid of him, because the whole crowd was spellbound by his teaching" (11:18). The stage is now clearly set for the passion narrative of Mark 14 and 15. As theologian Daniel Harrington summarizes it,

> Jesus recognizes the suffering that awaits him and struggles to accept it (14:33–35). He is betrayed by Judas and abandoned by the rest of the Twelve. He is arrested, tried, and executed under Pontius Pilate, with the collaboration of the Jerusalem leaders. The crowds, who once showed positive enthusiasm for him (11:1–11), now reject him in favor of Barabbas (15:6–15). He dies a cruel death of crucifixion, with the psalm of the righteous sufferer (Psalm 22; Mark 15:34) on his lips. Only a few women remain at the foot of the cross (15:40–41).[22]

If this were not suffering and abandonment enough, the original composition of the Gospel ends not with a triumphal proclamation of Jesus' resurrection but on this distressing note:

> Mary Magdalene, and Mary the mother of James, and Salome bought spices, so that they might go and anoint him. . . . When they looked up, they saw that the stone, which was very large, had already been rolled

---

21. "Beelzebul" is another name for Satan, the devil, or the chief of evil spirits. This particular title stresses that Beelzebul is the prince of demons.

22. Harrington, *Why Do We Suffer?*, 115.

back. As they entered the tomb, they saw a young man, dressed in a white robe, sitting on the right side; and they were alarmed. . . . They went out and fled from the tomb, for terror and amazement had seized them; and they said nothing to anyone, for they were afraid. (Mark 16:1–5, 8)[23]

The Gospels of Matthew and Luke adhere to the basic schema of Mark's Gospel and present similar dynamics leading to Jesus' suffering and death. Both Gospels reinforce the understanding of Jesus' suffering and death as the outcome of his prophetic ministry and include a piercing denunciation that Jesus leveled at the scribes and Pharisees. According to the Matthean text, Jesus instructs his disciples to "do whatever [the scribes and Pharisees] teach you and follow it," because they are teachers of the law. Nonetheless, Jesus cautions them, "do not do as they do, for they do not practice what they teach" (Matt. 23:2–3). In a scathing manner, Jesus denounces their scandalous and hypocritical practices:

They tie up heavy burdens, hard to bear, and lay them on the shoulders of others; but they themselves are unwilling to lift a finger to move them. . . . They love to have the place of honor at banquets and the best seats in the synagogues, and to be greeted with respect in the marketplaces, and to have people call them rabbi. (23:4–7)

Then Jesus directs his words to the religious leaders themselves:

Woe to you, scribes and Pharisees, hypocrites! For you cross sea and land to make a single convert, and you make the new convert twice as much a child of hell as yourselves. Woe to you, blind guides . . . ! For you . . . have neglected the weightier matters of the law: justice and mercy and faith. . . . Woe to you, scribes and Pharisees, hypocrites! For you clean the outside of the cup and of the plate, but inside they are full of greed and self-indulgence. . . . Woe to you, scribes and Pharisees, hypocrites! For you are like whitewashed tombs, which on the outside look beautiful, but inside they are full of the bones of the dead and of all kinds of filth. So you also on the outside look righteous to others, but inside you are full of hypocrisy and lawlessness. (23:15–28, passim)

In Luke's Gospel, this excoriation extends even to the scholars of the Mosaic law: "Woe to you lawyers! For you have taken away the key of knowledge; you did not enter yourselves, and you hindered those who were entering" (Luke 11:52).

Clearly such denunciations stung their targets to the heart! Luke's Gospel summarizes their response: "The scribes and the Pharisees began to be very

---

23. The Gospel of Mark that is part of the Christian canon has three different endings. This ending is most often attributed to the original author of the Gospel, but its abruptness led some to believe that a longer ending had been lost. There are two additional endings to the Gospel, designated as Mark 16:9–20, found in later manuscripts.

hostile toward him and to cross-examine him about many things, lying in wait for him, to catch him in something he might say" (Luke 11:53–54). Matthew, on the other hand, concludes the passage with a prophetic lament over the entire city of Jerusalem pronounced by Jesus himself:

> Jerusalem, Jerusalem, the city that kills the prophets and stones those who are sent to it! How often have I desired to gather your children together as a hen gathers her brood under her wings, and you were not willing! See, your house is left to you, desolate. For I tell you, you will not see me again until you say, "Blessed is the one who comes in the name of the Lord." (Matt. 23:37–39)

The connection between Jesus' teaching and healing ministry and his suffering and death is plain. In the words of theologian Gerald O'Collins, "A straight line led from his serving ministry to his suffering death."[24] This assertion is reinforced by New Testament scholar John Meier, who stated, "as a person lives, so that person dies."[25]

The Gospel of John, on the other hand, advances a somewhat different perspective on Jesus' suffering and crucifixion. In John's Gospel, "'the lifting up' of Jesus on the cross is really a part of his exaltation to his heavenly Father."[26] The key discourse in this regard begins with Jesus' confrontation with the scribes and Pharisees over a woman caught in adultery:

> The scribes and the Pharisees brought a woman who had been caught in adultery; and making her stand before all of them, they said to him, "Teacher, this woman was caught in the very act of committing adultery. Now in the law Moses commanded us to stone such women. Now what do you say?" They said this to test him, so that they might have some charge to bring against him. (8:3–6)

As the scribes, Pharisees, and others in the crowd continue to challenge Jesus' authenticity, John's Gospel points to the crucifixion as a demonstration of Jesus' truest self: "When you have lifted up the Son of Man, then you will realize that I am he, and that I do nothing on my own, but I speak these things as the Father instructed me" (8:28).

On one occasion of Jesus' preaching in the Temple, the chief priests and the Pharisees sent officers to arrest him (7:32); on another, "The Jews took up stones again to stone him . . . blasphemy," because he, "though only a human being," was "making [himself] God" (10:31, 33). Ultimately, although "many of

---

24. Gerald O'Collins, *Christology: A Biblical, Historical and Systematic Study of Jesus* (Oxford: Oxford University Press, 1995), 76.

25. John Meier, "Jesus," in *The New Jerome Biblical Commentary* (Englewood Cliffs, NJ: Prentice Hall, 1990), 1326.

26. Harrington, *Why Do We Suffer?*, 117.

the Jews . . . believed in him . . . some of them went to the Pharisees and told them what he had done."

> So the chief priests and the Pharisees called a meeting of the council, and said, "What are we to do? This man is performing many signs. If we let him go on like this, everyone will believe in him, and the Romans will come and destroy both our holy place and our nation." But one of them, Caiaphas, who was high priest that year, said to them, "You know nothing at all! You do not understand that it is better for you to have one man die for the people than to have the whole nation destroyed." . . . So from that day on they planned to put him to death. (11:45–50, 53)

The Gospel passages that frame the suffering and death of Jesus reveal an indisputable truth: According to the Gospel witness, the predominant impetus for the suffering and death of Jesus on the cross was his radical, prophetic, and challenging life, teaching, and ministry. Jesus transgressed religious and social boundaries; enacted a religious practice centered on the love of God for those who were victimized and marginalized by physical, psychological, religious, or social constraints; and constituted a new community of disciples whose numbers and fervor threatened religious and political authorities. Moreover, the way he spoke about his relationship with God as Father not only implicitly claimed his equality with God but also called into question the monotheism that was the cornerstone of Jewish belief.

From this perspective, the suffering and death Jesus endured were inescapable outcomes of the antagonism he drew from the religious and political establishments. Moreover, from this viewpoint, his death was not preordained by the will of God; it came to pass through the free will of those who condemned and crucified him. His death was not desired by God, but required by those whose authority and control was threatened by his liberating message. When faced with crucifixion, like the servant of Yahweh in Isaiah, Jesus steadfastly trusted in the faithfulness of God: "The Lord God helps me; therefore I have not been disgraced; therefore I have set my face like flint, and I know that I shall not be put to shame; he who vindicates me is near" (Isa. 50:7). His example calls those who suffer to the same trust in God, confident that God is near, that God is not responsible for their suffering, and that God will bring them through suffering and death to new and abundant life.

Reflect and Discuss

Does the discussion above change your thinking of why Jesus suffered and died? Why or why not?

The Cross as Willed by God

The Gospel passages discussed above seem to present a convincing case for the suffering and death of Jesus as an outcome of his radical fidelity to God and to the kingdom of God he proclaimed in word and deed. How is it then that Christians for two millennia consistently contend that Jesus' death was willed by God as a ransom for the forgiveness of sin? The first letter of John summarizes such thinking: "God's love was revealed among us in this way: God sent his only Son into the world so that we might live through him. In this is love, not that we loved God but that he loved us and sent his Son to be the atoning sacrifice for our sins" (1 John 4:9–10). While there is some evidence to support this claim in the Gospels, the cross as willed by God as reparation for human sin comprises a central theme in the Acts of the Apostles and in the epistles of Paul.

Evidence in the Gospels

The narrative of the agony in the garden provides a focal point in the Gospels for the belief that God willed Jesus' death. Most fully developed in Matthew's Gospel (cf. Mark 14:32–42; Luke 22:39–46), it tells the story of Jesus' struggle with his impending death in the context of prayer to his Father. "Deeply grieved, even to death," Jesus threw himself on the ground and prayed, "My Father, if it is possible, let this cup pass from me; yet not what I want but what you want." A second time, Jesus pleads with his Father, "If this cannot pass unless I drink it, your will be done." After praying a third time in the same words, Jesus rouses the disciples who were with him, saying, "See, the hour is at hand, and the Son of Man is betrayed into the hands of sinners. Get up, let us be going. See, my betrayer is at hand" (Matt. 26:38–46).

Interpretations of this passage suggest that what his Father "wants" and "wills" refers specifically to Jesus' suffering and death. As a result, most commentators conclude that Jesus' "course is fixed by the will of God, and this overrides whatever beliefs or feelings he has about death. For Jesus the issue is . . . submission to the divine will."[27] The use of the term "cup" is telling. In the Hebrew Scriptures, "'cup' is most often used figuratively in texts about suffering, especially suffering God's wrath or judgment."[28]

The suggestion that Jesus suffers God's wrath or judgment raises the other theme of the cross as reparation for human sins. From this viewpoint, Jesus is seen as an agent of atonement, a sacrificial substitute, who takes on the sins of a community or nation to expiate their wrongdoing. Echoes of this notion are found in the Suffering Servant Song of Isaiah 53. Like the servant, Jesus "has borne our infirmities and carried our diseases . . . struck down by God, and afflicted. . . . He

---

27. Dale C. Allison, "Matthew," in *The Oxford Bible Commentary*, ed. John Barton and John Muddiman (Oxford: Oxford University Press, 2001), 880.

28. Ibid.

was wounded for our transgressions, crushed for our iniquities. . . . The Lord has laid on him the iniquity of us all" (Isa. 53:4–6). In the Gospels, Jesus expresses his realization of the sacrificial nature of his death by telling his disciples that he would "give his life a ransom for many" (Matt. 20:28; Mark 10:45). Both Matthew's and Mark's Gospels situate this statement after Jesus' third prediction of his death and resurrection and immediately following what has sometimes been called "the dispute about greatness" (Matt. 20:20–28; Mark 10:35–45).

The dispute involves the request[29] that the sons of Zebedee, James and John, be given places of prominence at Jesus' left and right hands when he comes into his glory. Jesus challenges the brothers, asking if they are able to drink of the cup that he drinks, an allusion once again to his impending suffering and death. When the brothers reply in the affirmative, Jesus goes on to confirm that both brothers will indeed drink of the cup of suffering, but without any assurance that this will lead to the glory that each desires. When word of the brothers' request causes the other disciples to become angry at them, Jesus responds by clarifying for the disciples the meaning of true greatness:

> Whoever wishes to become great among you must be your servant, and whoever wishes to be first among you must be slave of all. For the Son of Man came not to be served but to serve, and to give his life a ransom for many. (Mark 10:43–45; cf. Matt. 20:25–28)

The final half-verse of Jesus' teaching "has given rise to great debate" and is "one of the very few verses in the synoptics where Jesus gives any kind of interpretation of his death."[30] Some contend that this may represent Jesus' own attitude, if the saying is seen against the backdrop of Isaiah 53, the song of the suffering servant.[31] Others state that there is no parallel in the language of the two.[32] Nonetheless, it is clear that this "ransom" will be accomplished by "one who must suffer, but who will then be vindicated."[33] The Last Supper as described in Mark 14:23–24, during which Jesus "took a cup, and . . . said to them, 'This is my blood of the covenant, which is poured out for many'" reinforces this interpretation. However, while this final verse in Mark depicts Jesus' death in sacrificial terms, only Matthew's Gospel includes the saying "for the

---

29. In Mark's Gospel, the request comes from the brothers themselves, while in Matthew it is their mother who makes the request.

30. C. M. Tuckett, "Mark," in *The Oxford Bible Commentary*, 908.

31. Lindsey P. Pherigo, "The Gospel according to Mark," in *The Interpreter's One-Volume Commentary on the Bible*, ed. Charles M. Laymon (Nashville: Abingdon, 1971), 663. Pherigo also notes that the idea of ransom is "contrary to the mainstream thinking of Matthew and Luke-Acts." As a result, "the ransom phrase is omitted in Luke 22:27 . . . and in Matt. 20:28 may be simply a carry-over from Mark."

32. Tuckett, "Mark," 908.

33. Ibid.

forgiveness of sins" (Matt. 26:28). Here, as in John 1:29, Jesus is seen as he "who takes away the sin of the world," implying that Jesus is the suffering servant "crushed for our iniquities . . . the iniquity of us all" (Isa. 53:5, 6).

Evidence in Acts of the Apostles

The Acts of the Apostles focuses more on the spread of the gospel Jesus proclaimed than on the meaning of his suffering and death on the cross. When speakers in the book of Acts like Peter and Stephen speak of Christ cruci-fied, they do so to admonish the obstinacy of their listeners in rejecting Jesus. In his speech in Solomon's Portico, Peter proclaimed, "you rejected the Holy and Righteous One . . . and you killed the Author of life, whom God raised from the dead" (3:14–15). When brought before the Sanhedrin, who asked by what power the disciples had healed, Peter responded, "Let it be known to all of you . . . that this man is standing before you in good health by the name of Jesus Christ of Nazareth, whom you crucified, whom God raised from the dead. This Jesus is 'the stone that was rejected by you, the builders; it has become the cornerstone'" (4:10–11). At the moment that the deacon Stephen staunchly debated with members of the Synagogue of Freedmen (6:9), a debate that would lead to his martyrdom, he placed the death of Jesus within the context of Israel's prophets and enraged his listeners with this accusation:

> You stiff-necked people, uncircumcised in heart and ears, you are for-ever opposing the Holy Spirit, just as your ancestors used to do. Which of the prophets did your ancestors not persecute? They killed those who foretold the coming of the Righteous One, and now you have become his betrayers and murderers. (7:51–53)

There is, however, a passage that presents a startling counterpoint to this line of thought. In Peter's speech after the Pentecost event, he implies a three-fold responsibility for the death of Jesus:

> You that are Israelites, listen to what I have to say: Jesus of Nazareth, a man attested to you by God with deeds of power, wonders, and signs that God did through him among you, as you yourselves know—this man, *handed over to you according to the definite plan and foreknowledge of God*, you crucified and killed by the hands of those outside the law. But God raised him up, having freed him from death, because it was impossible for him to be held in its power. (2:22–24, emphasis added)

The responsibility is first on the Israelites; second, on those who were the agents of Jesus' death; and third, "behind both, the divine plan."[34] This passage surfaces

---

34. Loveday Alexander, "Acts," in *The Oxford Bible Commentary*, ed. John Barton and John Mud-diman (Oxford: Oxford University Press, 2001), 1032.

the mystery of the relationship between the plan of God and the freedom of human beings, as well as the mystery of the relationship between the will of God and human suffering. While the latter mystery emerges only briefly in Acts, Paul develops it as a major theme in his writings.

Evidence in the Epistles of Paul

It is natural to raise questions about the historical reasons for the crucifixion of Christ. However, the Apostle Paul is unconcerned with such "historical causality," for "what dominates the texts that mention the death of Jesus is the stunning news that God is the protagonist."[35] Although Paul is keenly aware of those "who killed both the Lord Jesus and the prophets" (1 Thess. 2:15) and understands that Jesus fully exercised his human freedom in undergoing the suffering of the cross, in both cases, he believes that "the initiative comes in compliance with God's intention."[36] A number of Pauline passages attest to God's initiative in the event of the cross.

In the letter to the Romans, Paul points out that one is not justified through obedience to the law; rather, all who have sinned "are now justified . . . through the redemption that is in Christ Jesus, *whom God put forward as a sacrifice of atonement* by his blood" (3:24–25, emphasis added). Christ did so "*at the right time* . . . for the ungodly" (5:6, emphasis added) according to the will of God "*who did not withhold his own Son, but gave him up for all of us*" (8:32, emphasis added). Though this Son was blameless, God "*made him to be sin who knew no sin*, so that in him we might become the righteousness of God" (2 Cor. 5:21, emphasis added). In all of this, Christ "*became obedient* to the point of death— even death on a cross" (Phil. 2:8, emphasis added); thus Jesus' "dramatic display of selflessness . . . comes in coincidence with the divine purposes, not opposed to or outside them."[37]

Nonetheless, Paul interprets the cross theologically so that it is "possible to see Jesus' action as God's action."[38] In so doing, Paul illuminates that "Behind the drama of the self-giving of Christ is the self-giving love of God."[39] Furthermore, Paul not only gives believers the "Who" behind the tragedy of the cross but also for "Whom"—"for the ungodly" (Rom. 5:6), "for us" (Rom. 5:8), "for our sake" (2 Cor. 5:21)—and "Why"—"for our sins" (1 Cor. 15:3), "for our transgressions and . . . for our justification" (Rom. 4:25), "so . . . the many will be made righteous" (Rom. 5:19). In this way, the story of "the Son of God

---

35. Charles Cousar, *A Theology of the Cross: The Death of Jesus in the Pauline Letters* (Minneapolis: Fortress, 1990), 37. This section on Paul's theology of the cross and resurrection relies heavily and gratefully on this work.

36. Ibid.

37. Ibid.

38. Ibid.

39. Ibid.

'who loved me and gave himself for me'" (Gal. 2:20) becomes the story of one "who did not withhold his own Son, but gave him up for all of us" (Rom. 8:32). Although the greater purposes of God do not mitigate the responsibility of the religious and political leaders who condemned Jesus to death, for Paul, behind the folly of the cross lay the wisdom of God (cf. 1 Cor. 1:18 ff.).

There is a paradox here with which Christians have struggled for centuries: how is it that an all-loving and all-faithful God can intentionally will the suffering and death of the only Son? Paul strongly asserts that God can do so because of the great love God has for the world and the great desire God has for its "righteousness and sanctification and redemption" (1 Cor. 1:30). Rather than a source of shame and foolishness, the suffering and crucified Christ in Pauline theology is "the power of God and the wisdom of God" (1 Cor. 1:24). Human wisdom counted for nothing in the eyes of Paul. Rather, as he stated to the Corinthians, "I did not come proclaiming the mystery of God to you in lofty words or wisdom. For I decided to know nothing among you except Jesus Christ, and him crucified" (1 Cor. 2:1–2).

Reflect and Discuss

Every interpretation of the suffering and death of Jesus implies a particular understanding of God. What image of God stems from Jesus' death as a consequence of his life and ministry? What image of God stems from Jesus' death as willed by God? Explain the difference, if any, between the two images.

The Resurrection

Despite the significant testimony of the Gospels and the compelling arguments of Paul about the historical reasons and the divine purposes behind the cross of Christ, it is only in light of the resurrection that "the disclosive power of the cross comes into play."[40] The resurrection is the context through which the earliest Christians reflected on the life, suffering, and death of Jesus of Nazareth and in which they found its meaning and significance. This does not suggest, however, that all the New Testament writers viewed the resurrection and its relationship to the crucifixion in the same way. In the Acts of the Apostles, for example, the relationship between cross and resurrection is clear; the resurrection is God's vindication of Jesus after the disgrace of the cross: "This man . . . you crucified and killed by the hands of those outside the law. But God raised him up, having

---

40. Gerald O'Collins, *Christology: A Biblical, Historical, and Systematic Study of Jesus* (Oxford: Oxford University Press, 1995), 101.

freed him from death . . . [and] has made him both Lord and Messiah, this Jesus whom you crucified" (Acts 2:23–24, 36; cf. 3:13–15, 10:39–40, 13:28–30). Nonetheless, this pattern is largely absent from the letters of Paul, who focuses on a threefold meaning of the resurrection "as God's saving event, as promise of the future, and as operative in the life of believers."[41]

While the Gospels contain the narratives of the resurrection, the meaning of the resurrection for Christ and the Christian community is found in the letters of Paul. First Corinthians 15, in which Paul responds to the report that some in Corinth "say there is no resurrection of the dead" (15:12), contains the most fully elaborated teaching. Paul begins by reminding the community "that Christ died for our sins in accordance with the scriptures, and that he was buried, and that he was raised on the third day in accordance with the scriptures" (15:3). However, he continues,

> If there is no resurrection of the dead, then Christ has not been raised; and if Christ has not been raised, then our proclamation has been in vain and your faith has been in vain. We are even found to be misrepresenting God, because we testified of God that he raised Christ—whom he did not raise if it is true that the dead are not raised. For if the dead are not raised, then Christ has not been raised. If Christ has not been raised, your faith is futile and you are still in your sins. . . . If for this life only we have hoped in Christ, we are of all people most to be pitied. (1 Cor. 15:13–19)

In this passage, Paul points out that the resurrection is *God's saving event* because it is through the resurrection that God's forgiving act becomes effective in the lives of believers: "The juxtaposition between 'Christ died for our sins' (15:3) and 'if Christ has not been raised, you are still in your sins' (15:17) leaves no doubt about the indispensable role of both the crucifixion and resurrection for salvation."[42] Romans 10:9 reiterates the role of the resurrection for salvation in the form of a confessional statement: "If you confess with your lips that Jesus is Lord and believe in your heart that God raised him from the dead, you will be saved." Based on these and other passages (cf. Rom. 4:24–25, 8:34; 1 Thess. 4:14), "one is left with the profound impression that Jesus' resurrection, alongside the crucifixion, plays a decisive role in the drama of salvation."[43] This has led one biblical scholar to claim that "the cross of Christ is not a real saving act without the resurrection."[44]

---

41. Cousar, *A Theology of the Cross*, 85.

42. Ibid., 87.

43. Ibid., 90.

44. Gerhard Delling, "The Significance of the Resurrection of Jesus for Faith in Jesus Christ," in *The Significance of the Message of the Resurrection for Faith in Jesus Christ*, ed. C. F. D. Moule, trans. R. A. Wilson (Naperville, IL: A. R. Allenson, 1968), 98.

First Corinthians also points to the resurrection as *promise of the future*. In crafting his argument, Paul not only ties the significance of Jesus' resurrection to his crucifixion but also points to its consequences for believers. As Paul asserts, "Christ has been raised from the dead, the first fruits of those who have died. . . . For as all die in Adam, so all will be made alive in Christ" (15:20–22). In Christ's resurrection is the assurance of the future resurrection of the dead for all "who have died in Christ" (15:18). By calling Christ the "first fruits of those who have died," Paul "signifies both something incomplete and yet something hopeful. Christ's resurrection . . . assures the whole. . . . What has happened to Christ has not yet happened but will happen to 'all.'"[45] Christian faith in the resurrection of the body "anchors the promise of God's future"[46] and ultimately gives the suffering and the dying reason for hope.

Finally, Paul teaches that the resurrection must be *operative in the life of believers*. Although Paul closes his letter to the Corinthians with an admonition of how they are to live (15:58), the resurrection and Christian life are more noticeably linked in Paul's letters to the Romans and to the Colossians. Invoking the experience of their baptism, Paul questions the believers in Rome, "Do you not know that all of us who have been baptized into Christ Jesus were baptized into his death?" This being so, "as Christ was raised from the dead by the glory of the Father, so we too might walk in newness of life" (Rom. 6:3–4). In Romans, this newness of life involves rejecting the dominion of sin, impurity, and iniquity (6:12,19). However, in Paul's letter to the Colossians, this newness operative in the lives of believers is described not only in terms of renunciation of vices, but of living out specific virtues as signs of new life in Christ. Having been raised with Christ (Col. 3:1), the Colossians are counseled, "Set your minds on things that are above, not on things that are on earth. . . . seeing that you have stripped off the old self with its practices and have clothed yourselves with the new self, which is being renewed . . . according to the image of its creator" (Col. 3:2, 9–10). Moreover, Paul gives the Colossians a clear picture of what this new self in the image of its creator must look like:

> As God's chosen ones, holy and beloved, clothe yourselves with compassion, kindness, humility, meekness, and patience. Bear with one another and, if anyone has a complaint against another, forgive each other; just as the Lord has forgiven you, so you also must forgive. Above all, clothe yourselves with love, which binds everything together in perfect harmony. And let the peace of Christ rule in your hearts. . . . And be thankful. (Col. 3:12–15)

---

45. Cousar, *A Theology of the Cross*, 86, 87.
46. Ibid., 90.

In the lives of Christians, "the cross and resurrection form an inseparable unity. . . . Faith in the resurrection is really the same thing as faith in
the saving efficacy of the cross."[47] While the testimonies of the Gospels and
Epistles concerning the will and purposes of God in the event of the cross
raise poignant questions about the relationship between God and suffering
in the life of each person, there is no doubt about the will and purposes of
God in the resurrection. Whatever the intentions of God with regard to the
cross, it is clear that, in the resurrection, God acted decisively to overcome and
transform suffering and death into newness of life as a sign of the unconditional faithfulness and love that bring salvation. Because the Christian tradition never presumes one without the other, the connection between cross and
resurrection always looms as a critical issue. Excess emphasis on the cross—
even as "the divine embrace of suffering and defeat"—offers "no more than
continued despair, because God's suffering has no resolution, no redemptive
force." Conversely, excess emphasis on the resurrection inescapably verges on
triumphalism, as "the cries of human pain, rejection, and death exposed in
Jesus' passion are modulated by the exuberance of 'he is risen.'"[48] However, for
those afflicted, "to discover that Jesus has been raised from the dead and is the
'firstfruits' of the entire harvest is to be given a promise. The assurance that
there is something more, even though the 'more' defies description, nevertheless offer[s] hope, a sober and realistic hope."[49]

Reflect and Discuss

One author above claims that "the cross of Christ is not a real saving
act without the resurrection." Would you agree or disagree that this is
the intended biblical message of salvation? Explain your answer.

Suffering and Discipleship

Both the Gospels and the Epistles make clear the cost of discipleship. If the radical life and ministry of Jesus led to his suffering and death, as the Gospels clearly
indicate, then those who followed him as disciples could expect the same. Jesus'
own teachings also indicated that sharing wholeheartedly in his mission and
ministry demanded asceticism, which called for sacrifices and raised conflicts for
the disciple who responded to his call. Whether the ascetical style of discipleship

---

47. Rudolf Bultmann, "New Testament and Mythology," in *Kerygma and Myth: A Theological Debate*, ed. H. W. Bartsch, trans. R. H. Fuller (London: SPCK, 1957), 41.

48. Cousar, *A Theology of the Cross*, 83.

49. Ibid., 91–92.

that Jesus preached to his first-century followers is applicable to Christians today has long been subject to debate. Regardless of the answer to that debate, it is clear those who have dedicated their lives to Christian discipleship throughout the centuries have often found themselves at odds with their surrounding culture, not unlike the early Christians in the age of the Roman Empire.

Suffering and Discipleship in the Gospels

Shortly after the first prediction of his passion in the Gospel of Mark, Jesus presents this challenge to his disciples: "If any want to become my followers, let them deny themselves and take up their cross and follow me. For those who want to save their life will lose it, and those who lose their life for my sake, and for the sake of the gospel, will save it" (8:34–35; cf. Matt. 10:38–39, 16:24–27; John 12:25). Luke's Gospel embellishes this statement by describing this as a "daily" task of the disciple (Luke 9:23). Moreover, the Gospel writer also demands a total renunciation of family ties: "Whoever comes to me and does not hate father and mother, wife and children, brothers and sisters, yes, and even life itself, cannot be my disciple" (Luke 14:26). The reason for this was made clear earlier in the Gospel when Jesus bluntly describes the goal of his mission:

> Do you think that I have come to bring peace to the earth? No, I tell you, but rather division! From now on five in one household will be divided, three against two and two against three; they will be divided: father against son and son against father, mother against daughter and daughter against mother, mother-in-law against her daughter-in-law and daughter-in-law against mother-in-law. (Luke 12:51–53; cf. Matt. 10:34–35)

In addition, the disciples were to practice an ascetic lifestyle when sent out to preach the word of God and to heal the sick and exorcize demons. When Jesus sent out the seventy-two on mission, he instructed, "Cure the sick, raise the dead, cleanse the lepers, cast out demons. You received without payment; give without payment. Take no gold, or silver, or copper in your belts, no bag for your journey, or two tunics, or sandals, or a staff; for laborers deserve their food" (Matt. 10:8–10). Moreover, he cautioned them that they would not necessarily receive a warm reception!

> See, I am sending you out like sheep into the midst of wolves; so be wise as serpents and innocent as doves. Beware of them, for they will hand you over to councils and flog you in their synagogues; and you will be dragged before governors and kings because of me, as a testimony to them and the Gentiles. . . . Brother will betray brother to death, and a father his child, and children will rise against parents and

have them put to death; and you will be hated by all because of my name. . . . When they persecute you in one town, flee to the next; for truly I tell you, you will not have gone through all the towns of Israel before the Son of Man comes. (Matt. 10:16–23)

Sayings such as these highlight the complete commitment necessary to be a disciple of Jesus. According to one commentator, "Discipleship may be a response to grace . . . but it makes demands which mean that it should not be entered upon lightly. . . . Disciples are to 'carry the cross' in a manner of life which reflects that of Jesus and in a discipleship that goes with him all the way to Jerusalem."[50] In the Lukan Gospel, this manner of life requires renunciation of possessions: "So therefore, none of you can become my disciple if you do not give up all your possessions" (Luke 14:33). This is a point reinforced throughout that Gospel. On one occasion, for example,

A certain ruler asked him, "Good Teacher, what must I do to inherit eternal life?" Jesus said to him . . . "You know the commandments: 'You shall not commit adultery; You shall not murder; You shall not steal; You shall not bear false witness; Honor your father and mother.'" He replied, "I have kept all these since my youth." When Jesus heard this, he said to him, "There is still one thing lacking. Sell all that you own and distribute the money to the poor, and you will have treasure in heaven; then come, follow me." (Luke 18:18–22)

This he could not do, and he went away sad. Although the demand to renounce wealth and possessions ran counter to the Jewish understanding of riches as a sign of divine favor, Jesus assures his disciples that these and other renunciations do not go unrewarded: "Truly I tell you, there is no one who has left house or wife or brothers or parents or children, for the sake of the kingdom of God, who will not get back very much more in this age, and in the age to come eternal life" (Luke 18:29–30; cf. Matt. 19:28–29, Mark 10:29–30).

Reflect and Discuss

Does it seem to you that Christians today are called to the same asceticism Jesus demanded of his disciples? Can they expect the same reception to their teaching and preaching? Give an example to support your answer.

---

50. Eric Franklin, "Luke," in *The Oxford Bible Commentary*, ed. John Barton and John Muddiman (Oxford: Oxford University Press, 2001), 946.

Suffering and Discipleship in the Epistles

The suffering of the disciple foretold in the Gospels is actualized and described in the writings of Paul. However, Paul identifies the suffering of the disciple with the suffering of Christ. As he writes in the letter to the Corinthians,

> We are afflicted in every way, but not crushed; perplexed, but not driven to despair; persecuted, but not forsaken; struck down, but not destroyed; always carrying in the body the death of Jesus, so that the life of Jesus may also be made visible in our bodies. For, while we live, we are always being given up to death for Jesus' sake, so that the life of Jesus may be made visible in our mortal flesh. (2 Cor. 4:8–11)

Despite his forthright language, Paul does not glorify his suffering; the persecution suffered by the disciple is unjust, just as the death of Christ was unjust. Rather he invests it with a twofold meaning. "First, suffering allows for identification with Jesus, and, ultimately, resurrection with Jesus. . . . Secondly, Paul's suffering mirrors Jesus' suffering and hence makes Jesus' life visible to the world."[51] Paul not only suffers his own afflictions, but those of the churches where he has sown the seed of the gospel. He identifies with the sufferings of Christ and with those of the community: "And, besides other things, I am under daily pressure because of my anxiety for all the churches. Who is weak, and I am not weak? Who is made to stumble, and I am not indignant?" (2 Cor. 11:28–29). Paul also says that "a thorn was given me in the flesh, a messenger of Satan to torment me" (2 Cor. 12:7). Some commentators interpret this thorn as a physical ailment that Paul understands as Satan's ongoing influence in the world; others argue that it refers to an opponent of Paul or of the church. Although Paul continually sought to be rid of this thorn, in it he found the power of Christ.

> Three times I appealed to the Lord about this, that it would leave me, but he said to me, "My grace is sufficient for you, for power is made perfect in weakness." So, I will boast all the more gladly of my weaknesses, so that the power of Christ may dwell in me. Therefore I am content with weaknesses, insults, hardships, persecutions, and calamities for the sake of Christ; for whenever I am weak, then I am strong. (2 Cor. 12:8–10)

Once again, there is a great paradox in Paul's interpretation of his suffering. He finds strength in weakness, wisdom in folly, glory in affliction, freedom in imprisonment, gain in loss, life in death—resurrection in the cross. Moreover, he encouraged the early Christians to adopt a similar interpretation: "We are children of God, and if children, then heirs, heirs of God and joint heirs with Christ—if, in fact, we suffer with him so that we may also be glorified with him"

---

51. Margaret Macdonald, "2 Corinthians," in *The Oxford Bible Commentary*, ed. John Barton and John Muddiman (Oxford: Oxford University Press, 2001), 1139.

(Rom. 8:16–17). Clearly, the letters of Paul put an extraordinary emphasis on suffering to attain glory, an emphasis wholly in keeping with his vision of Christian discipleship.

> For Paul, the paradigm of Christian existence, of Christian reality, is the cross. . . . One's faithfulness to the crucified messiah is measured, not in gifts of power or wisdom, but in degrees of sacrifice and suffering. . . . God's locus in this world is disclosed in the cross. . . . Therefore, Paul can boast in his sufferings, in the very absence of earthly rescue, in the knowledge that he travels in the footsteps of the crucified messiah.

Many of the other New Testament Epistles include Pauline themes, most notably the Letter to the Hebrews and the First Letter of Peter. Both of them discuss suffering and glory, as well as other themes about God's relation to suffering explored in this text: suffering as a test of faith, as a means of perfection, and as a form of discipline.

The Letter to the Hebrews was addressed to a Christian community worn down by hostility, abuse, and even the demands of the Christian life.[52] Early on, the author draws the link from suffering to perfection and glory: "We do see Jesus . . . now crowned with glory and honor because of the suffering of death. . . . It was fitting that God . . . , in bringing many children to glory, should make the pioneer of their salvation perfect through sufferings" (Heb. 2:9–10). This verse makes clear that Jesus' "exaltation took place 'because of the suffering of death.'"[53] Moreover, Jesus was "tested by what he suffered, [and so] he is able to help those who are being tested" (2:18). This testing resulted in compassion and mercy and in reverent submission and obedience to God's will (5:7–8). Hebrews also speaks of suffering as a discipline from God who "is treating you as children; for what child is there whom a parent does not discipline?" (12:7). This verse makes the connection between God and suffering so clear that one commentator observed, "Such advice could then be construed as a principle of theodicy: suffering was meant for human education."[54] Moreover, this letter echoes a theme of Paul's that Christians become children of God through suffering with Christ (Rom. 8:17): "If you do not have that discipline in which all children share, then you are illegitimate and not his children" (Heb. 12:8). The message is clear: "suffering is particularly required for those who share the status of the Son."[55]

---

52. The authorship of Hebrews has long been disputed. While some references suggest Pauline authorship, overall evidence for this is scant and thus the author remains unknown.

53. Harold Attridge, "Hebrews," in *The Oxford Bible Commentary*, ed. John Barton and John Muddiman (Oxford: Oxford University Press, 2001), 1239.

54. Ibid., 1253.

55. Ibid.

Reflect and Discuss

The Letter to the Hebrews raises again the notion of suffering as a test, as discipline, and as a means to perfection. What is your thinking on these perspectives at this point in the book or course?

Like Hebrews, 1 Peter was crafted to encourage Christians experiencing personal and economic loss because of their conversion. The author of 1 Peter reminds the community that this is to be expected as disciples of Jesus. "Beloved, do not be surprised at the fiery ordeal that is taking place among you to test you. . . . But rejoice insofar as you are sharing Christ's sufferings, so that you may also be glad and shout for joy when his glory is revealed" (1 Pet. 4:12–13). Within the familiar themes of suffering as a path to glory and as a test of faith, however, commentators note a significant development: "The language of 'sharing Christ's suffering' represents an intensification of association with Christ that goes beyond that of imitation."[56] The letter of Peter seems to suggest that "believers participate in the reality of Christ and share in his redemptive work of bringing the world to glorify God."[57] At one point, in fact, the author of 1 Peter is quite explicit about it: "If you endure when you do right and suffer for it, you have God's approval. For to this you have been called, because Christ also suffered for you, leaving you an example, so that you should follow in his steps" (1 Pet. 2:20–21). The letter to the Colossians strikes a similar note: "I am now rejoicing in my sufferings for your sake, and in my flesh I am completing what is lacking in Christ's afflictions for the sake of his body, that is, the church" (1:24; cf. 2 Cor. 4:10–11). While 1 Peter hovers between imitation and identification, these words from Colossians carry no suggestion of imitation. The sufferings being endured are those of Christ because the ones who bear them are members of the body of Christ (the church) and reveal God's grace through their afflictions as Christ did.

Reflect and Discuss

Is a Christian required to undergo suffering to imitate Jesus? Why or why not? Support your answer.

---

56. Patricia McDonald, "The View of Suffering Held by the Author of 1 Peter," in *The Bible on Suffering: Social and Political Implications*, ed. Anthony J. Tanbasco (New York: Paulist, 2001), 177.

57. Ryan, *God and the Mystery of Human Suffering*, 71.

Case in Point: Romero

While the question of whether or not Christians are required to suffer and give their lives for Christ and for their faith remains open for intellectual discussion, the reality is that countless Christians have endured persecution, imprisonment, and suffering in the name of Christ because of their radical commitment to his way of life and teaching. Those who have made the supreme sacrifice of their lives for their religious faith come from every major religious tradition and are designated as *martyrs*. The term *martyr* itself actually means "witness," meaning one who gives testimony or witness to their religious belief. However, over time the title became synonymous with those who suffered unto death. The early Christian community applied the title of martyr first to Jesus himself because of his death on the cross.[58] In the centuries since and even to this day, numerous named and unnamed persons who have made the ultimate sacrifice in their imitation of Christ have had the name *martyr* bestowed on them.

This "Case in Point" examines a twentieth-century martyr whose life parallels that of Jesus in striking ways. Like Jesus, his words and actions on behalf of the poor and disenfranchised enraged both religious and political authorities. Like Jesus, he suffered a martyr's death for his radical commitment to the Gospel and to the poor and persecuted people of his community. Nonetheless, like Jesus, he believed in the resurrection not only for himself but also for the people whose cause he championed. His name was Óscar Arnulfo Romero y Galdámez (August 15, 1917–March 24, 1980), but his people referred to him as *Monseñor*.

Óscar Romero was a Roman Catholic priest who served the people of El Salvador for thirty-five years, first as a parish priest, then as bishop to the diocese of Santiago, and finally as archbishop of San Salvador in 1977. He came to the position of archbishop during a time of dramatic change in the Catholic Church in Latin America. In 1967, the Latin American Bishops met in Medellín, Colombia, to deliberate about how to implement the reforms of the Second Vatican Council in Latin America. They "resolved to abandon the hierarchy's traditional role as defender of the status quo and to side, instead, with the continent's poor in their struggle for social justice," a decision that created

---

58. Frances M. Young, *The Use of Sacrificial Ideas in Greek Christian Writers from the New Testament to John Chrysostom* (Eugene, OR: Wipf & Stock, 2004), 107.

Case in Point: Romero (continued)

division among both clergy and faithful.[59] Bishop Romero himself was skeptical of such reforms, which solidified his reputation as a religious conservative.

Romero also came to prominence during a bitterly violent time in El Salvador.

> Executions, kidnappings and torture of the rural poor and activists who opposed El Salvador's right-wing government had become commonplace in the late 1970s. The slogan "Be a Patriot—Kill a Priest" was written on many walls, indicating that the Catholic priests who had sided with the country's poor were also a target for the death squads that terrorised the country.[60]

Despite this milieu, Romero "held a strong belief that those in power were basically good."[61] His appointment as Archbishop of San Salvador, therefore, disappointed those clergy committed to social reform. By all accounts, "he was predictable, an orthodox, pious bookworm who was known to criticize the progressive liberation clergy so aligned with the impoverished farmers seeking land reform."[62] In contrast, Romero's appointment was welcomed by those in the Salvadoran government and society who expected him to go about "reining in the priests who . . . were stirring up the peasantry."[63] However, those who knew him realized that "Romero had been gradually awakening to the desperate poverty of the peasants and to the unjust wages and working conditions they had to accept."[64] This gradual awakening came to an abrupt climax when his dear friend Jesuit Father Rutilio

---

59. United Nations, "Archbishop Óscar Arnulfo Romero," available at *www.un.org/en/events/right totruthday/romero.shtml*.

60. Julian Miglierini, "El Salvador Marks Archbishop Óscar Romero's Murder," BBC News, available at *http://news.bbc.co.uk/2/mobile/americas/8580840.stm*.

61. "If they kill me, I will rise again in the Salvadoran people," *Salvanet: A Publication of Christians for Peace in El Salvador*, March/April 2000, available at *http://crispaz.org/salvanetarchive/0200.pdf*.

62. Renny Golden, "Oscar Romero: Bishop of the Poor," *USCatholic.org*, available at *http://www.uscatholic.org/culture/social-justice/2009/02/oscar-romero-bishop-poor*.

63. James R. Brockman, "Pastoral Teaching of Archbishop Oscar Romero," *Spirituality Today* 40 (June 1988), available at *http://opcentral.org/resources/2015/01/19/james-r-brockman-pastoral-teaching -of-archbishop-oscar-romero/*.

64. Ibid.

Grande, who had defended the rights of the *campesinos* to organize farm cooperatives, was ambushed and assassinated with two of his parishioners. At Grande's funeral, Archbishop Romero preached,

> What is the role of the Church in this universal struggle for liberation from so much misery? The Pope reminds us that . . . the voices of the world's bishops, represented especially by those bishops from the Third World, cried out on behalf of those who remain on the margin of life [*sic*] famine, chronic disease, illiteracy, poverty. The Church cannot absent itself from this struggle for liberation, but its presence in this struggle must lift up and respect human dignity.[65]

The death of Father Grande marked a turning point in the life and ministry of Archbishop Romero, who later stated, "When I looked at Rutilio lying there dead I thought 'if they have killed him for doing what he did, then I too have to walk the same path.'"[66] Deeply shaken by this event, Romero became a tireless and forthright advocate for the marginalized and oppressed.

Despite his efforts, the violence continued. Romero condemned the violence and persecution that would take the lives of more than seventy-five thousand Salvadorans in a civil war. He expressed his anguish to Pope John Paul II and made clear that support of the El Salvadoran government "legitimized terror and assassinations."[67] Romero wrote to then President Jimmy Carter, warning that continued American military aid to El Salvador would "undoubtedly sharpen the injustice and the repression inflicted on the organized people, whose struggle has often been for their most basic human rights."[68] His appeals were ignored. In a final effort to stop the bloodshed, on March 23, 1980, he delivered an impassioned speech that challenged the army of peasants who were terrorizing their fellow citizens.

65. Óscar Romero, "Homily for the Funeral Mass of Father Rutilio Grande," *Romerotrust.org*, March 14, 1977, available at *http://romerotrust.org.uk/index.php?nuc=homilies&id=7*.

66. Kurt Struckmeyer, "Óscar Romero," *FollowingJesus.org*, *http://followingjesus.org/companions/romero.html*.

67. Struckmeyer, "Óscar Romero."

68. Ibid.

Case in Point: Romero *(continued)*

Brothers, you came from our own people. You are killing your own brothers. Any human order to kill must be subordinate to the law of God, which says, "Thou shalt not kill." No soldier is obliged to obey an order contrary to the law of God. . . . It is high time you obeyed your consciences rather than sinful orders. The church cannot remain silent before such an abomination. . . . In the name of God, in the name of this suffering people whose cry rises to heaven more loudly each day, I implore you, I beg you, I order you: stop the repression.[69]

The next day, March 24, 1980, in the midst of saying Mass in the small chapel near the cathedral, Archbishop Óscar Romero was shot and killed by an assassin. More than 250,000 mourners attended his funeral, during which a bomb exploded and shots were fired into the crowd, killing thirty to fifty people. As his personal assistant said, "Archbishop Romero was the most loved person and the most hated person in this country. And as Jesus, he was crucified."[70] Nonetheless, Archbishop Romero, as Jesus himself, knew the meaning of the cross he would bear.

Those who surrender to the service of the poor through love of Christ, will live like the grains of wheat that dies. It only apparently dies. . . . The harvest comes because of the grain that dies. We know that every effort to improve society, above all when society is so full of injustice and sin, is an effort that God blesses; that God wants; that God demands of us.[71]

Like Jesus, Romero was aware that his impending death would not bring an end to the oppression of the people for whom he gave his life; however, he declared, "You can tell the people that if they succeed in killing me . . . [a] bishop will die, but the church of God, which is the people, will never perish."[72] Finally, while *Monseñor*

---

69. Michael Campbell-Johnston, SJ, "Romero: 'the voice of those who had no voice,'" *Thinking Faith*, March 23, 2011, available at *www.thinkingfaith.org/articles/20110323_1.htm*.

70. Miglierini, "El Salvador Marks Archbishop Oscar Romero's Murder."

71. Óscar Romero, "Catholic Social Justice Quotes," *Justicebeforecharity.org*, available at *http:// justicebeforecharity.org/quotes.php*.

72. Ibid.

Case in Point: Romero *(continued)*

Romero realized the inevitability of his death, he held firm to the certainty of resurrection. "I have frequently been threatened with death," Romero admitted. "I must say that, as a Christian, I do not believe in death but in the resurrection. If they kill me, I shall rise again in the Salvadoran people."[73]

On May 24, 2015, Óscar Arnulfo Romero y Galdámez was beatified by decree of Pope Francis in these words: "In virtue of our apostolic authority, we hereby grant the faculty whereby the venerable Servant of God Óscar Arnulfo Romero y Galdámez, bishop and martyr, pastor after the heart of Christ, evangelizer and father of the poor, heroic witness of the Reign of God, a reign of justice, fraternity and peace, from this day forward is to be called blessed and his feast day observed the 24 of March, in which he was born into heaven."[74]

Reflect and Discuss

Archbishop Romero's life mirrors that of Jesus in many ways. Choose some aspect of Romero's life discussed above and compare and contrast it with what you may know of the life of Jesus. How are they similar; how do they differ?

For Further Reading

Cousar, Charles. *A Theology of the Cross: The Death of Jesus in the Pauline Letters.* Minneapolis: Fortress, 1990.

Dodd, C. H. *Parables of the Kingdom.* New York. Scribner's Sons, 1961.

Harrington, Daniel. *Why Do We Suffer? A Scriptural Approach to the Human Condition.* Lanham, MD: Rowman & Littlefield, 2000.

---

73. Robert Ellsberg, "Oscar Arnulfo Romero (1917–1980) Archbishop and Martyr of San Salvador," in *All Saints: Daily Reflections on Saints, Prophets, and Witnesses for Our Time* (New York: Crossroad, 1997).

74. Roger Cardinal Mahony, "Beatification of Archbishop Oscar Romero," *Angelus*, May 28, 2015, available at *www.angelusnews.com/news/world/beatification-of-archbishop-oscar-romero-8041/#.VejV8pfJEQ2.* Beatification is a first step toward canonization or sainthood.

Romero, Óscar. *Voice of the Voiceless: The Four Pastoral Letters and Other State-ments.* Translated by Michael J. Walsh. New York: Orbis, 1985.

Films

Monseñor: The Last Journey of Oscar Romero. Directed by Ana Carrigan and Juliet Weber. South Bend, IN: University of Notre Dame, 2012.

Romero. Directed by John Duigan. Pacific Palisades, CA: Paulist, 1989.

CHAPTER 4

Classical Theologies of Suffering and Evil

I sought whence evil comes and there was no solution.
—AUGUSTINE OF HIPPO, CONFESSIONS

Introduction

Having examined the Christian biblical responses to the question of God and suffering, this exploration turns now to Christian theological traditions for their insights. This chapter investigates the proposals of theologians from the classical tradition. The writings from this tradition have significantly shaped and influenced many theologians and other people of faith who engage the mystery of God and suffering.

Three important considerations shape theologies of suffering and evil in the classical tradition. First, in this tradition, theologians offer proposals that are presumed to be applicable to all persons and situations. This universal approach was motivated by the ideal that truth is best established through abstract concepts rather than by the concrete situations and experiences of people in their daily lives. Second, theologians in the classical tradition represent Christian theology from a Western worldview. The Western worldview refers to cultural and philosophical perspectives that developed in the Western Hemisphere, including most of Europe, ancient Northern and Southern Africa, and the Americas. Third, theologians in the classical tradition accept and defend classical theism's understanding of God as omnipotent, omniscient, and omnibenevolent.[1] Their commitment to a classical concept of God exerts great influence on the conclusions they draw concerning the relationship between God and suffering.

For the most part, the insights of classical theologians concern the sources and nature of evil rather than the suffering that results from it. Nonetheless, their

---

1. See chapter 2.

writings clarify the relationship between God and evil in the world and apply to the question of God and suffering. This chapter considers the insights of three theologians whose work has had significant impact and enduring authority in classical theism: Augustine of Hippo, Irenaeus of Lyons, and Thomas Aquinas. From these theologians, two main themes emerge in the discussion of God, evil, and suffering: evil as privation of the good, espoused by Augustine and Aquinas, and evil as the grasping for divinity, espoused by Irenaeus.

Augustine and Aquinas: Evil as the Privation of Good

The theme of evil as the privation of good begins with the proposition "*Omnis natura bonum est*" —"every actual entity [something that exists in itself] is good." It is based on the divine refrain that echoes throughout the first chapter of the book of Genesis at the end of each day of creation: "And God saw that it was good. . . . And God saw that it was good. . . . And God saw that it was very good." It is also grounded in the understanding that a God who is all-powerful, all-knowing, all-loving, and all-good would not explicitly create that which is essentially evil or existentially opposed to the good of God's very nature. As conceived by the philosopher Plotinus, the Supreme Being is in essence the good, and thus evil cannot be part of this Ultimate Reality.

> If such be the Nature of Beings and of That which transcends all realms of being, Evil cannot have any place among Beings or in the Beyond-Being; these are good. There remains, only, if Evil exists at all, that it be situate in the realm of non-Being, that it be some mode, as it were, of the Non-Being, that it have its seat in something in touch with Non-Being or to a certain degree communicate in Non-Being . . . something of an utterly different order from Authentic-Being.[2]

Plotinus is making the point that, if Being Itself is in essence good, then evil cannot possess Being because evil is the opposite of good. As a result, Plotinus claims that evil has no actual being; it is a "no-thing," rather than a "something." Because of this, evil is defined as the *absence* of something, *not* the presence of something; evil is the absence or privation of the good (*privatio boni*). The principal theologians who advanced this perspective on evil were Augustine of Hippo and Thomas Aquinas. This section looks at each theologian in turn.

---

2. Plotinus, *Enneads*, trans. Stephen MacKenna (London: Faber and Faber, 1962), 1.8.3.

> ### Reflect and Discuss
>
> How do you respond to the idea that evil is simply the absence of the good, a "no-thing" rather than a something? Does this definition fit all kinds of evil in the world? What might be some exceptions?

Augustine of Hippo

The notion of evil as the privation of good was first formulated by Augustine, theologian and Bishop of Hippo in the Roman province of Africa, on the cusp of the fourth and fifth centuries. Augustine defended this idea through two principles. The first is the principle of plenitude and the second is the aesthetic principle.

The Principle of Plenitude

Augustine adapted the principle of plenitude from the philosophy of Plato and Plotinus. This principle proposes "that a universe containing every possible variety of creatures, from the highest to the lowest, is a richer and far better universe than would be one consisting solely of the highest kind of created being."[3] Augustine associates this principle with the conception of the universe as a Great Chain of Being that couples the Platonic principle of plenitude with the Aristotelian concept of the Ladder of Life:

> The Great Chain of Being derived from two Greek ideas. The first originated . . . in Plato and is called The Principle of Plenitude. It states that, since God is perfectly good, therefore He must have created all possible forms of life. Any deficiency in the created variety of the world would be a mark of incompleteness, something incompatible with God. The second idea derives from Aristotle and is called The Ladder of Life. It states that all forms of natural phenomena exist on a hierarchical scale, rising very gradually by degrees from the lowest forms of inanimate matter (like rocks), to simple forms of life, to more complex forms, to human beings, and (as later developed by Christian thinkers) to the planets and fixed stars through all the various orders of angels right up to God Himself. Thus, every natural and spiritual phenomenon has its own particular ranked place in the comprehensive scheme of God's creation.[4]

---

3. John Hick, *Evil and the God of Love* (San Francisco: Harper & Row, 1978), 72.

4. Ian Johnston, "Ancient and Modern Science: Some Observations," Vancouver Island College, BC, Can., available at *http://records.viu.ca/~johnstoi/essays/histsci.htm*.

According to Plotinus, the universe came about because of the supreme Plenitude or abundance of Being, "flowing out in the creation of the reality . . . in the order of possible beings . . . down to matter" at the very border of nonbeing.[5] This Plenitude flowed out into a hierarchy of forms in creation, each having its specific place and role in the scheme of reality. In the 1936 work, *The Great Chain of Being: A Study of the History of an Idea*,[6] A. O. Lovejoy argued that the notion of the Great Chain of Being was critical in the formation of the ancient and medieval worldview.

> This view saw all of creation existing within a universal hierarchy that stretched from God (or immutable perfection) at its highest point to inanimate matter at its lowest. . . . Indeed, each link in the Great Chain of Being represented a distinct category of living creature or form of matter. Those creatures or things higher on the Chain possessed greater intellect, movement, and ability than those placed below. Thus each being in the Chain possessed all of the attributes of what was below plus an additional, superior attribute:
>
> God: existence + life + will + reason + immortality + omniscient, omnipotent
>
> Angels: existence + life + will + reason + immortality
>
> Humanity: existence + life + will + reason
>
> Animals: existence + life + will
>
> Plants: existence + life
>
> Matter: existence
>
> Nothingness
>
> As a result of this hierarchy, creatures and things on a higher level were believed to possess more authority over lower ones.[7]

Hence, the closer a form of being is to Being Itself, the more it possesses the characteristics of the fullness of Being and, thus, the good. Conversely, the further away a form of being is from fullness of Being in the Great Chain, the less it possesses the characteristics of Being Itself and, thus, good itself.

Aside from its theological ramifications, this viewpoint had moral, political, and scientific implications as well. First, "it is a moral imperative for each creature to know its place in the Chain of Being and fulfill its own function without

---

5. Hick, *Evil and the God of Love*, 73–74.

6. A. O. Lovejoy, *The Great Chain of Being: The History of an Idea* (Cambridge, MA; Harvard University Press, 1936).

7. Steve Snyder, "The Great Chain of Being," *Faculty.Grandview.edu*, available at *http://faculty .grandview.edu/ssnyder/121/121%20great%20chain.htm*.

trying to rise above its station or lowering itself by behavior proper to the lower links in the chain." Furthermore, belief in the Chain of Being "meant that a monarchical government was ordained by God and inherent in the very structure of the universe. Rebellion against a king was not challenging the state; it was an act against the will of God itself." Finally, this concept endorsed "the idea that the physical world reflected God's ordained will . . . with a God-centered and God-controlled worldview . . . [and] an Earth-centered model for planetary rotation."[8] Hence, failing to fulfill one's function, to know one's place, to obey the monarch, or to affirm a geocentric universe was tantamount to causing evil or committing sin.

Reflect and Discuss

Can you think of any implications of the Great Chain of Being that still affect our worldview or influence morality, politics, or science? Give some examples.

Regrettably, the belief that evil derived from the failure of creatures to abide by a God-ordained plan for creation prompted Plotinus to equate evil with matter. He did so because he saw the "soul's entanglement in its material body as the cause of the evil which it both suffers and commits." According to Plotinus, "This bodily Kind, in that it partakes of Matter, is an evil thing."[9] Hence, although Plotinus makes the claim that evil is a *privation*, that is, a *no-thing*, his philosophy gives evil an existence by equating it with matter and making it a *something*. Augustine, however, remedied this deficiency by adapting the principle of plenitude to God's creative purposes.

In Augustine's theology of creation, in creative omnipotence, "God acts deliberately to form a universe, and He acts in terms of the principle of plenitude, considering it better to produce all possible forms of being, lower as well as higher, poorer as well as richer, all contributing to a wonderful harmony and beauty in His sight."[10] According to Augustine, God "has created 'out of nothing' all that exists other than Himself. And as the work of omnipotent Goodness, unhindered by any recalcitrant material or opposing influence, the created world is wholly good."[11] Yet Augustine saw that some things seemed deprived of full goodness. He likened this privation of good to the condition of blindness,

---

8. Ibid.

9. *Enneads*, 1.8.4.

10. Hick, *Evil and the God of Love*, 76–77.

11. Ibid., 44.

which is not the presence of something, but the absence of something—namely, sight. The same may be said of cold as the absence of warmth or darkness as the absence of light. However, in Augustine, "there is no Neo-Platonic descent from the goodness of pure being to evil matter"; there are only levels of lesser good.[12] All that God created is good, but to a greater or lesser extent according to the attributes a creature possesses in the Great Chain of Being.

> ### Reflect and Discuss
>
> What makes something a greater or lesser good? Give some quali-ties that differentiate one from another. Are there any qualities that change whether something is greater or lesser? Why?

Nevertheless, the nature of creation is not like the unchangeable nature of its all-good Creator. It is mutable and corruptible. In other words, it is liable to being deprived of its good. As Augustine understood it,

> evil is not any kind of positive substance or force, but consists rather in the going wrong of God's creation in some of its parts . . . every-thing, other than God . . . is made 'out of nothing' and is accordingly mutable and capable of being corrupted; and evil is precisely this cor-ruption of a mutable good.[13]

If evil derives from the corruption of a mutable good, how does this mutation take place? For Augustine, the corruption of the good can only occur through the exercise of free will. Only those creatures with free will can decide not to ful-fill their function or to know their place in the universe; only a creature with free will can refuse to obey the monarch or choose to affirm a geocentric universe. Only those creatures with free will can misuse their freedom, choosing the lesser good over the supreme good who is God. For Augustine, while it is possible that animals at certain levels of the Chain of Being may possess the attribute of free will, only in humans and in angels is that free will combined with reason. Only these creatures have the ability to freely reject the good. Thus, Augustine con-tends, human beings continue to bring evil into the world by turning away from God in imitation of their forebears, Adam and Eve, whose "original sin" affects all humankind.

> In the beginning man's nature was created without any fault and without any sin. . . . Indeed, all the good qualities which it has in its

---

12. Ibid.

13. Ibid., 46.

organization, life, senses, and understanding, it possesses from the most high God, its creator and shaper. On the other hand, the defect which darkens and weakens all those natural goods so that there is need for illumination and healing, is not derived from its blameless maker but from that original sin that was committed through free will.[14]

Reflect and Discuss

Is free will a sufficient proposal for the presence of evil in the world? Can you think of exceptions? What makes them evil?

The corruptibility of good that stems from original sin, however, was not limited to humans. Augustine points out that this original sin also corrupts the goodness of creation. Because of the sin of Adam and Eve, humans live in a "fallen world," rather than in a paradise ordered toward God. Thus even so-called natural evils, such as disease or death, can be traced to the original sin for which all creation justly deserves punishment. This line of thought is reflected in this remark from a person diagnosed with cancer:

> I don't know why I have cancer, and I don't much care. It is what it is—a plain and indisputable fact. Yet even while staring into a mirror darkly, great and stunning truths begin to take shape. Our maladies define a central feature of our existence: We are fallen. We are imperfect. Our bodies give out.[15]

His thinking on original sin leads to a rather controversial point in Augustine's discussion of God and suffering: his conviction that all suffering is essentially punishment.[16] According to Augustine, humanity's "criminal nature draws upon itself the most righteous punishment" as a result of original sin.[17] Thus, "whatever is called evil is either sin or the punishment for sin."[18] There is no such thing as "innocent suffering" for Augustine; all who suffer do so justifiably

---

14. Augustine, *On Nature and Grace* 3.3, in *Four Anti-Pelagian Writings*, trans. J. A. Mourant and William J. Collinge (Washington, DC: Catholic University of America Press, 1992).

15. Tony Snow, "Cancer's Unexpected Blessings," *Christianity Today*, July 20, 2007, available at *www.christianitytoday.com/ct/2007/July/25.30.html*.

16. An excellent resource for Augustine on evil and suffering is the doctoral dissertation of Samantha E. Thompson, "Augustine on Suffering and Order: Punishment in Context," University of Toronto, 2010, available at *https://tspace.library.utoronto.ca/bitstream/1807/26246/1/Thompson_Samantha_E_201011_PhD_thesis.pdf*.

17. Augustine, *Nature and Grace* 3.3.

18. Augustine, *De Genesi ad litteram imperfectus liber* 1.3, in *On Genesis*, trans. Edmund Hill (Hyde Park, NY: New City Press, 2002).

because of their sinful nature. The sources of this suffering as punishment are twofold: the first source is suffering inflicted by oneself and the second is suffering inflicted by God.

Reflect and Discuss

Do you agree with Augustine that there is no such thing as innocent suffering? Defend your point of view.

In the first case, suffering as punishment is self-inflicted: a natural consequence of the sin committed. To explain this, Augustine compares sin as withdrawing oneself from God to abstaining from food.

> Since we have already learned that sin is not a substance, let us consider . . . whether abstinence from food is also not a substance. One indeed abstains from a substance, since food is a substance. But to abstain from food is not a substance—yet nevertheless if we abstain entirely from food . . . our body languishes and is so impaired by frailty of health, so exhausted of strength, and so weakened and broken with weariness . . . it would barely be capable of being restored to the use of that food, by abstaining from which it became corrupted. Likewise, sin is not a substance, but God is a substance, the supreme substance, the only true nourishment of the rational creature. Listen to how the Psalmist expresses what it is to withdraw from him by disobedience and to be unable through weakness even to receive that in which one truly ought to rejoice: "My heart is withered and beaten like grass, because I forgot to eat my bread."[19]

Although God is the one rejected by the sinner, the suffering as punishment comes from the very act of "abstaining" or withdrawing from God, who is necessary for human well-being. In separating oneself from God, which is the very meaning of sin, the sinner "deprives himself of a good, and this is bad for him."[20]

However, in the second case, suffering is a punishment that is God-inflicted. In one of Augustine's most blatant statements on the subject, he writes, "We use the word 'evil' in two senses: first when we say that someone has done evil; and second, when we say that someone has suffered evil. . . . God is the cause of the second kind of evil, but in no way causes the first kind."[21] Here

---

19. Augustine, *Nature and Grace* 20.

20. Augustine, *De Genesi ad litteram imperfectus liber* 8.14.31.

21. Augustine, *Free Will* 1.1, in *Augustine: Earlier Writings*, trans. J. H. S. Burleigh (Philadelphia: Westminster, 1953).

Augustine makes clear that God is never the source of the evil, which results from human free choice; God never inspires a person to do wrong. However, if a person suffers as a result of sin, that evil could be construed as the penalty the sinner pays to God for disobeying God's commands: "No one overcomes the laws of the almighty Creator. Every soul must pay back what it owes. . . . If it does not pay its debt by doing justice, it will pay its debt by suffering misery."[22] As one Christian minister phrased it,

> Why do bad things happen to good people? The Christian answer is that there are no good people! None of us deserves the life that we have, which is a gratuitous gift from God. . . . Even though most people would not blame God for natural disasters that create suffering, it can be argued that even these sources of pain are all a result of judgment in a general sense for man's sin. No one [who] gets caught up in suffering due to natural events is truly innocent.[23]

This begs the question: how can God, who is all-good, be the source of suffering and evil? Augustine sets forth his argument in this way:

> Let no one think of this account that the punishment of the wicked, which is obviously evil to those who are punished, does not come from [God]. . . . "Death and life are from the Lord God" (Sir 11:14). Therefore the punishment of the wicked, which is from God, is indeed evil to the wicked; but it is counted among the good works of God.[24]

How can this be the case? According to Augustine, punishment of the wicked ranks among the good works of God because it springs both from God's justice and from God's desire to discipline and correct the sinner—to bring about good effects in the sinner even if it initially affects the sinner badly. However, this divine punishment also extends to creation. In *The City of God*, Augustine writes that sin has "moved God's indignation so that he has filled the world with dire calamities" and "caused God to give effect to his threats and warnings by bringing destruction on the earth."[25] Some commentators submit that Augustine's logic seems to fail at this point, arguing that much of creation does not possess the capacity to sin against God since, aside from angels and

---

22. Ibid., 3.15.

23. "How Can a Good God Allow Evil and Suffering?" *Faithfacts.org*, available at *www.faithfacts .org/search-for-truth/questions-of-christians/how-can-god-allow-evil-and-suffering*.

24. Augustine, *Retractations* 1.26, in *Retractations*, trans. Mary I. Bogan (Washington, DC: Catholic University of America Press, 1968).

25. Augustine, *The City of God* 1.9, in *St. Augustine: Concerning the City of God against the Pagans*, trans. Henry Bettenson (Harmondsworth: Penguin, 1972).

humans, creation possesses neither will nor reason. Nonetheless, a more central question surfaces: If such wickedness and affliction, dire calamities and destruction, fill creation and its creatures, how can the world be considered good? Or, in the words of Leibniz in an earlier chapter, how can this be "the best of all possible worlds"? This question links Augustine's principle of plenitude to his aesthetic principle.

Reflect and Discuss

Consider the idea that all suffering is either self-inflicted because of sin or God-inflicted because of punishment. Does this idea seem to neglect any type of suffering that might be from another source?

The Aesthetic Principle

Augustine's second foundation for evil as the privation of good derives from his aesthetic principle. This principle defends the existence of evil as part of the harmonious perfection of creation. For Augustine, the "aesthetic theme is his affirmation of faith that, seen in its totality from the ultimate standpoint of the Creator, the universe is wholly good; for even the evil within it is made to contribute to the complex perfection of the whole."[26] The "Case in Point" in chapter 1, from *The Brothers Karamazov*, noted this principle, and Gottfried Leibniz also used it in his assertion that God is responsible for creating both the positive and negative aspects of creation. According to Leibniz, it would be ludicrous, "to say that the painter is the author of all that is real [in a painting] . . . without however being the author of what is lacking. . . . In effect, what is lacking is nothing more than . . . an infallible consequence of that which is positive, without any need for a distinct author."[27] In Plotinus's analogy of the artist and the work of art, much of what the human person considers to be evil is "the appropriate tint to every spot" in the immense canvas of the universe. "We are like people ignorant of painting," Plotinus claimed, "who complain that the colors are not beautiful everywhere in the picture."[28] Augustine agreed: "All have their offices and limits laid down so as to assure the beauty of the universe. . . . The black color in a picture may very well be beautiful if you take the picture as a whole."[29]

---

26. Hick, *Evil and the God of Love*, 82.

27. Leibniz, *Sämtliche Schriften und Briefe*, 6.3.151, in Michael Murray and Sean Greenberg, "Leibniz on the Problem of Evil," *Stanford Encyclopedia of Philosophy* (Spring 2013 edition), available at *http://plato.stanford.edu/archives/spr2013/entries/leibniz-evil/*.

28. *Enneads* 3.2.11.

29. Augustine, *True Religion* 40.76, in Hick, *Evil and the God of Love*, 83.

Does this mean that evil is a necessity in the cosmos? As one commentator notes,

> It is difficult to reconcile the comparison here of evil to touches of black in a painting with Augustine's view of evil as a privation of good. Privative evil seems more akin to a hole or gash in the painting; the colour black, by contrast, is needed by the artist to complete the image he intends. Is Augustine therefore saying that evil is *needed* to make a beautiful and perfectly ordered world?[30]

In answer to such a question, Augustine points out that evil only appears to be evil when it is seen in isolation; when the universe is taken as a whole, what seems to be evil is actually good because it is a necessary aspect of a good universe.

> We, for our part, can see no beauty in this pattern to give us delight; and the reason is that we are involved in a section of it, under our condition of mortality, and so we cannot observe the whole design, in which these small parts, which are to us so disagreeable, fit together to make a scheme of ordered beauty.[31]

In this, the aesthetic principle coincides with the principle of plenitude. Not only is the universe finely ordered in a chain of being from God to insentient matter; it also requires both positive and negative aspects that fit together "to make a scheme of ordered beauty." In other words, to be as wonderful as possible—to be "the best of all possible worlds"—the universe must contain a diversity of creatures, each considered good in the *grand scheme* of things, but which may be considered less than good or beneficial in and of themselves.

Translated into terms of good and evil, Augustine is suggesting that "the universe even with its sinister aspects is perfect."[32] As the contrast of dark and light hues in a painting adds to its beauty and accents its features, as darkness enables one to better appreciate sunlight, and as sickness makes one more appreciative of health, everything in the universe has its proper place and function in the ultimate order of creation. In Augustine's words, "In the universe, even that which is called evil, when it is regulated and put in its own place, only enhances our admiration of the good; we enjoy and value the good more when we compare it with the evil."[33] As a novelist once wrote,

> Maybe it's the very presence of one thing—light or darkness—that necessitates the existence of the other. Think about it, people couldn't

---

30. Thompson, "Augustine on Suffering and Order: Punishment in Context," 152.

31. Augustine, *City of God* 12.4.

32. Augustine, *Soliloquies* 1.1.2, in Hick, *Evil and the God of Love*, 84.

33. Augustine, *Enchiridion* 11, in *The Enchiridion on Faith, Hope and Love*, trans. Henry Paolucci (Chicago: Regnery Gateway, 1961).

become legendary heroes if they hadn't first done something to combat darkness. Doctors could do no good if there weren't diseases for them to treat.[34]

Augustine's aesthetic view, therefore, gives him a particular approach to natural evil—those events like earthquakes and hurricanes that have harmful effects on human life and property. For Augustine, what does not disturb the order of the created universe is not seen as a manifestation of evil. Hence, earthquakes, hurricanes, tornadoes, and tsunamis should not be considered evils since they result from the natural order of creation. However, Augustine's approach to moral evil through the aesthetic principle differs markedly from this approach to natural evil. Rather than being grounded in the operation of the natural order, the root of moral evil is human sin. Human sin is not part of the natural order of human nature as created by God. It is a deviation that occurs through the misuse of free will, which Augustine teaches is naturally ordered toward the ultimate good that is God. Evil, therefore, cannot be attributed to the creative action or intention of God. Neither can it be viewed as innate or essential to God's good creation. Evil, for Augustine, has no other source but in human sin itself or in the justifiable punishment for that sin by God.

Reflect and Discuss

Is evil a necessary aspect of creation? Could we recognize what is good in the absence of evil?

Thomas Aquinas

The thirteenth-century writings of Thomas Aquinas, Dominican theologian and philosopher, echo many of the themes of Augustine concerning the question of God, suffering, and evil. Keenly aware of the problem that evil and suffering pose to belief in God, Aquinas raises the subject of evil at the very outset of his magisterial work *Summa Theologica* (*ST*) in the question that deals with "whether God exists."[35] The first objection to the existence of God raises two opposing arguments. The first contends that if God is infinite, then any other being would necessarily be destroyed because there would be no place for it to exist. The existence of the world and its creatures proves that argument wrong.

---

34. Jessica Shirvington, "Quotes about Good and Evil," *Goodreads.com*, available at *www.goodreads.com/quotes/tag/good-and-evil*.

35. The *Summa Theologica* is organized as a series of articles on different theological questions. Each article has a standard format: (1) a series of objections that anticipate the final conclusion, (2) a short counterstatement, (3) the actual argument, and (4) replies to each of the initial objections.

However, the second argument centers on the existence of evil: "But the word 'God' means that He is infinite goodness. If, therefore, God existed, there would be no evil discoverable; but there is evil in the world. Therefore God does not exist."[36] Clearly, this objection and conclusion have echoed down the centuries, even to the early chapters of this book. In reply to this objection, Aquinas cites the wisdom of Augustine and the omnipotence and goodness of God, both of which point to the belief that God can bring good even out of evil.

> As Augustine says (*Enchiridion*, xi): "Since God is the highest good, He would not allow any evil to exist in His works, unless His omnipotence and goodness were such as to bring good even out of evil." This is part of the infinite goodness of God, that He should allow evil to exist, and out of it produce good.[37]

While this argument may explain *why* evil exists, it does not explain *what* Aquinas considers evil. In discussing the nature of evil, Aquinas adheres strictly to the Augustinian tradition of evil as the absence or privation of good. To emphasize his point, Aquinas examines the nature of evil in the context of his discussion of creation itself. He first establishes the connection between created being and Being Itself—that is, God: "As existence is common to all . . . all created things, so far as they are beings, are like God as the first and universal principle of all being."[38] This does not suggest, however, that all created being is divine; only God possesses being and is Being in its fullness and most perfectly. Nonetheless, all other creatures *participate* in the Being of God because "every being in any way existing is from God."

> Now . . . God is the essentially self-subsisting Being. . . . Therefore all beings apart from God are not their own being, but are beings by participation . . . [and] are caused by one First Being, Who possesses being most perfectly.[39]

Moreover, creatures participate not only in the being of God but also in the goodness of God, who is the supreme good.[40] According to Aquinas, "it is absolutely true that there is something which is essentially being and essentially good, which we call God. . . . Everything is therefore called good from the divine goodness as from the first . . . and final principle of all goodness."[41] However,

---

36. Aquinas, *ST* 1.2.3, obj. 1. The *Summa* requires only internal citation, not page numbers or websites.

37. *ST* 1.2.3, rep. 1.

38. *ST* 1.4.3.

39. *ST* 1.44.1.

40. *ST* 1.6.2.

41. *ST* 1.6.4.

whereas "all the good that is in created things has been created by God," good is not simply a fixed state of being, but rather a dynamic movement toward the greatest good, who is God.

> In created things good is found not only as regards their substance, but also as regards their order towards an end and especially their last end, which, as was said above, is the divine goodness. . . . This good of order existing in things created, is itself created by God.[42]

This conclusion leads Aquinas to his definition of evil as the absence of good. As Aquinas has argued, *being itself* is good since God is Being Itself and being is ordered toward God as its ultimate good. Nonetheless, the question still arises of whether each and every being, that is, everything that has existence, is good. In reply, Aquinas asserts, "Every being, as being, is good. For all being, as being, has actuality and is in some way perfect." If this is the case, then, "No being can be spoken of as evil, formally as being, but only so far as it lacks being. Thus a man is said to be evil, because he lacks some virtue; and an eye is said to be evil [when] it lacks the power to see well."[43]

Reflect and Discuss

Do you agree that every actual entity—every being—is good? Can you think of any exceptions? By what criteria will you judge?

Aquinas develops his understanding of evil as the absence of good in tandem with his discussion of creation. Aquinas contends that "the perfection of the universe . . . consists of the diversity of things." This diversity did not come about by chance but from "the intention of the first agent, who is God."

> For He brought things into being in order that His goodness might be communicated to creatures, and be represented by them; and because His goodness could not be adequately represented by one creature alone, He produced many and diverse creatures that what was wanting to one in the representation of the divine goodness might be supplied by another. For . . . the whole universe together participates in the divine goodness more perfectly, and represents it better than any single creature whatever.[44]

---

42. *ST* 1.22.1.

43. *ST* 1.5.3, reply 2.

44. *ST* 1.47.1.

This diversity also includes inequality and "as the wisdom of God is the cause of the distinction of things, so the same wisdom is the cause of their inequality." This inequality of natural beings is "arranged in degrees,"

> as the mixed things are more perfect than the elements, and plants than minerals, and animals than plants, and men than other animals; and in each of these one species is more perfect than others. Therefore, as the divine wisdom is the cause of the distinction of things for the sake of the perfection of the universe, so it is the cause of inequality. For the universe would not be perfect if only one grade of goodness were found in things.[45]

As in Augustine, these statements by Aquinas concerning creation clearly reflect the principle of plenitude as well as the Great Chain of Being. However, whereas Augustine interpreted the plenitude of creation as demonstrating the creative omnipotence of God, Aquinas understands this plenitude as participating in and representing the supreme goodness of God. Through creation, God communicates aspects of the divine goodness that cannot be adequately communicated through only one finite creature. Hence the universe *taken as a whole* represents divine goodness, rather than any one part, "for the roof of a house differs from the foundation, not because it is made of other material; but in order that the house may be made perfect of different parts."[46] Furthermore, Aquinas asserts, "the perfection of the universe requires that there should be some which can fail in goodness."[47] This is reminiscent of the aesthetic principle in Augustine, which suggests that the existence of some things imperfect in themselves are actually necessary for the overall perfection of the world. Moreover, Aquinas teaches that created things are by their nature susceptible to corruption since they are composed of finite matter. This includes humans who, as embodied, have the potential for corruption. Therefore, it is perfectly reasonable and in fact necessary that humans and other material creatures "fail in goodness," since not doing so is inconsistent with their nature as finite and corruptible. Nonetheless, many Christians question this reasoning. One blogger wrote the following concerning the 9-11 terrorist attacks:

> If God wants us to suffer from such things as terrorist attacks to bring some sort of good out [of] it, why bother praying for such a thing as the protection and safety promised in the 91st Psalm, or asking him to heal those affected by the tragedy? The greater good theodicy also seems [to] muddy the waters in alleviating the suffering of our neighbors

---

45. *ST* 1.2.
46. *ST* 1.47, reply 3.
47. *ST* 1.48.2.

around us. For if God has allowed certain evils for a greater good, why should we work to stop injustices when greater goods will ultimately come about if we simply allow them to happen?[48]

Aquinas defends his thinking in his discussion of the providence of God. The objection is raised that "a wise provider excludes any defect of evil, as far as he can, from those over whom he has care. But we see many evils existing. Either, then, God cannot hinder these, and thus is not omnipotent; or else he does not have care for everything."[49] In response, Aquinas differentiates between one who has care over a particular thing and one whose care is universal in scope. While particular providers can exclude defects from what is under their care, "one who provides universally allows some little defect to remain, lest the good of the whole should be hindered. Hence, corruption and defect . . . are in keeping with the plan of universal nature, inasmuch as the defect in one thing yields to the good of another, or even to the universal good."[50] Thus Aquinas suggests that some incidences of evil are part of the divine plan for the universe, "for if all evil were prevented, much good would be absent from the universe." For example, "A lion would cease to live, if there were no slaying of animals [for food]; and there would be no patience of martyrs if there were no tyrannical persecution." Nonetheless, his reasoning, like that of Augustine, is contingent on one fundamental belief: that God is "so almighty and so good as to produce good even from evil."[51]

Reflect and Discuss

Aquinas suggests that corruption and defect are in keeping with the plan of universal nature. Does this ring true in your experience? Is it true of the cosmos as a whole?

Aquinas also incorporates the Augustinian idea that creatures are ordered in the Great Chain of Being and that particular degrees of goodness are proper to each creature. However, while goodness and perfection for Augustine involve each creature's fulfilling its proper role in the order of life, Aquinas does not understand goodness and perfection in this static, orderly way. Rather, he sees goodness and perfection as a dynamic teleological movement, a striving toward

---

48. "Did God Allow the Attacks on 9/11 for a 'Greater Good'?" *The Gospel according to Erik*, available at *http://thegospeloferik.wordpress.com/2011/09/10/did-god-allow-the-attacks-on-911-for-a-greater-good/*.

49. *ST* 1.22.2, obj. 2.

50. *ST* 1.22.2, reply 2.

51. Ibid.

the fulfillment of a goal. That goal is found in the goodness and perfection of God. When the creature makes progress toward its ultimate goal in God, the goodness of God is effectively communicated through that creature; the failure or absence of such progress constitutes evil. Thus, because "the being and the perfection of any nature is good . . . it cannot be that evil signifies being, or any form or nature. Therefore it must be that by the name of evil is signified the absence of good."[52]

Reflect and Discuss

Do you accept Aquinas's assertion that humans by nature are oriented toward God? What are some pros and cons to that position?

This leads Aquinas to examine more deeply the relation between God and evil, and his response approximates that of Augustine. Like Augustine, Aquinas concedes that God may be the source of what the creature would call evil; "as the surgeon cuts off a limb to save the whole body . . . , divine wisdom inflicts pain to prevent fault."[53] Here the term "pain" means penalty or punishment; hence, God does inflict suffering as discipline or punishment, but only for the greater good of reordering the creature toward its goal in God. However, while God may inflict suffering as a discipline, God does not motivate persons to cause the suffering of others. Hence, "God is the author of the evil which is penalty, but not of the evil which is fault."[54] As one Christian pastor explained it,

> God is not trying to solve the problem of our comfort, but of our rebellion to Him, our going our own way, and of our flesh, which scripture tells us is inherently antagonistic to the things of the Spirit (Gal. 5:17). Among those who are saved, He is trying to sanctify us, which involves the discipline of our flesh, and is contrary to our comfort in every way. God places such a high premium in forming Christ in us that He considers suffering but a small and temporary price to pay.[55]

Aquinas further presses the point to deal with whether God as the Supreme Good is the cause of evil. His response is twofold. On the one hand, Aquinas agrees with Augustine that evil resulting from a defect of action is caused by the defect of an agent. Humans, for example, are defective agents, first because

---

52. *ST* 1.48.1.

53. *ST* 1.48.6.

54. *ST* 1.49.2.

55. Greg Heesen, "Does God Inflict Suffering?" *Reclaim Your Church*, available at *http://reclaimyourchurch.org/worship-center-forum-leola-pa-lancaster-pa/does-god-inflict-suffering/*.

humans are finite, material creatures, and second, because they have been affected by original sin. Their defect of action is termed sin or the failure to do good. On the other hand, God is without defect, so evil of this kind cannot be attributed to God. Thus the evil associated with a defect of action derives from the freely chosen failure of corruptible creatures to do the good. Only humans and angels possess both freedom of choice and corruptibility, so this source of evil is peculiar to them. Moreover, because of their corruptibility, "it follows that sometimes they do fail"; so "it is in this that evil consists, namely, that a thing fails in goodness."[56]

Aquinas, like Augustine, traces the capacity for such failure in goodness to original sin. However, Augustine taught that "our first parents fell into open disobedience because they were already secretly corrupted; for the evil act had never been done had not the evil will preceded it."[57] This corruption is so complete that individuals "are not able to do justly and fulfill the law of righteousness in every part thereof" through the fallen will alone; they require God's grace even to desire the good.[58] Aquinas does not share Augustine's pessimism concerning human nature. According to Aquinas, in the state of original justice, before original sin, "reason itself was perfected by God and was subject to Him. Now this same original justice was forfeited through the sin of our first parent."[59] However, the loss of original justice does not take away "the natural inclination to virtue" that human beings possess because they are rational beings. The natural inclination to good "is diminished by sin . . . but is not entirely destroyed"; thus, the corruption of the will is not complete.[60]

Despite that evil derives from the human failure to will and do the good, Aquinas acknowledges that the full weight of responsibility may not rest on creatures alone. In fact, "the evil which consists in the corruption of some . . . natural things and voluntary things" have their cause in God. His rationale for this comes from his belief in God as the Creator of all things. If a creator produces something corruptible and defective, one can reasonably conclude that the corruption and defect was caused by the one who created it. God did not intend to create anything except for the "good of the order of the universe," but, as Aquinas has already argued, the order of the universe requires that some things can and therefore do fail. Thus God, by creating things for the good order of the universe, "consequently and as it were by accident, causes the corruption of things."[61] This corruption derives from the fact that creatures are, by their very nature, finite and liable to corruption. Nonetheless, God does not actively

---

56. *ST* 1.48.2.

57. Augustine, *City of God*, 14.13.

58. Augustine of Hippo, *On Merit and the Forgiveness of Sins, and the Baptism of Infants*, II.5, *Newadvent.org*.

59. *ST* 1a.2ae.85.3.

60. *ST* 1a.2ae.85.4.

61. *ST* 1.49.2.

will such evils or sufferings for their own sake, but permits them for the greater good of the whole. This can be comforting for those who suffer, as this Christian mother of two expressed:

> One of the most powerful words of comfort I received when we were grieving our baby's loss was from a friend who said, "Your pain may not be about just you. It may well be about other people, preparing you to minister comfort and hope to someone in your future who will need what you can give them because of what you're going through right now. And if you are faithful to cling to God now, I promise He will use you greatly to comfort others later." That perspective was like a sweet balm to my soul, because it showed me that my suffering was not pointless.[62]

Reflect and Discuss

Is there such a thing as pointless or senseless suffering? What would be some examples of this?

Irenaeus: Evil and Grasping for Divinity

In formulating their theologies of suffering, Augustine and Aquinas begin with a conception of creation as an original state of perfection and justice that human beings corrupted through their original sin. However, not all theologians accept that as their starting point. For some, like the second-century apologist Irenaeus, Bishop of Lyons, God created the world with only the *potential* for perfection. For Augustine, evil stemmed from humanity's disruption of the order of creation and, for Aquinas, from humanity's divergence from its orientation toward God. For Irenaeus, however, evil derives from humanity's impatience with the process of growth and development toward fulfillment in God, what one commentator calls the "haste of sin."[63] Hence, the original sin—which, Irenaeus asserts, humanity continues to repeat—is an "original act of haste . . . , a wish to be done with waiting . . . the decision to settle for far lower than what is intended for one as in a grasping after what is higher."[64] God's intention for creation and its creatures is to develop from immaturity to maturity in God's good time and come gradually to the fullness of each one's being for the glory of God. Thus, at

---

62. Sue Bohlin, "The Value of Suffering," *Bible.org*, available at *https://bible.org/article/value-suffering*.

63. Jeff Vogel, "The Haste of Sin, the Slowness of Salvation: An Interpretation of Irenaeus on the Fall and the Redemption," *Anglican Theological Review* 89 (2007): 443–59.

64. Ibid., 448.

creation, "God intended man to have *all* good, but in his, God's time; and therefore all disobedience, all sin, consists essentially in breaking out of time."[65]

Like Aquinas, Irenaeus taught that human beings were created in a state of original justice and in the image and likeness of God: "Through the *imago dei*, God bestows humanity with the capacity to reflect the divine attributes . . . thereby manifesting 'God's glory' in the world and *achieving perfection*."[66] Unlike both Augustine and Aquinas, however, Irenaeus stated that this perfection existed only in its nascent or undeveloped form, which meant that it had to mature to fullness over time. To do this, God endowed human beings with the gift of free will so that they could voluntarily obey God's commands and grow into full perfection.

> God made man a free [agent] from the beginning, possessing his own power . . . to obey the behests [commands] of God voluntarily. . . . For there is no coercion with God, but a good will is present with Him continually. . . . And in man . . . He has placed the power of choice . . . so that those who had yielded obedience might justly possess what is good, given indeed by God, but preserved by themselves. On the other hand, they who have not obeyed shall, with justice, be not found in possession of the good, and shall receive condign [appropriate] punishment.[67]

To provide for humans' nourishment and growth, the earth and all things in it were in a state of perfection at creation. God provided for them "a place better than this world, excelling in air, beauty, light, food, plants, fruit, water, and all other necessities of life, and its name is Paradise."[68] However, while the garden was perfect in every respect, human beings were not. According to Irenaeus, the first human beings were essentially immature, like children. While Irenaeus acknowledges that, in divine omnipotence, God could have created human beings as perfect, he nonetheless contends that humans could not be both created *and* perfect for two reasons. First, by definition, that which is created is finite and corruptible and therefore not perfect: "Created things must be inferior to Him who created them, from the very fact of their later origin; for it was not possible for things recently created to have been uncreated . . . for this very reason do they come short of the perfect."[69] The second reason follows

---

65. Hans Urs von Balthasar, *A Theology of History* (San Francisco: Ignatius, 1994), 37.

66. Christopher T. Bounds, "Irenaeus and the Doctrine of Christian Perfection," *Wesleyan Theological Journal* 45 (Fall 2010): 167, emphasis added.

67. Irenaeus, *Against Heresies*, 4.37.1; *NewAdvent.org*, available at *www.newadvent.org/fathers /0103437.htm*.

68. Irenaeus, *Demonstration of the Apostolic Preaching* 12, ed. L. M. Froidevaux, Sources Chrétiennes, 62 (Paris: Cerf, 1965).

69. Irenaeus, *Against Heresies* 4.38.1.

from the first: "as the latter [i.e., the human being] was only recently created, he could not possibly have received [perfection], or even if he had received it, could he have contained it, or containing it, could he have retained it."[70] This situation is such because, at creation, humans were "infantile."

> So are they unaccustomed to, and unexercised in, perfect discipline. For as it certainly is in the power of a mother to give strong food to her infant, [she does not], as the child is not yet able to receive more substantial nourishment; so also it was possible for God . . . to have made man perfect from the first, but man could not receive this [perfection], being as yet an infant.[71]

Humans were not yet capable of receiving the mature gifts of higher-level thinking, reasoning, and responsibility. As Irenaeus writes, "Being newly created, Adam and Eve were too weak to bear the fullness of perfection; they could only mature into God-bearers over a period of time."[72]

Reflect and Discuss

What are your thoughts on Irenaeus's assertion that humans were created immature and even infantile, with only the potential for perfection? Does this present a different perspective on the way Christians view original sin and its effects?

Unfortunately, before these first humans could fully mature into the image and likeness of God in which they were created, the tempter deceived them into disobeying God's command and they sinned. Irenaeus contends, "God made humanity to be master of the earth and of all which was there. . . . Yet humanity was little, being only a child . . . and its mind was not yet fully mature; and thus humanity was easily led astray by the deceiver."[73] While Augustine would speak of this sin as pride, Irenaeus points to humanity's *impatience*, as "unwilling to be at the outset what they have . . . been created . . . and before they become men, they wish to be even now like God their Creator."[74] Their choice led to consequences for all of human history—misery, suffering, oppression, and death. This death, moreover, was not simply physical death, but a spiritual death of separation from God.

---

70. Ibid., 4.38.2.

71. Ibid., 4.38.1.

72. Vogel, "The Haste of Sin," 446.

73. Irenaeus, *Demonstration of the Apostolic Preaching* 12.

74. Irenaeus, *Against Heresies*, 4.38.4.

Therefore, even as Irenaeus asserts that the first human beings were infantile and immature, needing growth and development, he is adamant that Adam's disobedience proved disastrous. Like Augustine and Aquinas, Irenaeus acknowledges that Adam and his progeny are under the dominion of death and Satan and cut off from full participation in God. However, Irenaeus's view of original sin contains features that mitigate its seriousness compared to those of Augustine and Aquinas. Because of his view that Adam and Eve were children in the garden, not adults, they were not made perfect in a static sense. Instead, they needed to develop by God's grace toward perfection over time. Their disobedience was not calculating adult rebellion, but the weakness and ineptitude of the young.

Irenaeus also taught that God knew that these newly created beings would fail: "By His prescience He knew the infirmity of human beings, and the consequences which would flow from it."[75] This sometimes provokes people to question why God would have made human beings if God knew they would sin. Consistent with Irenaeus's view of human beings at creation, one commentary describes God like a parent of immature children.

> When parents have children they know that their kids will eventually act in sinful and even harmful ways. Yet, that doesn't stop them from having children. Why? First of all, it is worth the risk of their rebellion to bring them into the world. Second, the nature of love is to give and by having children the parents can better express their love. Third, just because the children will sin and rebel doesn't mean they shouldn't exist. Fourth, children have their own wills and can freely choose to rebel. Knowing this, parents all over the world still have children.[76]

According to Irenaeus, although God knew that humans would fall, God did not cause humanity's disobedience and fall into corruption. Furthermore, in divine omniscience and goodness, God made provision for it. Not only did God arrange and prepare a plan of salvation in Christ but also God created the world with the end of helping humanity to achieve perfection through the trials, temptations, and hardships of life. God brought good out of evil by using humanity's fall as a means of perfecting humanity.[77] Hence, while Irenaeus's writings contain little hint of suffering as discipline and punishment, they do acknowledge that God may be responsible for the existence of evil and suffering.

---

75. Ibid.

76. "If God Knew People Would Sin Why Did He Make Them?" *Christian Apologetics and Research Ministry,* available at *http://carm.org/questions/skeptics-ask/if-god-knew-people-would-sin-why-did-he-make-them.*

77. Irenaeus, *Against Heresies* 3.20.1, "Long-suffering therefore was God, when man became a defaulter. . . . God [did] permit man to be swallowed up by . . . the author of transgression, not that he should perish altogether when so engulfed; but, arranging and preparing the plan of salvation."

> ## Reflect and Discuss
>
> How would you respond to the question, "Why did God make human beings if God knew that they would sin?"

Like Aquinas, Irenaeus imputes responsibility to God because God created humanity as imperfect and tasked humanity with the freedom and responsibility to choose to grow toward perfection. To do so, humans must endure hardships and suffering in life. Natural and moral evil exist, therefore, to help people develop faith in God, grow in virtue, and learn obedience to God through suffering. Furthermore, Irenaeus's theology of suffering includes a semblance of the aesthetic principle. Like Augustine, he points out that absence and loss, darkness and death make people recognize and appreciate their opposites.

> And indeed those things are not esteemed so highly which come spontaneously, as those which are reached by much anxious care. . . . For otherwise, no doubt, this our good would be irrational, because not the result of trial. Moreover, the faculty of seeing would not appear to be so desirable, unless we had known what a loss it were to be devoid of sight; and health, too, is rendered all the more estimable by an acquaintance with disease; light, also, by contrasting it with darkness; and life with death.[78]

While many think that making suffering and evil somehow necessary for human well-being is unfortunate, it seems to ring true in many a person's life experiences. A newspaper columnist explained it this way:

> I ran across a quote I liked . . . "The soul would have no rainbow if the eyes had no tears." I think this quote is talking about my belief that, if we never suffer, we forget how to be grateful or thankful. When you suffer bad health, you realize what a blessing good health is. When you lose a job, it's very clear what employment benefits and income means. Sometimes it takes a loss to remind us of the many blessings we forget to appreciate.[79]

Contemplating humanity's fall and its implications for human life, Irenaeus distinguished in his teaching between the *image* of God and the *likeness* of God in which humans are created.

---

78. Irenaeus, *Against Heresies* 4.37.7.

79. Bob Billingsley, "Suffering Helps Us to Appreciate the Blessings," *Village Life*, available at *www.villagelife.com/commentary/billingsleys-bullets-suffering-helps-us-to-appreciate-the-blessings/*.

"Natural" or unredeemed humanity consists of a body, mind, and soul. In physical composition, humanity bears God's image. However, in their natural state humanity lacks God's likeness, which is the Holy Spirit. . . . When people receive the Spirit . . . they are made perfect through the Spirit's infusion and union with the human body and soul.[80]

The image of God is manifest in humanity's nature as a free and intelligent being, while the likeness of God comes about only through spiritual maturation and final perfecting brought about by the Holy Spirit. According to Irenaeus, the human person

is rendered spiritual and perfect because of the outpouring of the Spirit, and this is he who was made in the image and likeness of God. But if the Spirit be wanting to the soul, he . . . shall be an imperfect being, possessing indeed the *image* [of God] in his formation, but not receiving the similitude [*likeness*] through the Spirit; and thus is this being imperfect.[81]

So, like small children, humanity—individually and collectively—has had to grow in wisdom and grace throughout the ages, reaching the perfection of likeness to God at the end of an existence well-lived and developed through the Spirit's nourishment and influence. This growth and maturation takes place through the experiences of good and evil in human life, through which people learn to value the good because of its benefits and to avoid evil because of its detriments. Hence, "instead of the Augustinian view of life's trials as a divine punishment . . . Irenaeus sees our world of mingled good and evil as a divinely appointed environment for . . . development toward the perfection that represents the fulfillment of God's good purposes."[82] When persons respond to this mingling of good and evil under the influence of the Spirit, they develop character and virtue. Thus, like Aquinas, Irenaeus envisions human existence in a teleological fashion; humanity "is in the process of becoming the perfected being who God is seeking to create."[83]

Reflect and Discuss

How do you evaluate Irenaeus's argument that each person's existence is a process of becoming? Is that a source of hope or despair?

---

80. Bounds, "Irenaeus and the Doctrine of Christian Perfection," 170.

81. Irenaeus, *Against Heresies* 5.6.1.

82. Hick, *Evil and the God of Love*, 215.

83. Ibid., 256.

As a result, Irenaeus presents the world as what philosopher John Hick terms a vale of soul-making[84] or of soul-breaking. Through human choices, one can either follow the promptings of God's Spirit and grow in wisdom and grace toward the likeness of God (soul-making) or remain hardened in heart, perpetuating the evil and suffering already afoot in the world (soul-breaking). In this view, human existence free of difficulties, perils, and hardships would never allow human beings to develop into the likeness of God, for moral and spiritual growth comes through the facing and overcoming of challenges. Since, in the logic of Irenaeus, the fullness of good comes when the individual and community continue to mature in obedience to the working of the Holy Spirit, moral evil derives from human free will exercised in resistance or disobedience to the Spirit's slow and deliberate activity in human life. Instead of patiently engaging the process of growth and maturation, humans try "to become gods too quickly."[85]

> Impatient with their own incompleteness . . . human beings try to break out of time and perfect themselves. By sinking themselves into those things they think will relieve them of the burden of waiting on God, they try to achieve a premature finality. This grasping after divinity is irrational because it removes them from the condition necessary to receive it. . . . As Irenaeus puts it, this disobedience has "alienated us contrary to nature."[86]

What is the result of such alienation and "grasping after divinity"? It could be argued that it is suspicion and arrogance, violence and oppression, injustice and persecution. One could argue, as German theologian Dietrich Bonhoeffer did, that this very dynamic can cause evil and suffering on a scale as massive and horrendous as the Holocaust.

> In a brief commentary on the book of Genesis, . . . Dietrich Bonhoeffer, known best for his failed plot to kill Hitler and his subsequent execution, points the spotlight on the smallest of phrases, "Sicut Deus" in Latin: "Like God." Genesis chapter three [states]. . . . "You will not die . . . you will be like God, knowing good and evil." We know Adam and Eve disobey God . . . and the rest is history. Bonhoeffer comments that our deepest vulnerability as human beings contained in the story of The Fall is our primal desire not to be a creature. We don't

---

84. According to John Hick, "The phrase 'the vale of Soul-making' was coined by the poet John Keats in a letter written to his brother and sister in April 1819. He says . . . 'Call the world if you Please "The vale of Soul-making." . . . Do you not see how necessary a World of Pains and troubles is to school an Intelligence and make it a Soul?'" Hick, *Evil and the God of Love*, 259, n. 1.

85. Vogel, "The Haste of Sin," 443.

86. Ibid., 458–59.

want to be a creature with all those icky, frustrating, creaturely limita-tions, those weaknesses, needs, desires—but instead we want to be sicut deus, like God. To be created in the image of God is not enough.[87]

Reflect and Discuss

In the Holocaust, Bonhoeffer gives a concrete example of what grasp-ing after divinity and failing to embrace our humanity can produce. Does this perspective fit other personal, societal, or global events of evil and suffering? Be specific in your analysis.

Case in Point: *Sicut Deus*, Dietrich Bonhoeffer

Dietrich Bonhoeffer (1906–1945) was a German Lutheran pastor and theologian who in word and action stalwartly resisted the dictator-ship of Adolf Hitler and the persecution of the Jews under the Nazi regime. His stance against the scourge of Nazism and his writings and preaching in opposition to this movement demonstrate his thinking on the sources of evil and suffering in the world and highlight sev-eral themes set forth in this chapter. This "Case in Point" examines a critical period in Bonhoeffer's life when he joined the Nazi resistance movement and paid for this decision with his life.

Bonhoeffer was an outspoken critic of Hitler's regime from its outset. He supported civil disobedience in the face of unjust politi-cal movements and insisted that the Church could not simply "ban-dage the victims under the wheel"; it must "jam the spoke in the wheel itself."[88] When key positions in the German Church went to Nazi-supported clergy, Bonhoeffer founded the "Confessing Church,"

---

87. Walter Smedley, "Wanting to Be Like God," *St. Chrysostom's Episcopal Church*, October 27, 2013, available at *www.saintc.org/blog/wanting-to-be-like-god*. Genesis 3:1–5: "Now the serpent was more crafty than any other wild animal that the Lord God had made. He said to the woman, 'Did God say, "You shall not eat from any tree in the garden"?' The woman said to the serpent, 'We may eat of the fruit of the trees in the garden'; but God said, 'You shall not eat of the fruit of the tree that is in the middle of the garden, nor shall you touch it, or you shall die.' But the serpent said to the woman, 'You will not die; for God knows that when you eat of it your eyes will be opened, and you will be like God, knowing good and evil.'"

88. Dietrich Bonhoeffer, *A Testament to Freedom: The Essential Writings of Dietrich Bonhoeffer*, ed. Geffrey B. Kelley and F. Burton Nelson (San Francisco: Harper Collins, 1995), 132.

Case in Point: *Sicut Deus*, Dietrich Bonhoeffer (continued)

which embodied Christian opposition to Nazi rule. Disheartened by the complicity of the German Church with Nazism, Bonhoeffer accepted a position as pastor of two German-speaking Protestant churches in London. He did so in the hope of raising the consciousness of the Christian international community to the events unfolding in his homeland. However, after a two-year stint in London, Bonhoeffer returned to Germany and began to train pastors for the Confessing Church, which the German government had driven underground.

Branded an enemy of the state and banned from Berlin, Bonhoeffer traveled from one small town to another, secretly educating seminarians. When war seemed imminent, Bonhoeffer, a committed pacifist and opponent of the regime, faced possible conscription into Hitler's army. Refusal could have consequences both for himself and for his Confessing Church. In the midst of this dilemma, Bonhoeffer received an invitation from Union Theological Seminary in New York to teach. At first, he accepted the invitation, but he immediately regretted it and decided to return to Germany. As he wrote to a friend,

> I must live through this difficult period in our national history with the people of Germany. I will have no right to participate in the reconstruction of Christian life in Germany after the war if I do not share the trials of this time with my people. . . . Christians in Germany will face the terrible alternative of either willing the defeat of their nation in order that Christian civilization may survive or willing the victory of their nation and thereby destroying our civilization. I know which of these alternatives I must choose; but I cannot make that choice in security.[89]

When he returned to Germany, Bonhoeffer was forbidden to preach or to publish any of his writings.

Throughout this critical period of his life, Bonhoeffer produced several theological works that were clearly influenced by events in Germany. One such work was a series of lectures he had given on

---

89. Dietrich Bonhoeffer, *The Cost of Moral Leadership: The Spirituality of Dietrich Bonhoeffer*, ed. Geffrey B. Kelley and F. Burton Nelson (Grand Rapids: Eerdmans, 2003), 27.

Case in Point: *Sicut Deus*, Dietrich Bonhoeffer (continued)

the first three chapters of Genesis entitled *Creation and Fall*. In them, Bonhoeffer explored evil and its sources from the biblical perspective of the fall of humanity. For Bonhoeffer, creation was not simply a point in time, but rather a fundamental orientation to God. Like Augustine and Aquinas, he viewed creation as essentially good; however, its goodness consisted not simply in being itself, but "in being *under the dominion of God*."[90] According to Bonhoeffer, God is both the orientation and the goal of all human life. While God gives life to all creatures, God's true creativity is reflected only in humanity, which is made in the image of God. Like Irenaeus, Bonhoeffer states that human freedom is the image of God in humanity. Nonetheless, this freedom must always be exercised under the sovereignty of God, because true freedom and fullness of life only exist in continuous obedience to God. From within this theological context, Bonhoeffer analyzes the nature of sin and evil.

He begins his analysis with Genesis 2 in the Garden of Eden. Here God demarcates the limits of human freedom and life: "God commanded the [human], 'You may freely eat of every tree of the garden; but of the tree of the knowledge of good and evil you shall not eat, for in the day that you eat of it you shall die'" (Gen. 2:16–17). According to Bonhoeffer, God sets the boundary between what it means to be a creature and what it means to be God. This narrative makes clear that the knowledge of good and evil belongs only to God. For creatures, it is enough to know God, who is the only Good and who orders and orients their lives. Nonetheless, in their vain desire to be *sicut Deus*, "like God," the first humans exercise their God-given freedom to disobey God's command and transgress their limitations. For Bonhoeffer, this does not simply constitute disobedience, but rebellion.

> The word disobedience fails to describe the situation adequately. It is rebellion, the creature's stepping outside of the creature's only possible attitude, the creature's becoming creator, the destruction of creatureliness, a defection, a falling away from being safely held as a creature. As such a defection

---

90. Dietrich Bonhoeffer, *Creation and Fall: A Theological Exposition of Genesis 1–3* (Minneapolis: Fortress, 2004), 46, emphasis added.

> it is a continual fall, a dropping into a bottomless abyss, a state of being let go, a process of moving further and further away, falling deeper and deeper.[91]

Moreover, like the classical theologians before him, Bonhoeffer contends that this rebellion affects not only humanity but "the whole created world."

> And in all this it is not merely a moral lapse but the destruction of creation by the creature. The extent of the fall is such that it affects the whole created world. From now on that world has been robbed of its creatureliness and drops blindly into infinite space, like a meteor that has torn itself away from the core to which it once belonged.[92]

Humanity's transgression of its limits signifies, for Bonhoeffer, "not wanting to be a creature."[93] Moreover, their rejection of their true nature as creatures distorts their vision of what it means to be "like God." Two consequences flow from their rejected creaturehood and their distorted vision of God. First, their disordered desire to transcend their limits places them in opposition to one another. No longer do they see themselves as limited creatures, able to coexist "in the unity of creaturely, free love."[94] Rather, in their decision to be "like God," they transgress the boundaries natural to creaturehood and fail to acknowledge and respect the freedom and autonomy of the other. As a result,

> one person claims a right to the other, claims to be entitled to possess the other. . . . [The] human being who transgresses his or her boundary is a refusal to recognize any limit at all; it is a boundless obsessive desire to be without any limits.[95]

Second, their rejected creaturehood and distorted vision compel them to cover their nakedness, lest any actual limitations or shortcomings be

---

91. Bonhoeffer, *Creation and Fall*, 120.

92. Ibid.

93. Ibid., 116.

94. Ibid., 122.

95. Ibid., 123.

Case in Point: *Sicut Deus*, **Dietrich Bonhoeffer** (continued)

revealed, for "Human beings with no limit . . . do not show themselves in their nakedness."

> Nakedness is the essence of unity . . . of being for the other, of respect for what is given, of acknowledging the rights of the other as my limit and as creature. Nakedness is the essence of being oblivious of the possibility of robbing others of their rights. Nakedness is revelation; nakedness believes in grace.[96]

While in faithfulness and love, God calls to Adam and Eve to come out of hiding, out of self-reproach, and out of self-torment—calling to them, "be yourself"—it is to no avail.[97] They have renounced their creaturehood. Bonhoeffer laments that "the fall drops with increasing speed for an immeasurable distance,"[98] throughout all generations, even to this day.

Like Irenaeus, Bonhoeffer saw the disastrous consequences of this grasping to be "like God" outside of God's time and outside of human nature. He saw it in the Nazi regime in Germany and its genocidal persecution of the Jewish people. This regime recognized no limits on its right to possess the other, to condemn the other, to put the other to death. It recognized no standards of good and evil other than its own will, no sovereignty other than its own power. This dire situation ultimately impelled Bonhoeffer to join a German intelligence organization that served as the hub of anti-Hitler resistance and that plotted the assassination of Hitler. After a failed attempt on Hitler's life, Bonhoeffer was arrested in April 1943. He was held first at Tegel military prison, and then at Buchenwald and Flossenbürg concentration camps after his involvement in the plot to kill Hitler was uncovered.

Bonhoeffer did not shrink from culpability for his actions, nor did he try to excuse himself. He believed

> when a man takes guilt upon himself in responsibility . . . he answers for it. . . . Before other men, the man of free

---

96. Ibid., 124.
97. Ibid., 129.
98. Ibid., 130.

> ### Case in Point: *Sicut Deus*, Dietrich Bonhoeffer (continued)
>
> > responsibility is justified by necessity; before himself he is acquitted by his conscience, but before God he hopes only for mercy.[99]
>
> Embracing his own creaturehood and his faith in Christ, Bonhoeffer believed that his hope in God would not be disappointed. As he expressed in his theological work entitled *Ethics*, which was unfinished at the time of his death,
>
> > God loves human beings. God loves the world. Not an ideal human, but human beings as they are; not an ideal world, but the real world. What we find repulsive in their opposition to God, what we shrink back from with pain and hostility, namely, real human beings, the real world, this is for God the ground of unfathomable love. . . . While we exert ourselves to grow beyond our humanity, to leave the human behind us, God becomes human; and we must recognize that God wills that we be human, real human beings. . . . Jesus Christ is . . . the Yes of God to real human beings. . . . In this Yes all the life and all the hope of the world are comprised.[100]
>
> Like Jesus, Bonhoeffer's "yes" to God and to real human beings led to his death. With his fellow conspirators, he was "hanged on a twisted cross" on April 8, 1945.[101]

For Further Reading

Aquinas, Thomas. "Treatise on the Creation." In *The Summa Theologica of St. Thomas Aquinas*. Translated by the Fathers of the English Dominican Province, 229–56. Allen, TX: Christian Classics, 1981.

---

99. Dietrich Bonhoeffer, *Dietrich Bonhoeffer: Witness to Jesus Christ*, ed. John W. de Gruchy (Minneapolis: Fortress, 1991), 251.

100. Dietrich Bonhoeffer, *Ethics*, ed. Clifford Green (Minneapolis: Fortress, 2005), 84–85.

101. This phrase is the title of a documentary on Bonhoeffer's life, *Hanged on a Twisted Cross: The Life, Convictions and Martyrdom of Dietrich Bonhoeffer*. The phrase refers to the swastika, the symbol of Nazism.

Augustine of Hippo. *City of God.* Garden City, NY: Image Books, 1958.

Bonhoeffer, Dietrich. *Letters and Papers from Prison.* Greenwich, CT: Touchstone, 1997.

Carmody, John. *Cancer and Faith.* Mystic, CT: Twenty-Third Publications, 1994.

Hick, John. *Evil and the God of Love.* New York: Palgrave Macmillan, 2007.

Internet Resources

Davies, Brian, Denys Turner, and Michael Kremer. "Thomas Aquinas on God and Evil." The Lumen Christi Institute. Available at *http://player.vimeo .com/video/41258996* (time: 1:05:43).

Kreeft, Peter. "The Problem of Evil and Suffering." The Veritas Forum. Iowa State University, 2010. Available at *https://vimeo.com/17694928* (time: 1:16:28).

Film

Hanged on a Twisted Cross: The Life, Convictions and Martyrdom of Dietrich Bonhoeffer. Directed by T. N. Mohan. Worcester, PA: Gateway Films/Vision Video, 1996.

Part II

Contextual Theologies of Suffering

Theology can never be neutral or fail to takes sides on issues related to the plight of the oppressed. For this reason it can never engage in conversation about the nature of God without confronting those elements of human existence which threaten anyone's existence as a person.

—JAMES CONE, *A BLACK THEOLOGY OF LIBERATION*

CHAPTER 5

Only a Suffering God Can Help

God lets himself be pushed out of the world on to the cross. He is weak and powerless in the world, and that is precisely the way, the only way, in which he is with us and helps us. . . . Christ helps us, not by virtue of omnipotence, but by virtue of his weakness and suffering. Here is the decisive difference between Christianity and all religions. Man's religiosity makes him look in his distress to the power of God in the world: God is the *deus ex machina*. The Bible directs man to God's powerlessness and suffering; only the suffering God can help.

—DIETRICH BONHOEFFER, *LETTERS AND PAPERS FROM PRISON*[1]

Introduction

"Only the suffering God can help." Dietrich Bonhoeffer made this claim from his prison cell just before his execution.[2] While his claim has become accepted among a growing number of theologians in the last two centuries, it could well be regarded as heretical according to the classical theology discussed in chapter 2, which considers suffering in God inconsistent with divine nature.[3] Although biblical descriptions of God are replete with language for divine actions, emotions, and relationships, classical Christian theism deemed this language symbolic or analogical and continued to affirm the immutability and impassibility of God.[4] In the last hundred years or so, however, this perspective has been subject to increasing criticism and revision by a number of theologians. This transformation has been so dramatic that it has been termed "one of the most striking developments in theology today," representing a "structural shift in the Christian

---

1. Edited by John W. de Gruchy (Minneapolis: Augsburg Fortress, 2009), 479. The phrase "*deus ex machina*" that Bonhoeffer uses refers to the belief of some that in the face of suffering and evil, God mysteriously enters the world to put an end to problems that seem impossible to solve.

2. See "Case in Point," chapter 4.

3. See also Geddes MacGregor, *He Who Lets Us Be: A Theology of Love* (New York: Seabury, 1975), 3–5.

4. Warren McWilliams, *The Passion of God: Divine Suffering in Contemporary Protestant Theology* (Macon, GA: Mercer University, 1985), 12.

mind."[5] Many contemporary theists admit that the inability of God to suffer "is perhaps the most questionable aspect of certain forms of orthodox Christian theism"[6] and has led to increasing criticism of the doctrine of impassibility in the last decade of the nineteenth century.[7]

In his exploration of "The Suffering God: The Rise of a New Orthodoxy," pastor and theologian Ronald Goetz proposed four factors that he believes contributed to the rise of this "new orthodoxy" of the suffering God. These factors include the decline of Christianity, the rise of democracy, the problem of suffering and evil, and the scholarly study of the Bible.[8] In discussing the first factor, Goetz associates the decline of Christianity with the spread of atheism. He also states that the decline of Christianity stems from the conspicuous absence of, for many Christians, "mighty acts of God" in the contemporary world. The second factor of rising democratic structures argues that an immutable and impassible God has no relevance to those concerned with the exercise of human freedom and agency in the world. The third factor of the problem of suffering and evil, made stark by the brutalities of two world wars, raised questions about God's role and responsibility in the suffering and evil so rampant in the twentieth century. Finally, the fourth factor of scholarly study of the Bible clearly revealed that the God of Israel and of Jesus Christ was by no means an unaffected deity, but one full of immense passion and anguish. This last factor led to a restored focus upon the theology of the cross, which viewed the passion of Christ as a revelation of the passion of God. So deep was this conviction that one theologian asserted that "the cross of Christ was no afterthought on the part of God but was the expression at a definite historical period of something which represented an eternal activity in the divine life."[9]

Advancements in philosophy and in science compounded these factors. Scholars in contemporary metaphysics proposed that God is an active participant in history. As a result, it deemed the image of an immutable and impassible God inadequate.[10] A further significant influence was the growth of an evolutionary view of science that envisioned God as immanent in the evolutionary

---

5. Daniel Day Williams, *What Present-Day Theologians Are Thinking*, 3rd ed. (New York: Harper & Row, 1967), 171–72.

6. Kenneth Surin, "The Impassibility of God and the Problem of Evil," *Scottish Journal of Theology* 35, no. 2 (April 1982): 97.

7. Richard Bauckman, "Only the Suffering God Can Help: Divine Passibility in Modern Theology," *Themelios* 9 (April 1984): 6.

8. Ronald Goetz, "The Suffering of God: Rise of a New Orthodoxy," *The Christian Century* 103 (April 1986): 385–89.

9. Vernon Storr, in Francis H. House, "The Barrier of Impassibility," *Theology* 83 (November 1980): 410.

10. Williams, *What Present-Day Theologians Are Thinking*, 173.

struggle between death and new life.[11] Moreover, phenomenologists contend that a God of unconditional love cannot but be affected by the suffering of the loved one: "To love is to rejoice with the joys and sorrow with the sorrow of others. Thus it is to be influenced by those who are loved."[12]

Despite growing acceptance of the concept of divine suffering, these theologies have their critics. Some feminist theologians object that the suffering and crucified Christ as the image of the suffering God tends to glorify violence and abuse and encourages the believer to follow his example of suffering in silence. Furthermore, they contend that theologies of atonement and redemption frequently communicate the message that suffering itself is salvific. These critics point to the advice given to women to "suffer in silence" or to "bear your cross" when afflicted by domestic abuse and societal oppression; based on the suffering and sacrifice of Jesus, this advice commends suffering as holy and redeeming, rather than encouraging women to resist and to raise their voices in protest.

In addition to these feminist critiques, many Catholic theologians have also raised criticism in keeping with the classical tradition discussed in chapter 2. They maintain that attributing suffering to God contradicts the divine nature as immutable and impassible; it inhibits divine freedom and subjects the Creator to the vicissitudes of the created order. Notable among the Catholic voices raised in critique is Dutch theologian Edward Schillebeeckx, who flatly maintains, "We cannot look for the *ground* of suffering in God."[13] For Schillebeeckx, God as "Being Itself" must be conceived as "pure positivity," the "benevolent, solicitous 'one who is against evil,' who will not admit the supremacy of evil and refuses to allow it the last word."[14] He firmly maintains that the Christian message does not attempt to justify evil or suffering and rejects the claims that God either required the death of Jesus or experienced Jesus' suffering within God's own self.[15] The German Catholic theologian Johann B. Metz also criticizes the concept of a suffering God. According to Metz, this theological position is too speculative, "with God behind the back of the human history of suffering."[16] Metz contends that suffering in God reduces divine power and compromises divine transcendence. Moreover, it militates against hope for change in this

---

11. J. K. Mozley, *The Impassibility of God: A Survey of Christian Thought* (Cambridge: Cambridge University Press, 1926), 124.

12. Charles Hartshorne, *A Natural Theology for Our Time* (LaSalle, IL: Open Court, 1967), 75. A phenomenologist is one whose research concentrates on the study of consciousness and objects of direct human experience.

13. Edward Schillebeeckx, *Christ: The Experience of Jesus as Lord*, trans. John Bowden (New York: Crossroad, 1999), 727, emphasis in the original.

14. Edward Schillebeeckx, *Jesus: An Experiment in Christology*, trans. Hubert Hoskins (New York: Seabury, 1979), 267.

15. Schillebeeckx, *Christ*, 728.

16. Johann Baptist Metz, *A Passion for God: The Mystical-Political Dimension of Christianity* (New York: Paulist, 1998), 69, emphasis in the original.

world and diminishes human motivation to work toward justice. In a series of questions that outline the primary objections to the notion of suffering in God, Metz relentlessly challenges this theological move.

> How is the discourse about a suffering God in the end anything more than a sublime duplication of human suffering and human power-lessness? How does the discourse about suffering in God . . . not lead to an eternalization of suffering? Do not God and humanity end up . . . under a . . . universalization of suffering that finally cuts off the counterimpulse resisting injustice?[17]

While acknowledging these feminist and Catholic critiques, many theologians and people of faith find it increasingly difficult to reconcile the scope and intensity of suffering in the last century with belief in an impassible God. In the wake of the Holocaust and the bombing of Hiroshima and Nagasaki, Jewish philosopher Hans Jonas asserts that extreme and incomprehensible suffering calls humanity to "rethink [the concept of God] so it remains thinkable."[18] It is this kind of rethinking that the theologians in this chapter have undertaken. Although "how God grapples with and overcomes [suffering] is a mystery,"

> it is one that we . . . must ponder over in the grasp of [God's] infinite love. We have the assurance of the victory of this love, but we cannot use this assurance . . . to provide easy consolation. If we do, we may become like the friends of Job, whose all too rational and plausible explanations of his plight only added to his torment.[19]

This chapter explores the theologies of the suffering God from the perspectives of four theologians: Jürgen Moltmann, Kazoh Kitamori, Jon Sobrino, and Sallie McFague. While each of these scholars uses the Scriptures as the source for their proposals about the God who suffers, each reflects on them through the lens of a particular historical or cultural viewpoint, which is called "context." In theology, context refers to the complex of social, cultural, religious, and personal influences on the worldview of a theologian or of a believer. It is the environment of particular struggles, concerns, and questions that give rise to theological investigation. While all theology is contextual because it is always influenced by the personal, social, and cultural history and worldview of the persons engaged in it, these theologies are intentionally and explicitly so. For example, the context in which Dietrich Bonhoeffer wrote was shaped in large part by the rise of Nazism, the suppression of Christianity, his association with the underground

---

17. Ibid., 70.

18. Hans Jonas, "The Concept of God after Auschwitz: A Jewish Voice," *Journal of Religion* 67 (January 1987): 3.

19. Surin, "The Impassibility of God," 115.

resistance movement, and his personal faith. In this chapter, the context that influences each theologian is a particularly significant historical event of suffering and devastation.

German theologian Jürgen Moltmann grounds his theology of the suffering of God in the context of Auschwitz and in the crucifixion of Christ. In the aftermath of the atomic bombings of Hiroshima and Nagasaki, Japanese theologian Kazoh Kitamori bases his thought on the writings of the prophets and on the crucifixion of Christ. Jesuit theologian Jon Sobrino writes against the backdrop of the slaughter of thousands in his country of El Salvador and throughout Latin America and focuses on the cross of Christ and the passion narrative in the Gospel of Mark. Finally, in response to the ecological crisis currently facing the planet and its inhabitants, Protestant theologian Sallie McFague grounds her theological reflections in the incarnation, crucifixion, and resurrection of Jesus.

> ### Reflect and Discuss
>
> At this preliminary stage of the chapter, what is your response to the proposal of the suffering God? What arguments from this introduction do you find compelling or lacking? Why?

The Crucified God

The Context: The Holocaust or Shoah[20]

In January 1933, Adolf Hitler was appointed chancellor of a German nation still reeling from the economic effects of World War I and a worldwide depression. Under Hitler, the leader of the National Socialist German Workers' Party and the author of *Mein Kampf,* Nazism became established as the political ideology of a totalitarian state in which Jews and other "undesirable" persons were oppressed, persecuted, and ultimately killed. In 1933, the Jewish population of Europe was more than nine million; by 1945, it was three million—nearly six million Jews living in Germany or in German-occupied countries had been executed as part

---

20. While usually referred to as the Holocaust, from the Greek meaning "burnt sacrifice or offering," the genocide of Jewish persons by the German Nazis in World War II is referred to in many Jewish sources through the biblical word *Shoah,* from the Hebrew meaning "catastrophe" or "destruction." One reason is the use of the word *Holocaust* as a more general reference to atrocities committed by the Nazis and to other events of mass devastation. Another is that *Holocaust* as a burnt sacrifice has the religious implication that this event of genocide represented an offering to God. The term *Shoah,* on the other hand, refers specifically to "the murder of and persecution of European Jewry" at the hands of the Nazis. See "The Holocaust: Definition and Preliminary Discussion," *Yad Vashem,* available at *www.yadvashem.org/yv/en/holocaust/resource_center/the_holocaust.asp#!prettyPhoto.*

of the "Final Solution," the Nazi policy to eliminate Jews throughout Europe. The tyranny and annihilation also spread to millions of other people including prisoners of war, intelligentsia, political opponents, religious dissidents, and those who did not meet prescribed social norms. In addition, more than 200,000 disabled patients living in German institutions were killed in the "Euthanasia Program," a radical plan to restore the "racial integrity" of the German nation. The program "endeavored to eliminate what eugenicists and their supporters considered 'life unworthy of life': those individuals who . . . because of severe psychiatric, neurological, or physical disabilities represented at once a genetic and a financial burden upon German society and the state."[21]

In the first years of the regime, the Nazi government established ghettos, as well as concentration camps and forced–labor camps to facilitate control and deportation of the Jews. To these were later added mobilized killing units (*Einsatzgruppen*) and killing centers. From 1941 through 1944, the Nazis deported millions of Jews from Germany and throughout Europe to these ghettos and extermination camps, murdering them in gassing facilities. At first, "the Nazis experimented with gas vans for mass killing. Gas vans were hermetically sealed trucks with engine exhaust diverted to the interior compartment." Later, in 1942, mass killing in stationary gas chambers began.

Until 1944, pleas from Jews throughout the world, as well as from those who had managed to escape the death camps, were frequently ignored by the Allied governments and evidence was often suppressed or "classified." Assisting European Jews was not a high priority of the Allied governments as they sought to defeat Hitler militarily. The courageous acts of individual rescuers and resistance members proved to be the exception, not the norm.[22] Church response to the Shoah was mixed. "The leaders of the [German] Churches spent a great deal of time delineating a 'viable' position: one that would conform to Christian doctrine, prevent their Church from dividing into opposing factions, and avoid antagonizing the Nazi authorities."[23] Outside Germany, many Christian Church and religious organizations issued statements condemning the persecution of the Jews by the Nazis.

Overall, the world response was slow and largely ineffective: "There is no question that the silence and inaction of the world community in the face of irrefutable evidence resulted in the senseless loss of millions of lives."[24]

---

21. "Euthanasia Program," *USHMM.org*, available at *www.ushmm.org/wlc/en/article.php?ModuleId =10005200*.

22. Victoria J. Barnett, "The Role of the Churches: Compliance and Confrontation," *Anti-Defamation League*, available at *http://archive.adl.org/braun/dim_14_1_role_church.html#.VgBg5O2FPyo*.

23. Ibid.

24. Gary M. Grobman, "The Holocaust—A Guide for Teachers," cited in "The Holocaust: World Response," *Jewish Virtual Library*, available at *www.jewishvirtuallibrary.org/jsource/Holocaust /worldres.html*.

What forms or events of genocide are taking place in today's world? What has caused or is causing them? How has the world responded?

The Crucified God

In the preface to his book *The Crucified God*, German theologian Jürgen Moltmann wrote,

> I experienced a . . . "dark night" in my soul, for the pictures of the Bergen-Belsen concentration camp and horror over the crimes at Auschwitz, had weighed on me and many other people of my generation ever since 1945. Much time passed before we could emerge from the silence that stops the mouths of people over whom the cloud of the victims hangs heavy. It was the Jewish survivors of the Holocaust and Jewish theologians who opened our lips. *The Crucified God* was said to be a Christian "theology after Auschwitz." That is true, inasmuch as I perceived Golgotha in the shadow of Auschwitz.[25]

Profoundly moved by this experience of the Holocaust and by the God of Jesus Christ revealed on the cross, Jürgen Moltmann grounds his theology of the suffering God in the Christian biblical tradition. Drawing on the prophetic tradition of Israel, the self-emptying of Christ (Phil. 2:6–8),[26] and the Pauline affirmation that "in Christ God was reconciling the world to himself" (2 Cor. 5:19), Moltmann most forcefully articulated his theology in the shadow of Auschwitz in his book *The Crucified God*. In it, he sets aside the God of classical theism who is unchangeable and unaffected, deeming it inconsistent with the biblical vision of God revealed by the prophets as a God of responsiveness and pathos.[27]

According to Moltmann, "At the heart of the prophetic proclamation there stands the certainty that God is interested in the world to the point of suffering." Divine pathos, therefore, "describes the way in which God is affected by

---

25. Jürgen Moltmann, *The Crucified God: The Cross of Christ as the Foundation and Criticism of Christian Theology*, trans. R. A. Wilson and John Bowden (Minneapolis: Fortress, 1993), xi.

26. "Though he was in the form of God, [Jesus] did not regard equality with God as something to be exploited, but emptied himself, taking the form of a slave, being born in human likeness. And being found in human form, he humbled himself and became obedient to the point of death—even death on a cross" (Phil. 2:6–8).

27. Pathos is an emotion of sympathy or pity. It comes from the Greek *paschein*, meaning to experience or suffer. The philosopher Søren Kierkegaard described pathos as a profound and unshakable commitment of the heart.

events and human actions and suffering in history."[28] In the covenant relationship proclaimed by the prophets, God is passionately invested in the history of God's people, active on their behalf in absolute freedom yet capable of suffering under humanity's disobedience. Because of this, Moltmann rejects both classical theism and modern atheism and grounds his theology of suffering in the event of the cross, "which understands God as the suffering God in the suffering of Christ. . . . For this theology, God and suffering are no longer contradictions . . . but God's being is in suffering and the suffering is in God's being itself."[29]

Reflect and Discuss

Can you think of any examples from the Scriptures or from the early chapters of this book where God shows emotion or experiences suffering? On what basis can Moltmann assert that the suffering of Christ is the suffering of God? Do you agree? Why or why not?

Moltmann's point of departure is a literal reading of the cry of abandonment[30] that Jesus utters from the cross to the God who has forsaken him: "Jesus cried out with a loud voice, '*Eloi, Eloi, lema sabachthani?*' which means, 'My God, my God, why have you forsaken me?'" (Mark 15:34). This cry was Jesus' anguished plea to God to demonstrate divine righteousness and power on his behalf, a plea that seemed to receive no answer. Because of this, Moltmann is convinced that the Father truly did abandon the Son on the cross. When divine intervention did not come, Moltmann claims, the torment of Jesus increased—intensified by the intimate relation of love that he had enjoyed with God, the love of a Father and Son. At this critical moment, Jesus is Godforsaken while the Father stands as the one who both wills and experiences the death of the Son. Thus, as "the Son suffers dying, the Father suffers the death of the Son."[31] The loving obedience of the Son even unto death is met by the grief-stricken love of the Father who has delivered and abandoned his Son unto death. For Moltmann, therefore, what happened on the cross must be understood as an event within the Trinity of God's own self. However, because of the distinction

---

28. Moltmann, *The Crucified God*, 270–71.

29. Ibid., 227.

30. Moltmann uses the term *dereliction* rather than *abandonment*. It means "the act of abandoning or the condition of being abandoned."

31. Moltmann, *The Crucified God*, 243. Cf. Mark 14:35–36: "[Jesus] went a little farther, he threw himself on the ground and prayed that, if it were possible, the hour might pass from him. He said, 'Abba, Father, for you all things are possible; remove this cup from me; yet, not what I want, but what you want.'"

of Persons within the Trinity, the Father's suffering is not the same as that of the Son:[32] "In the death of the Son, death comes upon God himself, and the Father suffers the death of his Son in his love for forsaken [humanity]."[33]

Reflect and Discuss

Moltmann claims that the Father literally abandoned the Son on the cross. What implications might this claim have for others who are in the midst of great suffering or who are facing death?

For both the Father and the Son, the capacity to suffer is eminently associated with the capacity to love: "God is unconditional love, because he takes on himself grief. . . . God suffers, God allows himself to be crucified and is crucified, and in this consummates his unconditional love that is so full of hope."[34] This hope, nonetheless, is future-oriented. In the present moment, suffering is relieved only by the recognition that God suffers with, for, and in humanity. In Moltmann's Trinitarian theology of suffering, the Father and the Son bear the suffering of humanity in solidarity with the afflicted and oppressed of history. It is the Spirit, however, who provides the hope that human suffering will one day be transformed into joy. The Spirit, who is the love between the Father and the Son, creates love for forsaken humanity and brings the dead to newness of life in the manner of the resurrection.

Hence, Moltmann's deity is a God of pathos and passion immersed in history and involved in the dynamics of the cosmos. Moltmann's God is also a Trinitarian God, which enables him to discuss different manners of suffering in God—namely, the distinctive suffering of the Father and the Son in the event of the cross. Furthermore, it enables him to propose how it is that God might both suffer with creation and its creatures and yet move them toward new life and liberation through the action of the Holy Spirit. Nonetheless, Moltmann's theology of suffering has several negative implications for the relationship between God and suffering. In his literal reading of Jesus' cry of anguish in Mark 15:34, Moltmann stresses the Father's deliberate abandonment of the Son on the cross, an emphasis that has been much criticized and that raises questions about God's role in the suffering of people today. Thus, while Moltmann undeniably provides a suffering world with the image of a God who knows its affliction and understands its pain, he risks the conclusion that the very God who suffers is the God who willed it so. Moreover, if transformation of suffering is solely

---

32. Moltmann, *The Crucified God*, 203.

33. Ibid., 192.

34. Ibid., 248.

future-oriented, it seems to imply that God is unable to change the plight of the suffering. So while Moltmann's concept of the crucified God offers ample compassion for humans who suffer, relief delayed seems to be relief denied. Consistent with the critique offered by Metz earlier in this chapter, attributing suffering to God can lead to accepting suffering for oneself, providing little motivation for action toward justice.

Reflect and Discuss

How does Moltmann's Trinitarian understanding of suffering and redemption in God address the criticisms of the suffering God set forth at the beginning of this chapter? Is Moltmann's argument credible for people of faith?

The Pain of God

The Context: The Atomic Bombing of Hiroshima and Nagasaki

While battles waged against Germany continued across Europe, the United States was also at war with Japan in the Pacific. Despite the distance, these two conflicts intertwined. With an eye on expansion in East Asia, Japan signed the "Tripartite Pact" with Germany and Italy in September 1940, forming the alliance known as the "Axis." In an attempt to stop this expansion, the United States imposed sanctions on Japan, which created severe economic conditions in the country. In retaliation, Japan launched an attack on the US Pacific Fleet at Pearl Harbor, Hawaii, and shortly after, the United States declared war on Japan, which had made steady military advances.

The US naval victory at the Battle of Midway in June 1942 marked the turning point in the war. Over the next year, Japan was forced to retreat from island after island. After the liberation of the Philippines in 1944, the United States began sustained bombing on Japan. By 1945, the Allied forces had defeated Germany in Europe, yet Japan doggedly continued to fight. Japan rejected the Allied demand to surrender, despite the Potsdam Declaration threat of "prompt and utter destruction" if Japan refused.[35]

United States military commanders planned continued bombing and a massive invasion. However, to avoid potential loss of life and bring the war to a speedy close, President Harry S. Truman decided to use the atomic bomb despite the reservations of a number of military advisors and scientists who had developed it. On

---

35. "Potsdam Declaration," *Hiroshima Peace Memorial Museum*, available at *www.pcf.city.hiroshima .jp/virtual/VirtualMuseum_e/visit_e/est_e/panel/A2_2/2201d.htm*.

August 6, 1945, an atomic bomb was dropped without warning on Hiroshima, a manufacturing center thought to have no Allied prisoner-of-war camps, with a blast equal to 12,000–15,000 tons of TNT. On August 9, 1945, a second atomic bomb, more powerful than that dropped on Hiroshima, was dropped on Nagasaki. It produced a blast equivalent to 22,000 tons of TNT. In addition to more than 100,000 initial casualties, thousands more eventually died of radiation exposure, which also caused infant mortalities, cancers, and chromosomal damage that would affect untold generations of Japanese to come. The decision of the supreme commander of the Allied Occupation to prohibit the publication of reports and studies of the damage caused by the bombings exacerbated these calamities.[36]

Because of this censorship, those citizens afflicted by the bombing not only struggled with their injuries and their terrors but also from ignorance of medical and social information and the toxic environment they lived in.

Reflect and Discuss

Can you think of military conflicts and their consequences today that compare with that of Hiroshima and Nagasaki? What are they? How do they compare? How does the world respond?

The Pain of God

Touched by the suffering and misery of Japan during World War II and especially by the bombing of Hiroshima and Nagasaki, Japanese theologian Kazoh Kitamori contextualizes his theology in the living reality of the Japanese people. In *Theology of the Pain of God*, he contends that periods and places wherein human suffering is most intense can witness to and be "a symbol of God's pain in the world."[37] Biblically, Kitamori claims that the pain of God is "the heart of the gospel."[38] Yet the principle foundation of his theology comes from the Hebrew Scriptures. He focuses on two specific prophetic passages—Jeremiah 31:20 and Isaiah 63:15[39]—especially their use of the word *hamah*, which means

---

36. The Atomic Bomb Museum, "Social Damages," *Atomicbombmuseum.org*, available at *www.atomicbombmuseum.org/3_social.shtml*.

37. Kazoh Kitamori, *Theology of the Pain of God* (London: SCM Press, 1966), 52–53, 137. This book was published in Japan in 1946.

38. Ibid., 19.

39. In Jeremiah 31:20, God speaks the word *hamah*: "Is Ephraim my dear son? Is he the child I delight in? As often as I speak against him, I still remember him. Therefore I am *deeply moved* for him; I will surely have mercy on him, says the Lord," emphasis added. In Isaiah 63:15, the one who prays applies the word to God: "Look down from heaven and see, from your holy and glorious habitation. Where are your zeal and your might? The *yearning of your heart and your compassion*? They are withheld from me," emphasis added.

to cry aloud, mourn, rage, or be troubled. The term *hamah* appears repeatedly throughout the Bible in reference to human beings and signifies human agony, anguish, suffering, and pain. However, the two passages highlighted by Kitamori are the only two in the Bible that use *hamah* in relation to God.

After surveying the multiple uses of *hamah* applied to human emotions and actions in the prophets and psalms, Kitamori proceeds by analogy to consider what this word might refer to in the inner heart of God. According to Kitamori, the use of *hamah* in Jeremiah is meant to convey the pain of God's heart in response to sinners, "the severest struggle of God's love which Jeremiah saw."[40] Kitamori warns against softening the impact of this divine reaction by reducing it to sympathy or emotion. He also differentiates it from divine empathy or grief. Following a translation done by Martin Luther, Kitamori understands *hamah* as a "severe pain" experienced by God, a grief or wailing, a pain or roaring in one's bowels; it is "'pain of God' [which] reflects his love toward those turning against it."[41] Kitamori then correlates this divine anguish with the love of God manifested in the cross, poured out upon those who had turned from God's immediate love. He concludes that both the "pain of God" and the "love of the cross" cancel the human sin of rejecting God's love, "the love of God who accepts as his own, sinners who are turning their backs on him."[42]

Reflect and Discuss

Kitamori correlates the pain of God with the love of God. Does this resonate with your human experience? Does pain sometimes result from the experience of love? In what ways?

Justifiably translated as "compassion," the *hamah* of God has an enduring nature, a love of "intent" that cannot be rejected by humankind. The apparent contrast between *hamah* as both pain and love is, according to Kitamori, "not simply a mystery of language, but also a mystery of grace."[43]

To demonstrate the critical relationship between divine love and divine pain, Kitamori delineates "three orders of divine love."[44] The first order is the love of God for those who are worthy, which includes Christ and those whose

---

40. Kitamori, *Theology of the Pain of God*, 153.

41. Ibid., 156.

42. Ibid.

43. Ibid., 157.

44. McWilliams, *The Passion of God*, 102.

relationship with God is not affected by sin. According to Kitamori, this is a parental love that is "smooth, flowing, and intense."[45] At creation, human beings were counted among those who were children of God by nature. Since the Fall, however, sin encompasses humanity; now only Christ is worthy of such love. The second order is the pain of God experienced in response to human sin. It has two aspects: "First, it is God's pain in the sense that he forgives and loves those who should not be forgiven; secondly, it is his pain in the sense that he sends his only beloved Son to suffer, even unto death."[46] Finally, the third order is love rooted in the pain of God. In this order, God continues to love sinful humanity, but now this love is mediated through the redemptive work of Christ on the cross, through which humans are sons and daughters of God through adoption, not nature. For this reason, the suffering of Christ corresponds to the pain of God; in Christ, "The pain of God is part of his essence. . . . The Bible reveals that the pain of God belongs to his *eternal being*."[47]

Thus the cross is no external act, but an act within God's own self; the pain of God is communicated in the pain of Christ. While the human situation of sin is such that God ought neither to forgive nor to abide human brokenness, the salvation effected by Jesus' death on the cross "is the message that our God enfolds our broken reality . . . [and] embraces us completely."[48] Jesus is the personification of the pain of God for human salvation, "the bitterest pain imaginable . . . of a father allowing his son to suffer and die."[49] This perception uniquely reflects the influence of his Japanese culture—namely, its "spirit of tragedy." Termed *tsurasa*, this spirit of deep anguish and pain is evoked "when one suffers and dies, or makes his beloved son suffer and die, for the sake of loving and making others live."[50] Although Kitamori considers the pain of God an eternal attribute and therefore discernible in any time or place, it is most readily discerned by those who have experienced devastating tragedy in life. This experience is particularly palpable for the Japanese in the post–World War II era, and Kitamori credits his cultural context for the development of his theology of the pain of God: "The pain of God can be discerned most vividly by the Japanese mind. . . . It is a truth acceptable all over the world. But this universal truth would not have been discerned without Japan as it medium."[51]

---

45. Kitamori, *Theology of the Pain of God*, 118.

46. Ibid., 120.

47. Ibid., 45, emphasis in the original.

48. Ibid., 20.

49. Ibid., 47.

50. Ibid., 135.

51. Ibid., 137.

Kitamori contends that God is immanent in human experience and "when the pain of God loves the human condition, it first makes human pain its own, becomes immanent with it, and then seeks to resolve the pain which is tangible."[52] Like the crucified God and the God of solidarity, this understanding of God can offer the compassionate companionship of one who deeply knows the pain one suffers and works through the circumstances of life to ease or eliminate it. Kitamori also sees human suffering as a service to God, a sacrifice for sin, a witness to the pain of God, or intercession for unbelievers.[53]

Unfortunately, these perspectives run the risk of glorifying or validating suffering, which may lead to apathy or indolence in counteracting the source of one's pain or suffering. They also tend to equate human suffering with divine punishment for sin, reviving the law of retribution that suffering is a result of sinfulness; it places the blame for suffering on the sufferer and the source of suffering in God. Such implications in Kitamori's theology of suffering may come from understanding that the real nature of human pain for Kitamori is rooted in humanity's estrangement from God. True pain arises when human beings become aware that they can no longer depend solely on themselves and need to seek salvation in the transcendent love of God. God's deepest pain is experienced when humanity fails to do so.[54]

God in Solidarity with the Oppressed of Latin America

The Context: El Salvador in Life and Death

Jon Sobrino, Jesuit Catholic priest and theologian, was born in Barcelona, Spain. However, in 1958, one year after entering the Jesuit order at eighteen, he was missioned to El Salvador, a country scarred by socioeconomic inequality, political oppression, and military violence since the 1930s. This state of affairs escalated into a full-scale civil war in 1980 after an election marked by fraud and

---

52. Ibid., 103.

53. Ibid., 62–64.

54. Ibid., 103.

intimidation and with a regime characterized by the systematic use of torture, abductions, and death squads to kill opponents of the government. As the *Report of the UN Truth Commission on El Salvador* characterized the period from 1980–1983, "violence became systematic and terror and distrust reigned among the civilian population. The fragmentation of any opposition or dissident movement by means of arbitrary arrests, murders and selective and indiscriminate disappearances of leaders became common practice."[55]

Throughout the 1980s, more than 75,000 Salvadorans were killed in massacres and executions and by landmines and bombing.[56] During this period Archbishop Oscar Romero was assassinated under orders from senior military officers (see "Case in Point," chapter 3). Commentators suggest that Romero's assassination "tipped the sporadic political violence of the 1970s into full-scale civil war."[57] When more than 250,000 mourners assembled for his funeral, they were attacked by snipers who killed forty-two and wounded more than two hundred.

This marked the beginning of a series of murders of religious men and women, perpetrated by military and paramilitary forces in El Salvador. In December 1980, four American churchwomen—Sisters Maura Clarke, MM; Dorothy Kazel, OSU; Ita Ford, MM; and lay missioner Jean Donovan—were raped and murdered for ministering to poor people and refugees in El Salvador. Then, in 1989, the Atlacatl Brigade, a counterinsurgency battalion created at the US School of the Americas,[58] entered the resident quarters at the Central American University José Simeón Cañas in San Salvador and brutally murdered six Jesuit priests, their housekeeper, and her daughter.[59] The Jesuits had been labeled as subversives by the El Salvadoran government. Jon Sobrino himself lived at the university but escaped assassination because he was traveling abroad.

Reflect and Discuss

What is the political situation in Latin America today and El Salvador in particular? What other civil wars rage throughout the world? How are the Church and the nations of the world responding?

---

55. United Nations Truth Commission on El Salvador, *From Madness to Hope: The 12-Year War in El Salvador, Derechos.org*, available at *www.derechos.org/nizkor/salvador/informes/truth.html*.

56. Ibid.

57. The Center for Justice and Accountability (CJA), "El Salvador: 12 Years of Civil War," *Cja.org*, available at *www.cja.org/article.php?list=type&type=199*.

58. The School of the Americas is a US Department of Defense Institute that provides military training to government personnel of Latin American countries.

59. The Jesuits were Ignacio Ellacuría, Segundo Montes, Ignacio Martín-Baró, Joaquín López y López, Juan Ramón Moreno, and Amado López; their housekeeper was Elba Ramos, and her daughter was Celia Marisela Ramos.

God in Solidarity

Like Moltmann and Kitamori, Latin American liberation theologian Jon Sobrino situates his discussion of the suffering of God in the cross of Christ and in the passion narrative of the Gospel of Mark, but he does so in response to the struggle of the oppressed persons of El Salvador and all of Latin America.[60] While Sobrino declares that the cross of Christ is a scandal, he insists that it is necessary for Christians to dwell upon the scandal of the cross to plumb the troubling mystery of God and suffering raised by the crucifixion. For Sobrino, this necessity is both theological and existential. To dwell upon the scandal of the cross is theologically necessary because it proclaims the God in whom one believes. Existentially, focus on the cross of Christ is necessary, "because history goes on producing crosses . . . and not even God changes things."[61]

In his theological reflection upon Mark 15:34 and upon the Son who dies abandoned by his Father, Sobrino centers on God's alleged absence to Jesus at his crucifixion. Sobrino suggests that the relationship between Jesus and the God he called Father was a balance of mystery and intimacy. The "infinite distance" of God was, by all Gospel accounts, accompanied by the "absolute closeness" of God, whom Jesus called Abba. This intimacy, however, seems to vanish on the cross, and Jesus' life apparently ends shrouded in the silence and inactivity of God his Father.

According to Sobrino, this sense of abandonment undoubtedly deepens the mystery of Jesus' relationship with God. However, it also weighs heavily upon the faith of each Christian who contemplates this mystery of abandonment, since it unavoidably "transforms and questions our ideas about God" and inevitably raises the issue of who God is and what God does about suffering.[62]

Probing the mystery of God in suffering, Sobrino indicates that individuals come to know God through God's words and deeds in history and in the Scriptures. Therefore, if, at the cross of Jesus, God neither speaks to console nor acts to intervene, one wonders how the absence of God's words and deeds may be a revelation of God. While such wonderment has drawn a variety of theological responses, Sobrino affirms what Jürgen Moltmann already proposed: "There is no substitute for calling this God 'the crucified God.'"[63] If the Gospels and human experience both indicate that, in the face of suffering and death, God by and large does not intervene, then Sobrino like Moltmann concludes that God participates in suffering, bears suffering, and reveals that suffering must be borne.

---

60. Jon Sobrino, *Jesus the Liberator: A Historical-Theological Reading of Jesus of Nazareth*, trans. Paul Burns and Francis McDonagh (Maryknoll, NY: Orbis, 2001).

61. Ibid., 234.

62. Ibid., 238.

63. Ibid., 235.

Reflect and Discuss

Sobrino writes that "history goes on producing crosses and not even God changes things." Do you agree with Sobrino? What crosses is history producing in the world today? What is God doing about them?

Sobrino cautions that speech about the way suffering affects God can only be speculative; it arises from the believer's faith and theological perspectives concerning the capacity of God to suffer. From his theological perspective, Sobrino echoes Aquinas's principle that one can only speak of God on the basis of experience linked to faith. Believers can accept positive attributes based on experience without much difficulty since they pose no threat of limitation on the nature of God.[64] However, according to Sobrino, the Incarnation introduced something radically new into the Christian conception of God; in the Incarnation, the unchangeable God "becomes" a human being with all the finitude and limitations that implies. Within this radically new experience, "Jesus is neither only what 'God has become,' nor only 'the firstborn' who points to God's future, but also the one who suffered on the cross and suffered specifically abandonment by God."[65] This reality impels believers to question the nature of God on the cross and to consider suffering as a possible mode of the being of God.

While the Christian Scriptures offer no specific words about the suffering of God, Sobrino points out that the writings of Paul intimate God's presence on the cross of Christ: "*in Christ* God was reconciling the world to himself" (2 Cor. 5:19, emphasis added). According to Sobrino, this divine presence cannot be separated from the cross; therefore, the experience of the cross mediates the experience of God.

> It is a feature of . . . revelation that the nature of the place in which God manifests himself is a mediation of God's own nature. . . . If this is the case, it is at least plausible to proceed in the opposite direction: in every place where Jesus' nature is present, something of God is revealed. It is therefore likely that God's presence on the cross, insofar as it is a cross, reveals something of God.[66]

On the basis of this reasoning, Sobrino concludes, "God suffered on Jesus' cross and on those of this world's victims by being their non-active and silent witness." Rather than implying a negativity, cruelty, or impotence in God, Sobrino claims

---

64. Ibid., 242.

65. Ibid., 243.

66. Ibid.

that this proposal must be seen as "a radical drawing near for love and in love, wherever it leads, without escaping from history or manipulating it from the outside."[67] This God who became incarnate and crucified reveals Godself as the "God of solidarity," the God who in a world of victims was prepared to become a victim in suffering love. Thus, "the cross presents a basic affirmation about God. It says that on the cross God himself is crucified . . . and takes upon himself all the sorrow and pain of history. This ultimate solidarity with humanity reveals God as a God of love in a real and credible way."[68]

Thus, from his stance in the midst of the suffering and oppressed of Latin America, Sobrino concludes, "If from the beginning of the gospel God appears in Jesus as a God *with* us, if throughout the gospel God shows himself as a God *for* us, on the cross he appears as a God *at our mercy* and, above all, as a God *like* us."[69] While theologians argue theoretically whether the symbol of a crucified God functions to justify suffering or to mount the strongest possible protest against suffering, Sobrino maintains the matter is not one of theory, but of practice. The symbol of the suffering, crucified God "makes clear in a history of suffering . . . that between the alternatives of accepting suffering . . . and eliminating it . . . we can and must introduce a new course, bearing it." In bearing this suffering, however, "God says what side he is on, what struggles he is in solidarity with."[70] The crucified God demands that one take a stance of hope and action in response to the suffering in the world, a movement toward the "'more' that leaves hearts forever restless, questioned and questioning."[71]

In his theology, Sobrino combines biblical and theological insights to arrive at the notion of the God who suffers in solidarity with the victims of history— an affirmation rarely made in Catholic theological tradition. For Sobrino, God is revealed in history through participation in suffering, but still has the power to liberate and transform within the present time. Nevertheless, Latin America's history of oppression and suffering leads Sobrino to the problematic conclusion that divine solidarity with suffering does not offer the options of eliminating or of accepting suffering, but rather of bearing suffering in the struggle for liberation. While this conception of God demonstrates divine solidarity with history's victims and signals God's intention of ending history's crosses, the liberating act of God seems delayed as long as crosses still rise up in history. Because his approach risks failing to inspire hope and commitment, Sobrino explicitly

---

67. Ibid., 244.

68. Jon Sobrino, *Christology at the Crossroads: A Latin American Approach*, trans. John Drury (Maryknoll, NY: Orbis, 1978), 371.

69. Sobrino, *Jesus the Liberator*, 245–46, emphasis in the original.

70. Ibid.

71. Ibid., 250.

challenges Christians to action for justice and to a stance of solidarity with the victims of history in imitation of the God in whom they believe. In so doing, Sobrino points to the example of Jesus Christ and urges a Christian discipleship that bears the suffering that often accompanies the quest for justice, a suffering borne by God's own self in the crucified Christ.

> ## Reflect and Discuss
>
> Like Moltmann, Sobrino indicates that something of the being of God is revealed in Jesus' suffering and death on the cross. What if Christians truly saw Jesus and his life and works as a revelation of the unseen God? Would that make a difference in how they think about God in the midst of suffering?

God at Risk

The Context: Global Environmental Crisis

It has been more than twenty years since theologian Sallie McFague published her works on theology in an ecological, nuclear age. Since that time, the environmental crisis has worsened rather than improved. Consider the following facts:

- In the last hundred years, the average temperature of Earth has risen by 1.4°F. Scientists project it to rise another 2 to 11.5°F over the next hundred years, resulting in significant and hazardous changes in climate and weather.[72]
- Since the 1980s, 30 percent of the world's natural environment has been destroyed, 50 percent of the world's populations of freshwater animal and plant species have disappeared, and 10 percent of Earth's natural forests have been lost.[73] Approximately 98 percent of the usable agricultural area of Earth has already undergone development.[74]
- Sixty-nine percent of the oceans' marine fish are caught commercially in quantities exceeding ecologically safe limits.[75]

---

72. US Environmental Protection Agency, "Climate Change: Basic Information," *Epa.gov*, available at www.epa.gov/climatechange/basics/.

73. World Health Organization, "Environmental Change," *WHO.int*, available at *www.who.int /trade/glossary/story023/en/*.

74. E. W. Sanderson, M. Jaiteh, M. A. Levy, K. H. Redford, A. V. Wannebo, and G. Woolmer, "The Human Footprint and the Last of the Wild," *Bioscience* 52 (October 2002): 891–904.

75. Claretian Publications, "Stat House," *Claretianpubs.org*, available at *http://salt.claretianpubs .org/stats/environment/enviro.html*.

- Forest-dependent species are becoming extinct at a rate of 40,000–60,000 species annually. It is expected that half of Earth's species will disappear within the next 75 years.[76] Eighty-seven percent of species endangerment can be explained by the single variable of human population density.[77]
- Around the world, thirty-one countries face long-lasting freshwater shortages. By 2035, that number will rise to more than fifty countries and nearly three billion people.[78]
- Oceans absorb about a quarter of carbon dioxide emissions, resulting in ocean acidification that critically modifies marine ecosystems.[79]

Theologically, this destruction of Earth has ramifications for human relationships with God, the created world, and its creatures. From the writings of Paul in his Epistles and the reflections of Augustine, through the scholasticism of Thomas Aquinas to the investigations of Karl Rahner, theologians assert that everything is full of sacred presence; everything has the capacity to reveal the Living God. As Aquinas wrote, "God is in all things . . . inasmuch as God is present to all as the cause of their being."[80] Because this perspective understands God not as being in opposition to nature, but rather truly present within it, Christian theology can claim that "Nature itself is symbolic or revelatory of God."[81] Thus exploitation and abuse of the natural world obscures and reduces the power of the environment to reveal God. Eco-theologian Thomas Berry bemoaned that "losing the richness of life around us will impoverish our sense of the God whose being is symbolically revealed to us through the extravagant diversity and beauty of nature."[82] Hence, "At the end of the day," beyond social, economic, or scientific considerations, "it may be essentially an ethical decision" that is required for the full flourishing of the environment in an ecological, nuclear age.[83]

---

76. Ibid.

77. J. K. McKee, P. W. Sciulli, C. D. Fooce, and T. A. Waite, "Forecasting Global Biodiversity Threats Associated with Human Population Growth," *Biological Conservation* 115 (2003): 161–64.

78. Eric Leech, "20 Gut-Wrenching Statistics about the Destruction of the Planet and Those Living upon It," *Treehugger.com*, available at *www.treehugger.com/clean-technology/20-gut-wrenching -statistics-about-the-destruction-of-the-planet-and-those-living-upon-it/page2.html*.

79. "The ocean is so acidic that it is dissolving the shells of our baby oysters." Michal Graham Richard, *Treehugger.com*, available at *www.treehugger.com/climate-change/ocean-so-acidic-it-dissolving -shells-our-baby-oysters.html*.

80. Aquinas, *ST* 1.8.3.

81. John Haught, "Ecology and Eschatology," in *And God Saw That It Was Good*, ed. Drew Christiansen and Walter Grazer (Washington, DC: US Catholic Conference, 1996), 47–64.

82. Thomas Berry, quoted in John Haught, "Ecology and Eschatology," 55.

83. E. O. Wilson, "Future of Life," keynote address at the Organisation for Economic Co-operation and Development Forum 2001 on Sustainable Development and the New Economy, in "Harvard Scientist Warns Environmental Damage Irreversible," *OECDobserver.org*, available at *www.oecdobserver .org/news/archivestory.php/aid/459/HARVARD_SCIENTIST_WARNS_ENVIRONMENTAL _DAMAGE_IRREVERSIBLE.html*.

Reflect and Discuss

What environmental issues are causing concern today? What do these concerns say about the relationship between human beings and the environment? How are human beings responding to these concerns?

God at Risk

In her theology of suffering, North American Protestant theologian Sallie McFague focuses upon the poor, oppressed, and ravaged of the world, but for her these include not only humanity but also nonhuman creation and Earth itself. McFague discusses her theology in two groundbreaking works in ecological theology: *Models of God: Theology for an Ecological, Nuclear Age* and *The Body of God: An Ecological Theology*.[84] Her ecological theology has the distinction of being one of the few theologies of suffering that includes the suffering of nonhuman creation within its concerns. In so doing, she clearly demonstrates that it is not enough to be concerned for the suffering of humanity alone; it is critical to adopt an ethic of care for the earth, the giver and sustainer of human life, in essential and practical ways. In her work, McFague grounds her theological reflections in significant moments in the life of Jesus of Nazareth. In *Models of God*, McFague's starting point is the resurrection of Jesus, which she interprets as the sign of God's promise to be always with the world in an embodied way. In *The Body of God*, McFague shifts from the resurrection to the incarnation as she invites believers "to imagine 'the Word made flesh' not as limited to Jesus of Nazareth."[85] Rather, she proposes, God's self-revelation comes through all of creation, which God brought into being with a divine word. In this vision of the God-world relationship, McFague emphasizes that all of creation communicates the divine presence and demonstrates the way in which God relates to the world.

McFague suggests that God's relation to the world is analogous to the relation of the human *person* to the human *body*. As the human body mediates human personhood, so the world mediates divine personhood. McFague therefore proposes that the world is analogous to the body of God. In this analogy, McFague insists that she does not identify God with the world any more than a human person identifies him- or herself solely with his or her body. The mere fact that one can speak of one's body objectively indicates that being human is more than the body alone. Therefore, her metaphor of the

---

84. Sallie McFague, *Models of God: Theology for an Ecological, Nuclear Age* (Philadelphia: Fortress, 1988), and *The Body of God: An Ecological Theology* (Minneapolis: Fortress, 1993).

85. McFague, *Body of God*, 131.

world as God's body does not limit or reduce God ontologically; the body of the universe remains finite, while God as its Creator and Life-giver transcends the world's limitations.

Nevertheless, McFague argues, "though God is not reduced to the world, the metaphor of the world as God's body puts God 'at risk.'" She contends that God, like human persons, is "made vulnerable" by what happens in and to the world as God's body.

> God will be liable to bodily contingencies. The world as God's body may be poorly cared for, ravaged, and . . . essentially destroyed . . . . In the metaphor of the universe as the self-expression of God . . . the notions of vulnerability, shared responsibility, and risk are inevitable.[86]

This metaphor underscores that the evil in the world occurs in and to God as well as to creation and its creatures. Moreover, it reveals the readiness of God to suffer for and with the world, a readiness embodied and demonstrated in "the inclusive, suffering love of the cross of Jesus of Nazareth." Because of this, McFague asserts that "God's suffering on the cross was not for a mere few hours . . . but is present and permanent. As the body of the world, God is 'forever nailed to the cross,' for as the body suffers, so God suffers."[87]

Reflect and Discuss

What is your response to McFague's metaphor of the world as God's body? How might we treat the planet differently if we envisioned God as immanent in the world and its creatures?

McFague indicates that her theology of the world as God's body may also imply that evil is a part of God's being; in an evolving universe, "much that is evil from various perspectives will occur, and if one sees this process as God's self-expression, then God is involved in evil."[88] In *The Body of God*, therefore, McFague modified her theology of the relationship between God and suffering and evil to include both divine immanence and divine transcendence.[89] Approaching her theological reflections through the mystery of the Incarnation and an evolutionary understanding of the universe, McFague asks, "Were

---

86. McFague, *Models of God*, 72.

87. Ibid.

88. Ibid., 75.

89. McFague, *The Body of God*, 131–32.

we to imagine 'the Word made flesh' as not limited to Jesus of Nazareth but as the body of the universe . . . might we not have an . . . awesome metaphor for both divine nearness *and* divine glory?"[90] God is immanently present in and through all bodies, yet transcends any one particular expression of divine presence. Therefore, "At one level . . . the universe as God's body moves us in the direction of contemplating the glory and grandeur of divine creation . . . while at another level it moves us in the direction of compassionate identification with and service to the fragile, suffering, oppressed bodies that surround us."[91]

Because she bases this model on the mystery of the Incarnation in which God becomes flesh in Jesus Christ, McFague states that Christianity is uniquely suited to embrace the paradigm of the world as God's body: "An incarnational religion, a bodily tradition, such as Christianity, should not have to strain to include the natural world and its creatures, for they epitomize the physical."[92] McFague terms her model "the Christic paradigm" and suggests that Christian faith and action must be "toward inclusive love for all, especially the oppressed, the outcast, the vulnerable" because, like the community of Jesus' disciples, *"the shape of God's body includes all, especially the needy and outcast."*[93] In an age of ecological devastation, moreover, the oppressed, the needy, and the outcast must include the "new poor," that is, nonhuman beings and the cosmos itself. McFague is clear that calling creation the "new poor" does not mean that the "old poor," that is, human beings, are being discounted. Furthermore, McFague still asserts the central place of humanity in the love of God; not "every microorganism is included in God's love in the same way as human beings are."[94] However, it does underscore both the intrinsic and the instrumental value of creation and its creatures. Creation has intrinsic value, in and of itself, because all life was lovingly created by God. Moreover, creation and its creatures have instrumental value because each member of the web of evolutionary life is interdependent on one another for its sustenance and well-being. Unfortunately, humans often see creation as having only instrumental value, "solely in terms of its usefulness to ourselves." When that happens, intrinsic value is often compromised and "we transgress the 'integrity of creation.'"[95] Because of this, McFague points out, *"we have made nature poor."*[96]

---

90. Ibid., 131, emphasis in the original.

91. Ibid., 135.

92. Ibid., 167.

93. Ibid., 160, 164, emphasis in the original.

94. Ibid., 165.

95. Ibid.

96. Ibid., 166, emphasis in the original.

Reflect and Discuss

How is the natural world the "new poor"? What have humans done to impoverish it?

McFague's Christic paradigm maintains that whatever suffering happens in creation happens to God as well. Nevertheless, in this Christic paradigm, McFague balances the crucified Christ with the resurrected Christ, whom she calls the Cosmic Christ. "Freed from the body of Jesus of Nazareth, to be present in and to all bodies" in the resurrection, God confirms the divine promise to be with creation always.[97] The appearance stories in the Gospels attest that "the liberating, inclusive love of God for all is alive in and through the entire cosmos."[98] While the crucified Christ assures the world of God's suffering love and presence with human and nonhuman victims in the body of the world, the resurrected Cosmic Christ assures creation of God's "compassion for the outcast and the vulnerable . . . when and where the oppressed are liberated, the sick are healed, the outcast are invited in."[99] This interplay acknowledges that God is both immanently capable of suffering and transcendently able to save. Each movement is a sign, however vague and fragmentary, that gives reason to hope and grace to endure.

Case in Point: *Night* by Elie Wiesel

Elie Wiesel is a Jewish-American professor, political activist, and survivor of the Shoah. Born in Sighet, Transylvania, in 1928, Wiesel has written more than fifty books, including *Night*,[100] which is based on his experiences during World War II and specifically as a prisoner in Auschwitz/Birkenau, Buna, and Buchenwald concentration camps. The genre of the book is a matter of some debate; some have called it a novel, an autobiography, a memoir, and a testimony. Wiesel himself called it his deposition.[101] Through the eyes and voice of the narrator Eliezer, an Orthodox Jewish boy of fifteen, *Night* offers an intensely

---

97. Cf. Matt. 28:20: "And remember, I am with you always, to the end of the age."

98. McFague, *The Body of God*, 179.

99. Ibid., 195.

100. Elie Wiesel, *Night* (New York: Hill & Wang, 1982).

101. Elie Wiesel, *All Rivers Run to the Sea: Memoirs* (New York: Schocken, 1996), 79.

Case in Point: *Night* **by Elie Wiesel** *(continued)*

personal, compelling, and frequently disturbing account not only of Eliezer's experiences of ghettoization, deportation, and imprisonment but also of his struggle with faith in God and in humanity. This "Case in Point" focuses strictly on Eliezer's struggle—and by extension, Wiesel's own—with God in the midst of the horrendous suffering and death of the Shoah.

At the outset of *Night*, the year is 1941. Eliezer is a pious young man who studies the Talmud by day and the cabala[102] by evening under the mentoring eye of Moshe the Beadle, who works at the Hasidic synagogue. During prayer, Eliezer would often weep over the destruction of the Temple at Jerusalem, a source of continuing grief for Orthodox Jews.[103] One evening, Moshe came to him.

"Why do you pray?" he asked me, after a moment. Why did I pray? A strange question. Why did I live? Why did I breathe? "I don't know why," I said, even more disturbed and ill at ease. "I don't know why."[104]

It is clear from this response that prayer and faith in God was part of the fabric of Eliezer's being, to the extent that it did not occur to him to ask "why" it was so. To him, it was as natural as life, as breath. There seemed no need to question. However, for Moshe, questioning was the heart of the matter, even questioning God.

"Man raises himself toward God by the questions he asks Him," he was fond of repeating. "That is the true dialogue. Man questions God and God answers. But we don't understand His answers." "And why do you pray, Moshe?" I asked him. "I pray to the God within me that He will give me the strength to ask Him the right questions."[105]

Some Jews in the camps did not question God, but interpreted their situation in terms of their ancestral faith. Lessons from the Hebrew Scriptures resonate through their interpretations.

---

102. Also spelled *kabbalah*, *cabala* is the ancient Jewish tradition of mystical interpretation of the Bible.

103. The most recent Temple of Jerusalem was destroyed by the Romans in 70 CE. It has not been rebuilt.

104. Wiesel, *Night*, 2.

105. Ibid., 2–3.

Case in Point: *Night* by Elie Wiesel *(continued)*

> God is testing us. He wants to find out whether we can domi-
> nate our base instincts and kill the Satan within us. . . . And
> if he punishes us relentlessly, it's a sign that he loves us all
> the more.[106]

However, Eliezer had grown dissatisfied with those answers. For him,
Auschwitz and the brutalities he experienced there shook not only his
faith in God but also in himself and in his future.

> Never shall I forget that night, the first night in camp, which
> has turned my life into one long night. . . . Never shall I for-
> get those moments which murdered my God and my soul
> and turned my dreams to dust. Never shall I forget these
> things, even if I am condemned to live as long as God Him-
> self. Never.[107]

While Eliezer questioned his faith because of the atrocities that
"murdered [his] God," he was surrounded by thousands of devout
Jews in the camps who continued daily devotions to God and com-
memorated the holy days of their tradition. One such commem-
oration was held on the eve of Rosh Hashanah, the start of the
Jewish New Year. According to the tradition, on Rosh Hashanah, God
inscribes who will live and who will die in books of God's decrees.
The books are then sealed on the feast of Yom Kippur, the Day of
Atonement, which is the last day to demonstrate repentance, to
make amends, and so to change the judgment God decreed. The
question of who would live and who would die had unparalleled
consequence in the concentration camps. It spoke to the existential
question that the imprisoned lived with each moment of each day.
Questions once again welled up inside of Eliezer as night fell on Rosh
Hashanah and "ten thousand . . . had come to attend the solemn
service, heads of the blocks, Kapos, functionaries of death."[108] It
seemed incongruous to him, even profane. The prayer began: "Bless

---

106. Ibid., 42.

107. Ibid., 32.

108. A *kapo* was a prisoner in the concentration camp assigned to supervise forced labor or do administrative tasks.

the Eternal. . . . Blessed be the Name of the Eternal!"[109] He defied the benediction with his whole being. "Blessed be God's name? Why, but why would I bless Him?"

> Because He caused thousands of children to burn in His mass graves? Because he kept six crematoria working day and night, including Sabbath and the Holy Days? Because in His great might, He had created Auschwitz, Birkenau, Buna, and so many other factories of death? How could I say to Him: Blessed be Thou, Almighty, Master of the Universe . . . for having chosen us to be slaughtered on Thine altar?[110]

There was a time in his life when he believed that "upon one solitary deed of mine, one solitary prayer, depended the salvation of the world."[111] Yet on this day he ceased to plead, no longer believing in the power of prayer or of God to save.

> I was no longer capable of lamentation. . . . I was the accuser, God the accused. My eyes were open and I was alone—terribly alone in a world without God and without man. Without love or mercy.[112]

> Clearly, the suffering and death witnessed by Eliezer in the concentration camps transformed his personal and religious worldview. At the outset of *Night*, belief was central to his identity; he even resisted Moshe's encouragement to question God. Later, all he has are questions. God has become a stranger to Eliezer, and he is a stranger even to himself. Yet in all the invectives he hurls at God, he does not ask the question "Where is God?" And yet another does ask the question, and the answer Wiesel offers in *Night* is enigmatic. It comes in a story about the execution on the gallows of "three victims in chains," one of them, a young boy.[113] Most commentators contend

---

109. Ibid., 63–64.

110. Ibid., 64.

111. Ibid., 65.

112. Ibid., 64–65.

113. Ibid., 61.

that the conclusion of the story refers to the death of God, the loss of innocence, or the demise of hope. However, could the God of the gallows stand like the crucified God, as the One at risk who suffers pain in solidarity with the victims?

> The SS seemed more preoccupied, more disturbed, than usual. To hang a young boy in front of thousands of spectators was no light matter. . . . The three victims mounted together onto the chairs. The three necks were placed at the same moment within the nooses. . . .
>
> "Where is God, where is He?" someone behind me asked.
>
> At the sign from the head of the camp, the three chairs tipped over.
>
> Total silence throughout the camp. On the horizon, the sun was setting. . . . We were weeping. . . .
>
> The two adults were no longer alive. . . . But the third rope was still moving; being so light, the child was still alive. . . .
>
> For more than half an hour he stayed there, struggling between life and death, dying in slow agony under our eyes. . . .
>
> Behind me, I heard the same man asking: "Where is God now?"
>
> And I heard a voice within me answer him: "Where is He? Here He is—He is hanging here on this gallows. . . ."[114]

Reflect and Discuss

How do you interpret the meaning of the response that Eliezer hears within him: God "is hanging here on this gallows"?

114. Ibid., 61–62.

For Further Reading

McFague, Sallie. *Models of God: Theology for an Ecological, Nuclear Age.* Philadelphia: Fortress, 1988.

Moltmann, Jürgen. *The Crucified God: The Cross of Christ as the Foundation and Criticism of Christian Theology.* Translated by R. A. Wilson and John Bowden. Minneapolis: Fortress, 1993.

Sobrino, Jon. *Jesus the Liberator: A Historical-Theological Reading of Jesus of Nazareth.* Translated by Paul Burns and Francis McDonagh. Maryknoll, NY: Orbis, 2001.

Wiesel, Elie. *Night.* New York: Hill & Wang, 1982.

Internet Resources

McFague, Sallie. "A New Climate for Theology: God, the World, and Global Warming." Lecture at Yale Divinity School Symposium, "Renewing Hope: Pathways of Religious Environmentalism." February 28, 2008. Available at *www.youtube.com/watch?v=QjK4d8ci1e0* (time: 1:02:13).

Moltmann, Jürgen. "'Sun of Righteousness, Arise!' The Justification of Sinners and Victims, from Martin Luther to Martin Luther King." Candler School of Theology, Emory University. Reformation Day 2011. Available at *www.youtube.com/watch?v=uun00U_QKzU* (time: 1:14:06).

Winfrey, Oprah. "Interview with Elie Wiesel at Auschwitz." *Harpo Productions, Inc.* Available at *www.youtube.com/watch?v=KugVjbq6Si8&list=PLm6yk2UM 7aMLlR7kF981w62sWkPVYyDx1&index=2* (time: 55:08).

Film

Roses in December [*The Women Martyrs of El Salvador*]. Directed by Anna Carrigan and Bernard Stone. New York: VIACOM Media Networks, 1982.

CHAPTER 6

God in the Silence of Sexism

> The reality of women's lives has been invisible to men. This invisibility
> persists at all levels, from the family to the nation. Though they share
> the same space, women and men live in different worlds.
> —UNFPA, *LIVES TOGETHER, WORLDS APART:*
> *MEN AND WOMEN IN A TIME OF CHANGE*

Introduction

In *Faith, Religion, Theology*, theologian William Madges defines theology as "a dynamic, thoughtful activity that seeks to bring a religious tradition into genuine conversation with some aspect of contemporary experience."[1] The last chapter made this clear in its discussion of contextual theologies shaped by contemporary experiences of genocide, war, and environmental destruction. Regardless of whether a theologian recognizes or acknowledges how influential context is on the process of his or her theology, context inevitably affects the product of theology—the texts, rituals, doctrines, and ethics that emerge from theological reflection. Therefore, "'Pure objectivity,' that is, an interpretation without presuppositions and without historical, cultural, or personal 'coloring' . . . is impossible."[2] As a result of their historical or cultural context, there are inherent limitations to specific theological insights and how a particular theological insight may apply. One limitation on theological insight—present throughout this book, but unacknowledged until this point—is that, prior to the twentieth century, the preponderance of Christian theology about God and suffering was produced almost exclusively by men. This near absence of women's voices and experiences in theology is part of the more pervasive and systemic silence and suffering experienced by women throughout the world as a result of the institution of patriarchy and the pattern of belief called sexism.

---

1. Brennan Hill, Paul Knitter, and William Madges, *Faith, Religion, Theology: A Contemporary Introduction* (Mystic, CT: Twenty-Third Publications, 2002), 287.

2. Ibid., 290.

> ### Reflect and Discuss
>
> Did you notice the near absence of women's theological voices in the text thus far? What difference does this absence make? Do men and women "live in different worlds"?

The Context: Global Patriarchy and Sexism

In its broadest definition, patriarchy is any system—social, religious, economic, philosophical, or familial—that rests upon male privilege and power and that perpetuates a model of relationship between men and women characterized by male superiority and female submission. Patriarchy stems from a family system "in which the father is the head of the family and men have authority over women and children."[3] Its influence spread beyond the family, as communities and societies became structured according to this system. Scholars trace the beginnings of patriarchy to a variety of factors that occurred at the juncture of the Stone Age and the beginning of civilization. Based on this estimate, the institution of patriarchy has existed since 3000 BCE.

Over time, the societal structures of patriarchy led to particular patterns of thought concerning men and women. Male authority in the family and ultimately in society spawned a system of beliefs and behaviors that assumed and then asserted the superiority of males over females not only culturally but ontologically—that is, solely on the basis of biological sex. As a general rule, society frequently regarded men as assertive, logical, powerful, and independent. On the other hand, society often stereotyped women as passive, emotional, weak, and dependent. These general presumptions about men and women in the absence of particular experiences stemmed from and then further shaped a system of distorted beliefs and behaviors termed *sexism*. Sexism is "discrimination based on gender, especially discrimination against women; attitudes, conditions, or behaviors that promote stereotyping of social roles based on gender."[4]

As the definition suggests, stereotyping on the basis of sex is more than an attitude or a pattern of thought. Sexist stereotyping often leads to relationships in which males exercise dominance and females respond with submission. Distorted belief in male superiority and female inferiority has led to male privilege and power in the global society and has frequently deprived women of equal standing, participation, and access to every sphere of economic, educational,

---

3. "Patriarchy," in *The American Heritage Dictionary of the English Language*, 4th ed. (New York: Houghton Mifflin, 2009), available at *www.thefreedictionary.com/patriarchy*.

4. "Sexism," *The American Heritage Dictionary of the English Language*, 4th ed. (New York: Houghton Mifflin, 2009), available at *www.thefreedictionary.com/sexism*.

political, and religious life. It has also resulted in suffering, hostility, and violence against women, from which women frequently have little or no legal or religious recourse. Unfortunately, these stereotypes have become such a part of the social fabric, cultural context, and human consciousness that their validity often goes unquestioned.

> ### Reflect and Discuss
>
> What sexual or gender stereotypes can you think of? Have you experienced being stereotyped in some way? What effect did it have on you?

Consider the following facts:

- Of the world's people, 855 million are illiterate; of these, 70 percent are female.
- As children, girls are often undervalued, fed less, and given inadequate health care.
- Parents in countries such as China and India sometimes use sex determination tests to find out if their fetus is a girl. Of 8,000 fetuses aborted at a Bombay clinic, 7,999 were female.
- There is no country in the world where women's wages are equal to those of men.
- Women produce nearly 80 percent of the food on the planet but receive less than 10 percent of agricultural assistance.
- Of the refugees and internally displaced in the world, 75 percent are women who have lost their families and their homes.
- In the former Yugoslavia, 20,000 women and girls were raped during the first months of the Serbo-Croatian War.
- The majority of the world's women cannot own, inherit, or control property, land, and wealth on an equal basis with men.[5]

These facts give only the barest outline of the tragic and life-shattering circumstances under which many of the world's women exist. Despite the awareness of these tragedies, a 2013 report by the World Health Organization concluded that these events of suffering, cruelty, and oppression are neither isolated nor decreasing; they are epidemic.

---

5. "Human Rights Facts and Figures," *Women's Learning Partnership for Rights, Development and Peace*, available at *www.learningpartnership.org/en/resources/facts/humanrights*.

Violence against women is not a new phenomenon, nor are its consequences to women's physical, mental and reproductive health. What is new is the growing recognition that acts of violence against women are not isolated events but rather *form a pattern of behaviour that violates the rights of women and girls, limits their participation in society, and damages their health and well-being.* When studied systematically, as was done with this report, it becomes clear that violence against women is a global public health problem that affects approximately one third of women globally.[6]

Despite such facts and reports, many people dismiss the idea that women experience inequality or subordination at this point in history. Nonetheless, stories not only of inequality but often of suffering, brutality, and death fill news reports each day.

In 1993 young women from Juarez started disappearing and turning up in fields and rubbish dumps, mutilated, sexually abused and murdered. Many of the victims were factory workers who disappeared while travelling to or from work. Others were teenage students, migrants and other vulnerable young women. . . . Femicide occurs . . . countrywide: at least 34,000 women were murdered in Mexico between 1985 and 2009, according to figures produced by the UN and local rights groups.[7]

A 14-year-old girl who became a national heroine when she protested the Pakistani Taliban's ban on education for girls in her home district was in critical condition Tuesday after she was shot in the head as she waited for a ride home from her beloved school, according to officials and witnesses. Malala Yousafzai, who was only 11 when she stood up to the Taliban over their ban, was sitting in a school van in Swat with other students on Monday, waiting to go home, when an assailant approached, asked which student was Malala, then opened fire.[8]

According to accounts, armed members of Boko Haram overwhelmed security guards at a school . . . , pulled the girls out of bed and forced them into trucks. . . . Nigerian authorities updated the

---

6. World Health Organization, "Global and Regional Estimates of Violence against Women: Prevalence and Health Effects of Intimate Partner Violence and Non-Partner Sexual Violence," *WHO.int*, available at *http://apps.who.int/iris/bitstream/10665/85239/1/9789241564625_eng.pdf*, emphasis added.

7. Olivia Kirkpatrick, "Femicide in Mexico: The Cotton Field Case and Its Sequels," *Third World Resurgence* 271/272 (March/April 2013), 41–42, available at the website of Third World Network.

8. Saeed Shah and McClatchy Newspapers, "Girl Who Defied Pakistani Taliban Shot for 'Promoting Western Culture,'" *Christian Science Monitor*, October 9, 2012, available at *www.csmonitor.com/World/Asia-South-Central/2012/1009/Girl-who-defied-Pakistani-Taliban-shot-for-promoting-Western-culture*.

number of girls kidnapped to 276. . . . Families had sent their girls to the rural school in Chibok for a desperately needed education.[9]

In the United States, in particular, many people believe that women have advanced beyond such misery and violence; however, it is frequently "a mirage of equality."

> Women are still being raped, trafficked, violated and discriminated against—not just in the rest of the world, but here in the United States . . . . And it's not just strangers who are killing women; more than 1,000 women were killed by their partners in 2005, and of all the women murdered in the United States, about a third are killed by a husband or boyfriend.[10]

Evidence that the structures of patriarchy and sexism continue to produce suffering and tragedy abounds in the lives of women every day in every country of the world.

Reflect and Discuss

Were you aware of such brutality against women? How would you explain the prevalence of such violence?

Women's Theologies and Suffering

In the movement from the context of women's suffering to the theology it engenders, it is important to recognize there is much in the biblical tradition and in the history of Christian thought that has perpetuated discrimination against women, producing rather than alleviating suffering. Traditional interpretations of the story of creation in Genesis 2, for example, claim that woman was created along with the animals for the benefit of man (Gen. 2:18); women are considered inferior because, while the Bible states that man was made complete in himself, the woman was made from the rib of the man (Gen. 2:21–22). A popular interpretation of Genesis 3 lays the burden of human sinfulness on the actions of the first woman because "Eve ate the apple" (Gen. 3:6). Moreover, the punishment pronounced by God on woman after the "original sin" clearly states that man "shall rule over" woman (Gen. 3:16). Regrettably, this leads to many women in

---

9. Need footnote here.

10. Jessica Valenti, "For Women in America, Equality Is Still an Illusion," *Washington Post*, February 21, 2010, available at *www.washingtonpost.com/wp-dyn/content/article/2010/02/19/AR2010021902049.html*.

the Bible being offered in prostitution or rape (Gen. 12:13–19, 19:1–8), considered as property (Exod. 20:17), taken as spoils in war (Deut. 20:14), abducted for wives (Judg. 21:21), silenced in church (1 Cor. 14:34; 1 Tim. 2:11–15), and subordinated to their husbands (Eph. 5:22–24; Col. 3:18; 1 Pet. 3:1).

Based on biblical passages such as these, Christian apologist Tertullian, writing toward the beginning of the third century CE, said of women,

> *You* are the devil's gateway: *you* are the unsealer of that (forbidden) tree: *you* are the first deserter of the divine law: *you* are she who persuaded him whom the devil was not valiant enough to attack. *You* destroyed so easily God's image, man. On account of *your* desert—that is, death— even the Son of God had to die.[11]

This line of thought continued into classical theological discourse.[12] Augustine taught that women could image God only in relation to a male.[13] Aquinas viewed a woman as a misbegotten or defective male,[14] lacking in good order and discretion.[15] Arguably the most vicious result of this oppression in Christian thought and practice was the European witch trials, which spanned more than two hundred years and resulted in the violent death of hundreds of thousands of women. A manual for the treatment of witches was written in 1486 and called the *Malleus Maleficarum* or the "Hammer of Witches." It provided directives for detecting and persecuting witches, the rules of evidence for condemning witches, and the procedures ordered by the religious authorities by which to torture witches and put them to death.[16]

---

11. Tertullian, "On the Apparel of Women," from *Ante-Nicene Fathers*, ed. Alexander Roberts, James Donaldson, and A. Cleveland Coxe (Buffalo: Christian Literature Publishing Co., 1885), 4.14. Revised and edited for New Advent by Kevin Knight, available at *www.newadvent.org/fathers/0402 .htm*, emphasis in the original. A Christian apologist is one who presents a basis for the Christian faith founded on reason, historical evidence, or philosophical argument in an attempt to defend the faith against objections.

12. A sampling can be found at the site "Statements on Women by Church Fathers, Doctors, and Saints," *Spring Hill College Theology Library*, available at *www.shc.edu/theolibrary/resources/women.htm*.

13. Augustine, *On the Trinity*, 12.7.10: "The woman together with her own husband is the image of God, so that that whole substance may be one image; but when she is referred separately to her quality of help-meet, which regards the woman herself alone, then she is not the image of God; but as regards the man alone, he is the image of God as fully and completely as when the woman too is joined with him in one."

14. Aquinas, *ST* 1.92, reply 1: "As regards the individual nature, woman is defective and misbegotten, for the active force in the male seed tends to the production of a perfect likeness in the masculine sex; while the production of woman comes from defect in the active force or from some material indisposition, or even from some external influence."

15. Ibid., 1.92, reply 2: "Good order would have been wanting in the human family if some were not governed by others wiser than themselves. So by such a kind of subjection woman is naturally subject to man, because in man the discretion of reason predominates."

16. "Introduction," *Malleus Maleficarum* (1486), trans. Montague Summers, available at *www .sacred-texts.com/pag/mm/*.

Compounding the subjugation of women in Christianity—and in other monotheistic religions—is that God is almost exclusively imaged as male. To be clear, Christianity has never explicitly assigned a sex to God and has always maintained that language about God is analogical and not literal. However, the overwhelming majority of personal images for God in scripture, ritual, song, and art have been drawn from male roles and experiences. Because of this, the Christian tradition seems to communicate the understanding that the Christian God is male. This understanding is reinforced by the reality that God became flesh through the male person of Jesus of Nazareth, who himself referred to God as Abba (Father) and told his disciples to call God "Our Father." This results in the Trinitarian naming of God as Father, Son, and Spirit, with no person of this Triune God in the female image.

For some, the question of the gender or sex of God is irrelevant, and many wonder what difference it makes whether one images God as male or female. The difference is twofold. First, when God is imaged almost exclusively in the personhood of one sex—the male—it implies that the personhood of the other sex—the female—does not adequately image God. Second, the way one understands *divine* authority and power affects the way one conceives *human* authority and power. If God, the ultimate source of authority and power in the universe, is imaged as male, then males are more likely to be envisioned as sources of authority and power in human life. This syllogism has had deleterious effects for the development of autonomy and leadership for many women.

Reflect and Discuss

Have you ever heard these or other religious arguments for the subjugation of women? Do you agree or disagree with them? Defend your position.

Women, of course, share many of the classical Christian responses to evil and suffering examined in earlier chapters of this book. They have seen suffering as a test of faith, as an educative process, and as a form of punishment; they have held fast to the belief that God has sent suffering in view of some greater good or for a reason beyond human comprehension. Added to these more universal responses, however, women have characteristically demonstrated an extraordinary willingness to bear suffering for the sake of others, especially for children and spouses. Stemming from socialization, from religious training, or from a combination of both, women become expert at "turning the other cheek, patiently enduring whatever suffering comes one's way rather than taking action to eliminate the cause."[17] Unfortunately, this tendency has led to situations that keeps women immersed in their own and others' suffering and militates against their well-being and flourishing.

Women's secondary status in society and church, and the suffering it has caused, have led women theologians over the past fifty years to reflect upon the Christian God and Christian doctrine through the experiences of women. This reflection revealed not only the sexual inequality and injustice that subjugate women but also that gender-bias is not the only source of oppression for women. For women who are not Caucasian and Euro-American, gender-bias comprises only one prong of the "triple oppression" of sexism, racism, and classism that frequently results in poverty and social injustice. The realization of how racism and classism shape women's experiences of suffering has resulted in a complex of theologies that respond to women's suffering, including Euro-American feminist theology, US black womanist theology, and US Hispanic/Latina *mujerista* theology.

These theologies consider scripture, Christian tradition, and the experiences of women within society and Church as essential theological sources. Black womanist theologians also mine slave narratives, autobiographies, and testimonies to capture the meanings and values of the African American community.[18] *Mujerista* theologians incorporate stories shared by Latinas as they struggle against the oppressions of class and economic injustice. Their theologies are by nature theologies of suffering; they begin with experiences of oppression and seek to speak rightly of God in the midst of them. Their fundamental task consists of analyzing the suffering and subjugation of women in specific social, cultural, and religious contexts; searching for sources that affirm women's dignity and worth; and risking new interpretations that prove healing and liberating for women's lives.

This chapter examines three theologies that address the suffering of women: feminist theology, womanist theology, and *mujerista* theology. These theologies do not claim to represent how all women within their context envision God's presence and action in their suffering. Nonetheless, each theological perspective recognizes a core of experiences as a particular source of suffering within that particular context; it then explores the presence and action of God in the midst of it to offer hope and bolster faith. Moreover, although each emerges from within the context of the United States, their theological insights are broad

---

17. Patricia L. Wismer, "For Women in Pain: A Feminist Theology of Suffering," in *In the Embrace of God: Feminist Approaches to Theological Anthropology*, ed. Ann O'Hara Graff (Maryknoll, NY: Orbis, 1995), 143.

18. Womanist theology is a liberationist theological approach that reflects upon Christian traditions, practices, scriptures, and biblical interpretation through the lens of African American women in America. It dialogues with and distinguishes itself from feminist theology and black theology because it focuses on the experiences of African American women and other women of color.

enough to bear on the plight of many women throughout the world who suffer the oppressions of sexism, racism, and classism with the abuse, exploitation, and injustice that accompany them.

> ### Reflect and Discuss
>
> Do you think women experience God differently than men? Have you ever thought of God in female terms? What female experiences might translate well in describing God's presence and action?

A Feminist Theology of Suffering: Suffering God, Compassion Poured Out

The feminist theology of suffering proposed by Catholic theologian Elizabeth Johnson stems from her study of God as Trinity through the lens of women's experience. In her book *She Who Is: The Mystery of God in Feminist Theological Discourse*, Johnson focuses on the biblical figure of Divine Wisdom, called *Hok-mah* in Hebrew, *Sophia* in Greek, and *Sapientia* in Latin, all nouns of female gender. Appearing as a sister, mother, hostess, preacher, and judge in the Hebrew Scriptures, Wisdom "pervades the world, both nature and human beings, interacting with them all to lure them along the right path to life" and to bring them to justice.[19] While sometimes construed as an attribute of God or as a mediator between God and the world, Wisdom is most often interpreted as a female personification of God in creative and liberative relationship with the world.[20] As Johnson describes, "Active in creation, she also works in history to save her chosen people, guiding and protecting them through the vicissitudes of liberating struggle."[21] Because of this, Wisdom, whom Johnson calls *Sophia* from the Greek, is central to her feminist theology of suffering.

Johnson begins with the question "What is the right way to speak about God in the constant happening of woe?"[22] Recognizing grief and lament as appropriate human responses to suffering and loss, she asserts that these emotional responses are also fitting for God who so loves the world. Johnson acknowledges that such responses conflict with the omnipotence and impassibility of God; she

---

19. Elizabeth A. Johnson, *She Who Is: The Mystery of God in Feminist Theological Discourse* (New York: Crossroad, 1993), 87.

20. This interpretation is supported by the equivalence between the deeds done by Wisd. of Sol. and those done by God. See Prov. 1:20–33, 3:18, 4:5–9, 8:1–36, 9:1–6; Wisdom 6:12–17, 7:7–14, 22–30, 8:1–8, 9:9–11, 10:1–21, 11:1–26; and Sir. 1:9–10, 4:12–18, 6:18–31, 14:20–27, 15:1–10, 24:1–29, 51:13–22.

21. Johnson, *She Who Is*, 91.

22. Ibid., 246.

is also mindful of the arguments proposed by classical theism to reconcile God and suffering.[23] Nonetheless, she points out the suffering that exists "in our history of barbarous excess . . . that does not simply punish or test or educate or work a greater good. Instead, it destroys."[24]

In the shadow of that kind of suffering, Johnson considers it scandalous to cling to an image of God who is either unaffected by or complicit in cruelty and destruction of such magnitude. As a result, Johnson finds the proposal of a suffering God persuasive, but remains cautious about attributing suffering to God if it means that suffering becomes a value in itself or leads to an acceptance of suffering rather than resistance to it. Nonetheless, she suggests that a feminist perspective "may contribute to a new realization of the power of the suffering God [which] . . . may in turn promote the full and equal humanity of women."[25]

Johnson explores four experiences of women's suffering as an entry point into her feminist theology of suffering. These include the pain of labor and childbirth, the penalty incurred for the sake of justice, the grief over misery endured by others, and the anguish of personal degradation. Johnson sees the first two experiences as "the coin of creative advance." Through the pain of labor and the price of just action, new life and liberation often emerge. However, in the latter two experiences, women "face the pit of darkness";[26] the affliction to self and others is beyond reason and redemptive value. How might these experiences of women's suffering shed light on the presence and action of a suffering God?

The Creative Suffering of God

Johnson focuses first on what may be termed the creative suffering of God. Creative suffering is goal-directed, a difficult means to a positive end. It is a suffering that can be borne in anticipation of the new life that will emerge. Drawn first from women's experiences of "bearing and birthing each new generation," this kind of suffering portends an outcome "woven round with a strong sense of creative power and joy."[27] The scriptures speak of God's creative suffering, laboring to bring forth new life to the beleaguered exiles of Israel:

> For a long time I have held my peace,
> I have kept still and restrained myself;
> now I will cry out like a woman in labor,
> I will gasp and pant.
> (Isa. 42:14)

---

23. See chapter 2 of this text, "The Claims of Classical Theism."

24. Johnson, *She Who Is*, 248–49.

25. Ibid., 254.

26. Ibid.

27. Ibid., 255.

Hearing the cry of her children for renewal and rebirth, Holy Wisdom rises up, straining to deliver a new world order of justice in a new heaven and a new earth. With her, "the whole creation has been groaning in labor pains until now" (Rom. 8:22). Nonetheless, she considers "that the sufferings of this present time are not worth comparing with the glory about to be revealed to us. For the creation waits with eager longing for the revealing of the children of God" (Rom. 8:18–19).

In like manner, God suffers creatively on behalf of all victims of injustice, who yearn for a future full of hope. Citing the courage of women from South Africa who protested apartheid, women from Guatemala who organized widows to protest the political violence, and activists like Rosa Parks, whose action sparked the civil rights movement, Johnson lifts up the image of the suffering God who hears the outcry of the afflicted, who is "moved to pity by their groanings because of those who afflicted and oppressed them" (Judg. 2:18). This is the God who said of the enslaved people of Israel, "I have observed the misery of my people who are in Egypt; I have heard their cry on account of their taskmasters. Indeed, I know their sufferings, and I have come down to deliver them" (Exod. 3:7–8). This is Divine Wisdom who burns with a passion that flames up in righteous anger against what is oppressive, injurious, or abusive to humanity and to creation itself. Embodied in the women of South Africa, Guatemala, and the civil rights movement, this is the God whose creative suffering acts to liberate those who are bowed down and to raise up those who are violated.

Reflect and Discuss

Are there other examples of creative suffering that occur to you? Might any of these apply to divine suffering?

The Compassionate Suffering of God

Johnson then turns to the kind of suffering provoked by injury and mistreatment to oneself or to loved ones—what may be termed compassionate suffering. Borne out of love and characterized by accompaniment, compassionate suffering keeps vigil with the anguished and sustains them in the movement through the darkness to light. The biblical tradition offers numerous examples of the suffering God of compassion. God is deeply moved by the suffering of the exiled families of Israel; God vows to have compassion on them, to restore their fortunes, and to bring them back to their own land (Jer. 31:1–26). Of the people wracked by war and strife, God says, "I weep with the weeping of Jazer . . . I drench you with my tears" (Isa. 16:9). In these and similar passages, divine compassion and love move God to take up "the cry of lament for beloved people who are broken and land that is devastated."[28]

This divine response resonates with the Shekhinah, another female image of God from the Jewish tradition. The Shekhinah is found in the Talmud, the Midrash, and the mystical tradition of Judaism and connotes a female personification of God's presence in the world, especially among the poor and suffering.[29] The Shekhinah is experienced as an ever-constant presence when Israel is in trouble, one that even feels the pain of the people: "When a human being suffers, what does Shekhinah say? 'My head is too heavy for me; my arm is too heavy for me.'"[30] This personal presence of God is most often associated with the exile. Shekhinah goes with people into captivity, sharing their misery and their wanderings; She weeps for the sufferings of the people and undergoes their persecutions with them.

Finally, those whose suffering "yields no discernible good but rather violates and destroys human dignity"[31] experience the compassionate suffering of God. Johnson asserts that woman in particular suffer this type of physical, social, and psychological affliction because of patriarchy and sexism around the world. As noted earlier, the scriptures chronicle stories of the abuse of women with no condemnation of those who perpetrated the violence.[32] The symbol of God's compassionate suffering with these victims is the crucified Christ, where "Wisdom participates in the suffering of the world and overcomes, inconceivably, from within through the power of love."[33]

Johnson points out that God's identification with the suffering world neither begins nor ends with the cross of Christ. As Jon Sobrino observed in the last chapter, history goes on producing crosses. On each of these, God faithfully keeps vigil "as pure unbounded love, utterly set against evil, totally on the side of the good."[34] It is this unconditional love—rather than the divine power to instantaneously change the situation of suffering—that represents the omnipotence of God in this theology of suffering. When one conceives of omnipotence as love, suffering in God is not an imperfection as classical theism would judge, but rather an excellence born of "an act of freedom, the freedom of love

---

28. Ibid., 260.

29. For a fuller development of this divine manifestation, see Gloria L. Schaab, "The Power of Divine Presence: Toward a *Shekhinah* Christology," in *Christology: Memory, Inquiry, Practice: Proceedings of the College Theology Society 2002*, ed. Anne Clifford and Anthony Godzieba (Maryknoll, NY: Orbis, 2003), 92–115.

30. J. Abelson, *The Immanence of God in Rabbinic Literature* (New York: Hermon, 1969), 104.

31. Johnson, *She Who Is*, 261.

32. See Phyllis Trible, *Texts of Terror* (Philadelphia: Fortress, 1984).

33. Johnson, *She Who Is*, 263.

34. Ibid., 265.

deliberately and generously shared" by Holy Wisdom.[35] While sharing intimately in this suffering, Wisdom is not overcome by it, for She is divine, not human. Rather, the compassion and creativity of Holy Wisdom moves the sufferer inexorably through affliction and pain to healing and new life. As Johnson phrases it, "If Holy Wisdom is in compassionate solidarity with suffering people in history, a future is thereby opened up even through the most negative experience. This is because we are speaking about *God*, than whose power of love nothing greater can be conceived." [36]

Reflect and Discuss

Does the idea of God's suffering in compassion for God's people resonate with you? Have you ever thought of God mourning or raging when God's creatures are afflicted?

A Womanist Theology of Suffering: Survival in the Wilderness

Womanist theologian Delores Williams constructs her theology of suffering in dialogue with the community and cultural context of African American women.[37] In so doing, Williams distinguishes her approach from both Euro-American feminist theology and from black liberation theology, first by focusing on the lives of *African American* women and second by focusing on African American *women*. While she sees commonalities between these theological approaches and womanist theology, she criticizes feminist theology for its silence on class privilege and white supremacy, and black theology for its predominantly liberation focus and androcentric bias. By failing to recognize and address the "invisibilization" of African American women in society and church, Williams contends, both approaches have perpetuated the oppression of black women rather than ameliorated it.

---

35. Ibid., 266.

36. Ibid., 268, emphasis in the original.

37. According to Williams, "Womanist theology is a prophetic voice . . . concerned about the well-being of the entire African American community, male and female, adults and children. . . . Womanist theology attempts to help black women see, affirm, and have confidence in the importance of their experience and faith for determining the character of the Christian religion in the African American community. Womanist theology challenges all oppressive forces impeding black women's struggle for survival and for the development of a positive, productive quality of life conducive to women's and the family's freedom and well-being. Womanist theology opposes all oppression based on race, sex, class, sexual preference, physical ability, and caste." Delores Williams, *Sisters in the Wilderness: The Challenge of Womanist God-Talk* (Maryknoll, NY: Orbis, 1999), xiii–xiv.

In her book *Sisters in the Wilderness: The Challenge of Womanist God-Talk*, Delores Williams identifies two approaches to biblical interpretation concerning God and suffering appropriated within the African American community. The first Williams terms the "liberation tradition." Found in songs, slave narratives, and preaching, this approach focuses on stories of principally male biblical figures engaged in struggle and liberation.[38] This tradition emphasizes the event of the Exodus when God freed the Israelites from slavery as well as the passage from Luke 4 in which Jesus describes his ministry in terms of liberation of the oppressed. Black liberation theologians used this tradition to envision God's response to human suffering as "God the liberator of the poor and oppressed."[39]

However, in her research Williams discovered an alternative tradition of African American biblical interpretation that presented a different picture of God's response to suffering. Passed down by writers, poets, sculptors, scholars, and preachers over a hundred years or more, this tradition focuses on the biblical figure of Hagar, "a female slave of African descent who was forced to be a surrogate mother, reproducing a child by her slave master because the slave master's wife was barren."[40] As Williams plumbed the African American sources, she discovered remarkable parallels between the history of African American women in America and Hagar:

> Hagar's heritage was African. . . . Hagar was a slave . . . brutalized by her slave owner. . . . Hagar had no control over her body. It belonged to her slave owner, whose husband . . . ravished Hagar. . . . Mother and child were eventually cast out . . . without resources for survival. . . . Hagar was a single parent.[41]

The similarities between Hagar's story and the history of African American women in America afforded Williams a starting point from which to construct her womanist theology of suffering. She named this Hagar-centered tradition of biblical interpretation the "survival/quality-of-life tradition." In this tradition, black women did not focus on the hopelessness of their situation; rather they emphasized God's response to their misery and oppression. Because of this, Williams centered on the questions "What was God's response to Hagar's predicament? Were her pain and God's response to it congruent with African American women's predicament and their understanding of God's response to black women's suffering?"[42]

---

38. Biblical figures include Moses and Aaron (Exod. 5–15); Shadrach, Meshach, and Abednego (Dan. 3); Daniel in the lion's den (Dan. 6); Paul and Silas (Acts 16:16–40); and, of course, Jesus of Nazareth.

39. Williams, *Sisters in the Wilderness*, 2.

40. Ibid.

41. Ibid., 3.

42. Ibid., 4.

The Hagar Tradition

The Bible tells the story of Hagar through two narratives in the book of Genesis. The first is Genesis 16:1–16, which tells the story of the patriarch Abram, his wife Sarai, and her Egyptian slave-girl Hagar. Because Sarai was unable to bear any children for Abram, she gave her slave-girl Hagar as a wife to Abram so that he and Sarai could "obtain children by her." Hagar did conceive a child by Abram, but afterwards Hagar "looked with contempt on her mistress." In return, Sarai "dealt harshly with her" and Hagar ran away (16:1–6).

Williams sees in these verses the history of African American women's suffering: "The slave woman's story . . . has been shaped by the problems and desires of her owners."[43] Hagar's experience is one of coercion and violation; she is caught between power and powerlessness, her life and future determined by a man and a woman of higher social status. In Hagar's experiences, Williams identifies significant issues also found in the history of African American women—sexual exploitation, domestic abuse, rape, surrogacy, poverty, homelessness, and single-parenting. Nonetheless, Hagar acts to free herself from this oppressive situation; pregnant and abused, she flees into the wilderness. It is in this wilderness experience that Williams perceives God's involvement not only in the life of a suffering Hagar, but in African American women's suffering and struggle for survival and for a better quality of life.

> The angel of the Lord found [Hagar] by a spring of water in the wilderness. . . . And he said, "Hagar, slave-girl of Sarai, where have you come from and where are you going?" She said, "I am running away from my mistress Sarai." The angel of the Lord said to her, "Return to your mistress, and submit to her." The angel of the Lord also said to her, "I will so greatly multiply your offspring that they cannot be counted for multitude." And the angel of the Lord said to her, "Now you have conceived and shall bear a son; you shall call him Ishmael, for the Lord has given heed to your affliction."(Gen. 16:7–11)

Reflect and Discuss

Were you familiar with the story of Hagar? Had you noticed her abuse at the hands of Abram and Sarai or the response of God in the wilderness? If not, what may have prevented you from taking note of her suffering?

---

43. Ibid., 15.

Divine Response to Hagar

This passage discloses the key to Williams's womanist theology of suffering. Although God recognizes and responds to Hagar's suffering, God neither actively alleviates it nor liberates Hagar from it. Rather, God sends Hagar back to the abusive situation and directs her to submit to Sarai! Moreover, the narrative represents the critical points on which Williams takes issue with black liberation theology and feminist theology in their theologies of suffering. Unlike the claim of black theology that God is a God of liberation who vindicates the oppressed and abused, a reading of the story of Hagar from the perspective of the female slave reveals that "the oppressed and abused do not always experience God's liberating power." From that viewpoint, moreover, "one quickly discerns a non-liberative thread running through the Bible."[44] In this story, God not only favors the rights of Sarai but also upholds her enslavement of Hagar. For Williams, this represents the position of white Euro-American feminist theology, which she criticizes for failing to recognize how white women in the society are also complicit in the oppression and suffering of African American women.

So one must ask, "Why would God act in such a way?" One could contend that God in fact is "partial and discriminating."[45] However, Williams has a different reading of the relation between God and Hagar. According to Williams, God aims not to assure Hagar's liberation, but rather to ensure Hagar's *survival* and that of her unborn son. Although returning to Sarai and Abram means returning to life as a slave, it at least bodes a *quality of life* for Hagar and her soon-to-be-born son that surely exceeds that of the wilderness. God gives hope for a further quality of life as well; God pledges to multiply Hagar's progeny beyond counting, beginning with her son, Ishmael. In all these acts, Williams discerns the kind of "serious personal and salvific encounters with God" experienced by African American women, "encounters that have helped them and their families survive."[46]

The second Hagar narrative in Genesis 21:8–21 confirms the validity of Williams's interpretation of God's response to a suffering Hagar. After the birth of Ishmael, Sarai, now *Sarah*, conceived and bore her own son, named Isaac.[47] However, when Sarah saw Ishmael playing with Isaac, she demanded that Abram, now *Abraham*, cast out both Ishmael and Hagar. Abraham was distressed, but not for Hagar the slave; rather, he was concerned for Ishmael and the line of children he would provide. In his reluctance to send his son Ishmael away, Abraham nonetheless received a promise from God that great nations would arise from "the son of the slave woman" (21:13). So, with a

---

44. Ibid., 144.

45. Naim Stifan Ateek, *Justice and Only Justice* (Maryknoll, NY: Orbis, 1989), 77.

46. Williams, *Sisters in the Wilderness*, 3.

47. Genesis 18:1–15 and 21:1–7.

measure of bread and a skin of water, Abraham sent Ishmael and Hagar to wander in the wilderness.

> When the water in the skin was gone, she cast the child under one of the bushes. . . . And as she sat opposite him, she lifted up her voice and wept. And God heard the voice of the boy; and the angel of God called to Hagar from heaven, and said to her, "What troubles you, Hagar? Do not be afraid; for God has heard the voice of the boy where he is. Come, lift up the boy and hold him fast with your hand, for I will make a great nation of him." Then God opened her eyes and she saw a well of water. She went, and filled the skin with water, and gave the boy a drink. (Gen. 21:15–19)

God is moved by the cry of the boy, rather than Hagar's voice and weeping; nonetheless, God reiterates the promise to make of Ishmael a great nation. As in the last wilderness experience, God does not liberate Hagar and Ishmael, but rather provides for their survival and quality of life in the wilderness through the vision and initiative of Hagar: "When Hagar and her child were finally cast out of the home of their oppressors and were not given resources for survival, God provided Hagar with a resource. God gave her new vision to see survival resources where she had seen none before."[48] While God promises to provide for their quality of life as well as for their survival (Gen. 21:20), it is Hagar who assures the boy that he would not grow up with the culture of her oppressors. Instead, she chose for him a wife from her homeland of Egypt (Gen. 21:21).

Reflect and Discuss

How would you describe the God whom Hagar encounters in the wilderness? Is God's treatment of Hagar equal to God's treatment of Sarai? If not, what difference do you note?

Experiencing God in the Wilderness

Rooted in her interpretation of the biblical tradition of Hagar, Williams proposes the paradigm of the wilderness experience for her womanist theology of suffering. For black women, Williams contends, the wilderness experience of suffering results not only from encounters with racism but also from the oppressions of sexism, classism, and poverty experienced by black women in family and society.

---

48. Williams, *Sisters in the Wilderness*, 5.

> [The wilderness-experience] is a symbolic term used to represent a near-destruction situation in which God gives personal direction to the believers and thereby helps her make a way out of what she thought was no way. . . . [The] wilderness experience meant standing utterly alone, in the midst of serious trouble, with only God's support to rely upon.[49]

From a theological perspective, Williams acknowledges that black women in the wilderness may find themselves caught in the tension between the God of the Hebrew slaves, who liberates in the Exodus event, and the God of Hagar who does not liberate in the wilderness. She does not advocate that African women eschew the identification with Israel in the Exodus, for this theme has pervaded the African American community and has provided hope throughout its history from the time of its enslavement. Nonetheless, Williams asserts that it cannot be used as the sole paradigm for understanding God's relationship with the black community. Doing so focuses inordinately on the slave period of the African American experience, putting it in "a kind of historical stalemate" that denies the prospect of change and development in the community's experience of God and God's relation to the community.[50]

In addition, Williams recognizes the transforming and healing relationship that the black community has had with Jesus in the wilderness "where one received from Jesus the strength needed to rise above one's ailments."[51] Nonetheless, their experience of Jesus also includes the doctrines of atonement and redemption. According to Williams, black women's experiences of surrogacy in the slave period raise serious questions about Jesus' atoning, redemptive, and liberative status for African American women. Like Hagar, a surrogate was a slave woman who bore a child on behalf of another.[52] If one asserts that "Jesus died on the cross in the place of humans, thereby taking human sin upon himself," Jesus is, in effect, "the ultimate surrogate figure." Because of this, surrogacy and the suffering and death that attend it "takes on an aura of the sacred."[53] When interpreted in this way, it may serve to signify and spiritualize the exploitation and oppression of black women, rather than to represent and effect salvation for them.

Because of these reservations, Williams turns to Hagar's experience of God in the wilderness for her theology of suffering. Rather than the experience of surrogacy, the wilderness paradigm attends to a different aspect of black women's "re/production history." Shaped and transformed in the wilderness experience,

---

49. Ibid., 108–9.

50. Ibid., 151.

51. Ibid., 112.

52. In the case of slave surrogates, mothers bore the children for the slave owners, who took possession of the children to sell them as slaves.

53. Williams, *Sisters in the Wilderness*, 162.

black women's re/production history is about "creating modes of resistance, sustenance, and resurrection from despair."[54]

The wilderness experience inspires initiative and enables black women to realize resources for survival and quality of life within themselves and their community where they had not seen them before. Their "absolute dependence" on God in the wilderness influences black women's being and doing in their lives as they shape the strategies "to deal with or resist difficult life-situations and death-dealing circumstances."[55] Ultimately, in a womanist theology of suffering, the wilderness experience is not a transient occurrence; it is the ordinary landscape of the lives of those who try to "make a way out of no way."[56] A womanist theology of suffering empowers women to seek God and God's word about survival and quality of life amid women's struggle to build lives while dwelling in the wilderness of their daily lives.

Reflect and Discuss

Which biblical paradigm of black theology resonates with you—the liberation paradigm or the survival paradigm? Which rings true in your experience of suffering or trial?

A *Mujerista* Theology of Suffering: *En la Lucha y el Exilio*

In her essay "In Search of a Theology of Suffering, *Latinamente*," Nancy Pineda-Madrid echoes an observation made at the beginning of this chapter: "Far too often, 'Christian' reflections on suffering have advanced the idealization of the passive, uncritical resignation to suffering. Unfortunately, this idealization and its corresponding distorted 'theology' have long plagued Latinas."[57] Hispanic/Latina theologies of suffering have arisen to address this distortion and to offer life-affirming theological alternatives. Two paradigms shape the Hispanic/Latina experience of suffering. The first is captured by the phrase *en la lucha*, which means "in the struggle." The second is the experience of *el exilio*, which means "the exile."

54. Ibid., 158.

55. Ibid., 159.

56. Ibid., xi.

57. Nancy Pineda-Madrid, "In Search of a Theology of Suffering, *Latinamente*," in *The Ties That Bind: African-American and Hispanic-American/Latino Theology in the United States*, ed. Anthony Pinn and Benjamin Valentin (New York: Continuum, 2001), 197.

God en la Lucha *(in the Struggle)*

Conceived *en la lucha*, Hispanic/Latina theology focuses its efforts upon the struggles and suffering of Hispanic women against ethnic prejudice, sexism, and classism. It recognizes sexism as an evil within its communities "that plays into the hands of the dominant forces of society . . . to repress and exploit us in such a way that we constitute a large percentage of those in the lowest economic stratum."[58] However, like womanist theology, it found itself at odds with "Anglo" feminism, which it critiqued because of ethnic prejudice and inattention to inequality. It therefore sought a name for itself that would distinguish its project from that of feminism. Because of its preferential option for *mujeres*, for *women*, Hispanic/Latina theologians in the United States adopted the name *mujerista* for their theological enterprise and centered their efforts on *mujerismo*, the struggles of Hispanic women against oppression. The task of *mujerista* theology is to render Hispanic women more conscious of the oppressive structures at work *en lo cotidiano*, in their everyday lives, and to discern the presence, action, and revelation of God therein. As a result, a *mujerista* theology of suffering is "not so much about God as about how we understand and relate to God" in the midst of the lived-experiences of Latinas in the struggle for survival and justice.[59]

According to *mujerista* theologian Ada María Isasi-Díaz, the God whom Hispanic women encounter *en la lucha* is a God who accompanies them in their daily struggle. Their relationship with God is intimate: "We argue with God, barter with God, get upset with God, are grateful and recompense God, use endearing terms for God. This intimate relationship with the divine is what is at the heart of our *comunidad de fe* [the community of faith]."[60] For some Latinas, this relationship centers on Jesus Christ as Savior. While his resurrection represents a victory over suffering and death, *mujerista* theologian Alicia Vargas contends that "for Latinas it is most significant that he suffered," not simply for the sake of suffering itself but for the sake of liberation.[61] Jesus continues to walk with Latinas each day, "hidden in, with, and under our suffering," leading them to resurrection and abundant life day by day.[62]

Hence, Latinas discover and discern the ongoing revelation of God in the struggle and accomplishments of their daily lives. As a Hispanic woman named Olivia put it,

---

58. Ada María Isasi-Diáz, "*Mujeristas*: Who We Are and What We Are About," *Journal of Feminist Studies in Religion* 8 (Spring 1992): 106.

59. Ada María Isasi-Diáz, *En la Lucha (In the Struggle): Elaborating a Mujerista Theology* (Minneapolis: Fortress, 1993), 175.

60. Ibid., 39.

61. Alicia Vargas, "The Construction of Latina Christology: An Invitation to Dialogue," *Currents in Theology and Mission* 34 (August 2007): 274.

62. Ibid.

> My faith is so strong that I figure that if [something] is God's will, that
> is what it's going to be. . . . If not, God was going to find a way, a
> way . . . I do not know how God does it. . . . What blows my mind
> is that I do my part and he [God] does the rest.[63]

Nonetheless, God does not act alone; God provides Latinas themselves with
the strength to endure difficulties and inspires them to make the best decision
for themselves and their loved ones. For this reason, dependence upon God is
inextricably bound up with Latinas' ability to depend on themselves. This combination of self-reliance and intimate relationship with God enables Latinas to
see themselves as persons of value:

> I always thank God for being the way I am. . . . I think I am some-
> body of value, because I am valued by God even if I am not valued by
> anyone else.[64]

According to Isasi-Díaz, "Authentic love of self becomes the basis for a relationship with the divine, with God transformed from one who is radically beyond
the person as agent, to one radically immanent to the agent."[65]

While this relationship with God in the struggle proves personally
life-giving and empowering, the fruits of it are never for the individual alone.
One's personal relationship with God is always in the context of the broader
Hispanic community immersed in its own labor of liberation. It is in and
through this oppressed community that God speaks. As a Latina named Lupe
described it,

> I am beginning to understand what I have heard for many years, for
> many years. God speaks more through the poor and in the poor and
> with the poor than in anybody else because they do not have anything.[66]

Because poor and oppressed women and men are the privileged locus of God's
revelation, a *mujerista* theology of suffering insists that they resist being passive
objects at the mercy of their oppressors. Rather they are called to become active
subjects in the struggle, intentional participants in the work of liberation even
in the midst of their poverty and distress. Therefore, liberative praxis born of
theological reflection and social analysis is central to a *mujerista* theology of suffering. Through such praxis, *las mujeres latinas* advance their understanding of
the forces and structures that alienate and marginalize them and deepen their
relationship to the God who liberates them.

---

63. Isasi-Diáz, *En la Lucha*, 101.

64. Ibid., 127.

65. Ibid., 158.

66. Ibid., 129.

God en el Exilio *(in the Exile)*

While the theme of exile also figures prominently in the theology of Ada María Isasi-Díaz,[67] it evokes a particular theology of suffering in the writing of theologian Elaine Padilla. In her essay "Border-Crossing and Exile: A Latina's Theological Encounter with Shekhinah," Padilla retrieves the Jewish figure of Shekhinah as "the one who accompanies the exiled and dispossessed of the land, becoming a tent-like divine mobile dwelling in which images of a better future can be nurtured."[68] Born in Puerto Rico, Padilla has a profound experience of not-at-homeness in the United States despite the fact that, as a Puerto Rican, she is a US-born citizen. Nevertheless, she intentionally adopts the stance of exile on behalf of herself and all immigrants because it enables her to "speak of resistance to the gaze that inspects and classifies to totalize, control, and dominate those who like me choose to remain in the liminal space as border-crossers."[69]

In Shekhinah, Padilla sees the divine Spirit as a source of energizing hope. In Jewish literature, Shekhinah "emerged as the wandering divine presence in the desert," as a God of accompaniment, as female in nature. In exile herself, Shekhinah is essentially separated from the Godhead; she "wanders in exile . . . as a suffering Mother, [who] takes upon herself human suffering," and, in so doing, "mends the world's brokenness as God joins the efforts of broken humanity."[70] According to Padilla, Shekhinah "is the one who helps realize common dreams of justice and freedom, one who raises voices of protest along with acts of kindness, one who engages in the struggles of life with lament and wisdom."[71] Through her, Latinas in the exile of suffering, abuse, oppression, and violence can discover open-ended possibilities for a new future and a new order where new forms of being may spring forth.

---

67. Ada María Isasi-Díaz was born in Havana, Cuba, and immigrated to the United States seventeen years later. See her "By the Rivers of Babylon: Exile as a Way of Life," in *Reading from this Place*, ed. Fernando F. Segovia and Mary Ann Tolbert (Minneapolis: Fortress Press, 1995) 1:149–63.

68. Elaine Padilla, "Border-Crossing and Exile: A Latina's Theological Encounter with Shekhinah," *Cross Currents* 60 (December 2010): 527. See the discussion of Shekhinah in the section on feminist theology.

69. Ibid., 529.

70. Ibid., 533.

71. Ibid., 534.

Padilla calls Shekhinah *una mestiza-mulata*, a woman of mixed origin—one with God, yet separated from God to dwell among God's exiled people. She suggests that Shekhinah exists as one who has "*un pie a cada lado*," one foot in each side of her divide, each side defining her identity. For her sister Latinas, "Shekhinah empowers and energizes a faith that faces life's conflicts and contradictions" and stirs in Latinas a vision of a preferred future characterized by *liberdad, comunidad de fe*, and *justicia* (liberty, faith community, and justice).[72] In the movement toward this future through the chaos of torture in the homeland, of sexual exploitation at the border, or of marginal survival in the United States, Latina women find a hospitable space in the Divine Shekhinah, a home in the not-at-home experience of exile. In this space, they find consolation in their suffering and encouragement for their quest as they risk becoming, belonging, and building a better future for themselves and their communities.

Reflect and Discuss

Have you ever had an experience of "exile," feeling not at home or out of place? Can you describe what it felt like? What did you desire during that time from others or from God?

Case in Point: *The Color Purple* by Alice Walker

Alice Walker—African American author, poet, and civil rights activist—was born in 1944 in Eatonton, Georgia. She was the youngest daughter of sharecroppers and so experienced poverty and discrimination firsthand. Walker lived much of her life in the racially divided South and attended segregated schools. She later studied at Spelman College in Atlanta and Sarah Lawrence College in New York, graduating from the latter in 1965. In that same year she published her first short story. Since then, she has authored seven novels, four collections of short stories, and four children's books, in addition to other volumes of essays and poetry. Her official biography describes her in this way:

---

72. Padilla, "Border-Crossing and Exile," 539. As Isasi-Díaz describes it, *liberdad* relates to self-fulfillment without self-promotion, *comunidad de fe* relates to recognizing and rejecting personal and social sin, and *justicia* relates to the establishment of political, economic, and social structures that negate the possibility of oppression. See *En la Lucha*, 34–45.

Case in Point: *The Color Purple* by Alice Walker (continued)

Walker has been an activist all of her adult life. . . . She is a staunch defender not only of human rights, but of the rights of all living beings. She . . . tirelessly continues to travel the world to literally stand on the side of the poor, and the economically, spiritually and politically oppressed.[73]

Of her many writings, Walker is arguably best known for *The Color Purple*, her 1983 epistolary novel set in the 1900s.[74] It centers on the life of its narrator, fourteen-year-old Celie, a poor, uneducated, black girl in Georgia, through whom Walker probes the female African American experience of sexism and racism. Suffering terrible sexual, physical, and psychological abuse from the men in her life, Celie has no one to turn to but God, to whom she pours out the pain of her life and struggles over a span of twenty years. The gripping novel gained Walker the Pulitzer Prize for Fiction—making her the first African American woman to earn that honor—and the National Book Award for Fiction in 1983. It was later adapted for film in 1985 and for theater in 2005.

This "Case in Point" focuses on Celie's relationship with God in her acute suffering. Like Hagar, Celie lives her life "in the wilderness," that place of suffering and struggle from which there seems to be no way out. Admonished to "not never tell nobody but God" about the sexual abuse she is enduring in that wilderness, Celie begins to write letters to God, hoping that God could give her "a sign letting me know what is happening to me."[75] Nonetheless, unlike the relationship between God and Hagar, there is no indication that Celie receives an answer from God when she cries out, but that does not seem to shake her faith. She tells her sister Nettie, "Never mine, never mine, long as I can spell G-O-D I got somebody along."[76] Clearly, Celie's God does not liberate her from her suffering by some divine intervention; nevertheless, like the God of Hagar, Celie's God helps her to survive.

---

73. *Alice Walker: The Official Website*, "Alice Walker—Official Biography," *AliceWalkersGarden.com*, available at *http://alicewalkersgarden.com/about-2/*.

74. An epistolary novel is one that tells a story through the medium of letters.

75. Alice Walker, *The Color Purple*, 7, available online from *https://www.scribd.com/book/171083362/The-Color-Purple*. This text retains the spelling, grammar, and colloquialisms used in *The Color Purple*.

76. Ibid., 25.

Although counseled to fight against the rape and abuse she receives, Celie states, "I don't know how to fight. All I know how to do is stay alive. . . . I don't fight, I stay where I'm told. But I'm alive."[77]

In the tension between safety and self-assertion that threads throughout the novel, Celie adopts the stance of many believers: suffering in this life can be endured in view of the reward to come in heaven. When her marriage shifts the pattern of abuse from her father to her husband, Celie resigns herself to it as the way of the world and looks to a better life hereafter. "I have to talk to Old Maker. . . . This life soon be over, I say. Heaven last all ways."[78] Despite the lack of response from her "Old Maker," Celie does not question her experience of God; she remains unreflective and unchanged—until she meets the fascinating Shug Avery.

Shug is a blues singer and the mistress of Celie's husband. Having fallen ill, Shug comes to stay in the home of Celie and her husband. During that time, Shug recovers letters from Celie's sister Nettie that her husband had hidden from Celie for years. In them, Celie learns things about herself and her past that shake her faith in God. She discovers long-held secrets about the death of her biological father, the stepfather who abused her, and the children she thought were her biological siblings. Celie is suddenly struck by God's silence and inaction; she says to God, "You must be sleep."[79] As a result, Celie writes to Nettie, "I don't write to God no more. I write to you."[80] Celie is ready to turn her back on the God that the dominant culture has given her, but as yet, has no God to replace it.

In this wilderness moment of God's apparent absence, Shug challenges Celie about her rejection of God and questions her about the God whom she rejects.

Shug: What happen to God?

Celie: Who that? What God do for me?

Shug: Celie! (Like she shock.) He gave you life, good health, and a good woman that love you to death.

---

77. Ibid., 23, 29.

78. Ibid., 49.

79. Ibid., 183.

80. Ibid., 198.

Case in Point: *The Color Purple* **by Alice Walker** *(continued)*

> **Celie:** Anyhow the God I been praying and writing to is a man. And act just like all the other mens I know. Trifling, forgitful and lowdown. . . . If he ever listened to poor colored women the world would be a different place, I can tell you. . . . But deep in my heart I care about God. What he going to think. And come to find out, he don't think. Just sit up there glorying in being deef, I reckon. . . .
>
> **Shug:** Tell me what your God look like, Celie.
>
> **Celie:** Aw naw, I say. I'm too shame. Nobody ever ast me this before, so I'm sort of took by surprise. Besides, when I think about it, it don't seem quite right. But it all I got. I decide to stick up for him, just to see what Shug say. . . . He big and old and tall and graybearded and white. He wear white robes and go barefooted.[81]

Here, Celie clearly names the God of the dominant culture. She reveals that God is not only male but also white! While she does not see God as abusive, Celie does feel that God is "deef" to her pleas and glories in being that way—just like the men and the white people in her life. She feels voiceless and unheeded, yet she needs and desires an intimate relationship with God. Like Hagar, she knows her survival and her quality of life depend on God and "trying to do without him is a strain."[82] Shug admits that she had to contend with the same experience.

> **Shug:** When I found out I thought God was white, and a man, I lost interest. You mad cause he don't seem to listen to your prayers. Humph! . . . Here's the thing. . . . The thing I believe. God is inside you and inside everybody else. You come into the world with God. But only them that search for it inside find it. . . . Trouble do it for most folks, I think. . . .
>
> **Celie:** But what do it look like?
>
> **Shug:** Don't look like nothing. It ain't a picture show. It ain't something you can look at apart from anything else, including yourself. I believe God is everything.[83]

---

81. Ibid., 198, 200, passim.
82. Ibid., 198.
83. Ibid., 202.

Case in Point: *The Color Purple* by Alice Walker (continued)

Despite Shug's conviction, Celie still finds herself in the wilderness. She writes to Nettie, "Well, us talk and talk bout God, but I'm still adrift. Trying to chase that old white man out of my head. . . . He been there so long, he don't want to budge. He threaten lightening, floods and earthquakes. Us fight. I hardly pray at all."[84] However, clearly a critical transformation in Celie's relationship with God is taking place. No longer is God deaf or silent; Celie experiences God in the struggle, but does not recognize that the struggle itself is prayer. Moreover, God is not only in the Bible, or in church, or in prayer, but all around her, and the spiritual life is not just about pleasing God.

> **Shug:** People think pleasing God is all God care about. But any fool living in the world can see it always trying to please us back. . . . It always making little surprises and springing them on us when us least expect.
>
> **Celie:** You mean it want to be loved, just like the bible say. . . . I been so busy thinking bout him I never truly notice nothing God make. Not a blade of corn (how it do that?) not the color purple (where it come from?). Not the little wildflowers. Nothing.[85]

However, like Hagar, Celie's encounter with God in the wilderness struggle has begun to open her eyes and to give her a new sense of self and a new vision of the life she could lead.

In her suffering and pain, Celie recognizes that she can discover her own concept of God and replace the images of God thrust on her by others. This realization contributes to her sense of self and advances her movement toward self-reliance and self-respect. Moreover, it enables her to seek a better quality of life than she had in Georgia; she decides to leave her abusive and oppressive life and move to Memphis. When her husband tries to derail this movement by telling Celie that she is poor, black, and ugly, and will amount to nothing, she asserts the self she has gained in the wilderness struggle. In words that seem to her to come from beyond

---

84. Ibid., 203.
85. Ibid.

> ### Case in Point: *The Color Purple* by Alice Walker *(continued)*
>
> her own person, she stands her ground: "Look like when I open my mouth the air rush in and shape words. . . . I'm pore, I'm black, I may be ugly and can't cook, a voice say to everything listening. But I'm here."[86]
>
> Celie's last letter in *The Color Purple*—a letter once again to God—demonstrates the extent of her personal and spiritual transformation. God is no longer a deaf and unresponsive male deity, but a God totally present to her in all of creation. In her salutation she triumphantly writes, "DEAR GOD. DEAR STARS, DEAR TREES, DEAR SKY, DEAR PEOPLES. DEAR EVERYTHING. DEAR GOD." As one commentator describes her, Celie "understands that the only thing God requires of people is the appreciation of everything [God] creates, and in return, God and humanity become inseparable."[87]
>
> In the end, this inseparability enables Celie to not only love herself as part of God's creation but also to reconcile with her husband and to reunite with the children who were taken from her at birth and now return as adults. She returns to Georgia as "a triumphant, independent, happy, lively woman"[88] who has gained financial and personal independence by starting her own business. Celie has become a "womanist," as Alice Walker describes it:
>
> > A woman who loves other women. . . . Appreciates and prefers women's culture, women's emotional flexibility (values tears as natural counterbalance of laughter), and women's strength. . . . loves individual men. . . . Committed to survival and wholeness of entire people, male and female. Not a separatist, except periodically, for health. . . . Loves music. Loves dance. Loves the moon. *Loves* the Spirit. Loves love and food and roundness. Loves struggle. *Loves* the Folk. Loves herself. *Regardless.*[89]

86. Ibid., 215.

87. Patricia Andujo, "Rendering the African-American Woman's God through *The Color Purple*," in *Alice Walker's The Color Purple*, ed. Kheven LaGrone (New York: Rodopi, 2009), 73.

88. Ibid.

89. Alice Walker, *In Search of Our Mothers' Gardens: Womanist Prose* (Boston: Houghton Mifflin Harcourt, 1983), ix, emphasis in the original.

For Further Reading

Isasi-Díaz, Ada María. *En la Lucha = In the Struggle: Elaborating a Mujerista Theology.* Minneapolis: Fortress, 1993.

Johnson, Elizabeth A. *She Who Is: The Mystery of God in Feminist Theological Discourse.* New York: Crossroad, 1993.

Walker, Alice. *The Color Purple.* New York: Mariner Books, 2006.

Williams, Delores. *Sisters in the Wilderness: The Challenge of Womanist God-Talk.* Maryknoll, NY: Orbis, 1999.

Internet Resources

Hayes, Diana. "Standing in the Shoes My Mother Made: Womanist Theology." Tolton Lecture, Catholic Theological Union, March 4, 2012. Available at *www.youtube.com/watch?v=OLjyfFCSPPM* (time: 58:49).

Isasi-Díaz, Ada María. "Religion and the Feminist Movement Conference: Panel IV." Harvard Divinity School, November 2, 2002. Available at *www.youtube.com/watch?v=HhSk4UHWUec* (time: 23:11).

Williams, Delores S. "Religion and the Feminist Movement Conference: Panel IV." Harvard Divinity School, November 2, 2002. Available at *www.youtube.com/watch?v=hltJgzbXPFI* (time: 17:00).

Films

The Color Purple. Directed and produced by Steven Spielberg. Burbank, CA: Warner Bros. Pictures, 1985.

CHAPTER 7

God in the Darkness of Xenophobia

> For Jesus, the universality of the saving nearness of God was made present through a life of care for all his fellow humans, through a selfless championing of suffering humanity. For Jesus, all human suffering was contrary to God's plan. God and suffering are diametrically opposed, and God always seeks to remove it.
>
> —JOHN MCNEILL, *TAKING A CHANCE ON GOD: LIBERATING THEOLOGY FOR GAYS, LESBIANS, AND THEIR LOVERS, FAMILIES AND FRIENDS*

Introduction

This chapter is about fear and the suffering it causes in the lives of particular persons living in the United States. Specifically, it considers xenophobia, which, in its broadest sense is defined as "an unreasonable fear, distrust, or hatred of strangers, foreigners, or anything perceived as foreign or different."[1] It is first and foremost an attitude directed toward a specific racial, ethnic, or social group. Persons holding such intense prejudices usually believe they have rational reasons for doing so. Nonetheless, xenophobia is often rooted in unfounded, distorted, or even reflexive patterns of belief that spawn fear, distrust, and hatred.

While most often associated with fear of particular ethnic groups, the term *xenophobia* also includes fear or distrust of persons who are of a different race, who speak a different language, who have a different sexual orientation, or who have different cultural or religious practices than one's own. Xenophobia, therefore, subsumes the prejudices of racism and heterosexism. Racism is "a belief or doctrine that inherent differences among the various human races determine cultural or individual achievement, usually involving the idea that one's own race is superior and has the right to rule others."[2] It has deep and tangled roots in the

---

1. "Xenophobia," *American Heritage New Dictionary of Cultural Literacy*, 3rd ed. (Orlando, FL: Houghton Mifflin Company, 2005), available at *http://dictionary.reference.com/browse/xenophobia*.

2. "Racism," Dictionary.com, *Dictionary.com Unabridged*, Random House, available at *http://dictionary.reference.com/browse/racism*.

United States dating back to the forcible importation of slaves more than four hundred years ago. Heterosexism describes a "system of bias regarding sexual orientation . . . that denotes prejudice in favor of heterosexual people and connotes prejudice against bisexual and, especially, homosexual people."[3] Reinforced by social and religious assumptions, it asserts that heterosexuality is the norm of human sexuality and that homosexuality is an aberrant orientation and behavior.

Both racism and heterosexism extend beyond an individual's fears or biases and infect political, economic, educational, and ecclesial policies and practices. As a result of such institutionalized prejudice in the United States, personal and communal rights, behaviors, and opportunities are severely restricted or eliminated for its victims, which results in immense personal and communal suffering. This chapter explores the theological responses to the suffering created by racism toward African Americans, xenophobia toward Hispanics/Latinos, and heterosexism toward gay and lesbian persons.

Reflect and Discuss

Have you ever been a victim of any of these prejudices or types of discrimination? What was your experience? Have you ever victimized others in this way? Why?

Black Liberation Theology and Suffering

Context

Black liberation theologies address suffering that has its roots in the slave experiences of black Americans. Therefore, the context of black theology in the United States dates from the seventeenth century when the first slaves were brought to Virginia. While slavery as an institution was ended by law in 1865 with the passage of the Thirteenth Amendment, racism toward black men and women in the United States has endured into the twenty-first century. Although the Civil Rights Act of 1964 legally prohibited segregation and discriminatory practices in businesses, in public places, and in employment, prejudice has proven far more difficult to uproot.

> In July of 1999, 10% of the African-American population in . . . a small town of 5,000 in the Texas Panhandle, was arrested on drug charges solely on the testimony of a single undercover officer. The arrests of 46 people, 39 of them black, resulted in 38 convictions

---

3. Patricia Beattie Jung and Ralph F. Smith, *Heterosexism: An Ethical Challenge* (Albany, NY: State University of New York Press, 1993), 13.

for various drug charges with sentences of up to 90 years in prison. In early April 2003, a . . . judge threw out all 38 drug convictions . . . because they were based on questionable testimony from a single undercover agent accused of racial prejudice.[4]

On February 26th, seventeen-year-old Trayvon Martin left a house in a town outside Orlando and walked to a store. He was seen by a twenty-eight-year-old man named George Zimmerman, who called 911 to report that Martin, who was black, was "a real suspicious guy." Zimmerman got out of his truck. Zimmerman was carrying a 9-mm. pistol; Martin was unarmed. What happened next has not been established, and is much disputed. . . . Zimmerman shot Martin in the chest. Martin did not survive.[5]

Beyond these specific instances, racism also manifests systemically in the lives of the forty-two million African American men, women, and children in the United States, who comprise 13.2 percent of the overall population in the country. Consider the following statistics:

- The poverty rate for all African Americans in 2012 was 28.1 percent.
- African Americans had a 10.7 percent unemployment rate in 2012, which is almost double that of the overall population.
- Of people who are homeless, 37 percent are black.
- Black Americans accounted for 49 percent of all homicide victims in 2005.
- African Americans are incarcerated at nearly six times the rate of whites.[6]
- In 2012, 51 percent of Americans expressed antiblack sentiments in a poll; 3 percent more than in 2008.[7]

Black liberation theology developed as a response to the pervasive experiences and debilitating effects of racial prejudice and discrimination suffered by African Americans in the United States.

---

4. American Civil Liberties Union, "Racist Arrests in Tulia, Texas," *ACLU.org*, available at *www .aclu.org/racist-arrests-tulia-texas*.

5. Jill Lepore, "Battleground America," *New Yorker*, April 23, 2102, available at *www.newyorker .com/magazine/2012/04/23/battleground-america?currentPage=all*.

6. Statistics may be obtained from the website of the US Department of Health and Human Services' Office of Minority Health at *www.omhrc.gov*; the US Census Bureau at *www.census.gov/*; the American Cancer Society at *www.cancer.org/research/cancerfactsstatistics/cancer-facts-figures-for-african -americans*; and the *Bureau of Justice Statistics Special Report*, August 2007, at *http://www.bjs.gov/index .cfm?ty=pbdetail&iid=400*; and NAACP, at *www.naacp.org/pages/criminal-justice-fact-sheet*.

7. Sonya Ross and Jennifer Agiesta, "AP Poll: Majority Harbor Prejudice against Blacks," *Associated Press: The Big Story*, October 27, 2012, available at *http://news.yahoo.com/ap-poll-majority-harbor -prejudice-against-blacks-073551680--election.html*.

The God of the Oppressed and the Black Christ

Like all liberation theologies, black theology is intrinsically a theology of suffering. It identifies itself with the concerns of black men and women in America and seeks to empower the black community to recognize and to break the chains of oppression that bind it. It is firmly grounded in the belief "that the liberation of the black community *is* God's liberation."[8] Black theology finds its voice through the Christian tradition; its task, according to theologian James Cone, is "to analyze the nature of the gospel of Jesus Christ in the light of oppressed blacks so they will see the gospel as inseparable from their humiliated condition."[9] He finds Christianity particularly suited to the goal of liberating the suffering and oppressed because the gospel derives from Jesus' ministry to and with persons who were poor, sick, despised, marginalized, and ostracized in their society. Hence, black theology has the life and mission of Jesus Christ as its point of departure and sees Jesus at work within the black community. For Cone, "The Jesus-event in twentieth century America is . . . an event of liberation taking place in the black community."[10]

Reflect and Discuss

What forms of oppression exist in the black community? What fuels these oppressions? How might one counteract them in practical ways?

The fundamental question posed by black liberation theology is "How do we *dare* speak of God in a suffering world, a world in which blacks are humiliated because they are black?"[11] This question serves as the touchstone by which all black theology is evaluated since it "forces us to say nothing about God that does not participate in the emancipation of black humanity."[12] Cone points out that the Christian understanding of God begins in God's liberation of the oppressed of Israel and comes to completion in the Incarnation of Jesus Christ. Revealed in the history of the oppressed of Israel and definitively in "the Oppressed One, Jesus Christ," black theology speaks of "the God who comes into view in their liberation."[13] To speak of God as one who condones or participates in the suffering of oppressed peoples denies the self-revelation of God in scripture.

---

8. James Cone, *A Black Theology of Liberation* (Maryknoll, NY: Orbis, 2010), 5, emphasis in the original.

9. Ibid.

10. Ibid., 5–6.

11. Ibid., 63, emphasis in the original.

12. Ibid.

13. Ibid., 64.

Reflect and Discuss

How might Jesus be considered "the Oppressed One"? How does the oppression that Jesus suffered relate to the black experience of oppression? How does it relate to black liberation?

According to Cone, "Blacks have heard enough about God." They now have more particular questions to ask: "What they want to know is what God has to say about the black condition. Or, more importantly, what is God doing about it?"[14] Cone begins the search for an answer to these questions in the Hebrew Scriptures, most notably in the event of the Exodus. Through this liberating activity, God reveals Godself as actively working in human history to release humans from the bonds of slavery. God's concern for the oppressed was also central to the prophetic tradition of the Hebrew Scriptures. The prophets reminded people of the centrality of justice in the concerns of Yahweh. This justice was not an abstraction; it was expressed through God's "making right what humans have made wrong."[15] The prophets proclaimed that God will not abide injustice toward the needy, but will act to defend their lives.

Reflect and Discuss

If God is the liberator of the suffering and needy, why does such oppression exist today? How is the liberating action of God to be understood in the lives of those who suffer?

The biblical tradition of God's liberating activity is deepened in the life of Jesus of Nazareth. Jesus is the Incarnation of the God of the oppressed who proclaimed freedom and set the captive free (cf. Luke 4:18–19). However, Jesus did more than free others from their burdens and bondage; Jesus took upon himself the humiliation and pain of the cross, "suffering for and with us so that our humanity can be liberated for freedom in the divine struggle against oppression."[16] Furthermore, "The resurrection conveys hope in God."

[It] is hope which focuses on the future in order to make us refuse to tolerate present inequities. To see the future of God, as revealed in

---

14. Ibid., 38.

15. Ibid.

16. James Cone, *God of the Oppressed* (Maryknoll, NY: Orbis, 1997), 128.

the resurrection of Jesus, is to see also the contradiction of any earthly injustice with existence in Jesus Christ.[17]

Their focus on the crucifixion of Christ, however, has also prompted black theologians to challenge how Jesus Christ has been perceived in the Christian tradition. Does the image of Jesus as Suffering Servant imply that affliction should be endured rather than transformed and alleviated? Does Jesus as the innocent Lamb who was slain convey the idea that violence should be passively accepted rather than actively resisted? What if Jesus were recognized as the Liberator of the oppressed who died in solidarity with the victims of violence and rose as a sign of hope and promise? These questions have stirred black theologians to plumb the significance of the historical and resurrected Christ to offer a variety of answers concerning his significance for a black theology of suffering.

Reflect and Discuss

What difference does a particular image of Jesus make in Christian life? Does the Christian image of Christ affect the way believers respond to suffering? Why or why not?

Martin Luther King Jr. believed that following Jesus Christ required a Christian to protest all forms of social and racial injustice that inflicted suffering on the black community. King did not interpret Jesus' salvation as reserved solely for the world to come, but preached that the freedom Jesus promised could be experienced as an earthly possibility.[18] He urged black persons to imitate Jesus' nonviolence, to bear Jesus' cross in this life, and to endure a "season of suffering" for justice.[19]

Other black theologians have insisted on proclaiming the blackness of Christ as the basis of his solidarity with the suffering community. J. Deotis Roberts maintained that Christ identified with each person in his or her unique race, gender, and historical context. Therefore, each and every person has the right to image Christ in her or his own likeness. According to Roberts, it is particularly critical to image Christ as black; doing so enables black persons to accept, affirm, and find meaning in their lives and "know true inner freedom" that enables them "to stand up to life."[20]

---

17. Cone, *A Black Theology of Liberation*, 4.

18. Kelly Brown Douglas, *The Black Christ* (Maryknoll, NY: Orbis, 2005), 37–45.

19. Martin Luther King Jr., *Stride toward Freedom: The Montgomery Story* (New York: Harper and Row, 1958), 220.

20. J. Deotis Roberts, "Black Theology and the Theological Revolution," *Journal of Religious Thought* 28, no. 1 (1972): 16.

For James Cone, the blackness of Christ "was a symbol of Jesus' existential commitments."[21] Throughout his life and ministry, Jesus identified with the suffering and oppressed of his time. In a racist society, therefore, Jesus identifies with black persons to the full extent of their blackness. The blackness of Christ proclaims that Christ struggles side by side with black men and women in America and bears their suffering. In the Black Christ, "God *really* enters into our world where the poor, the despised, and the black are, disclosing that he is with them, enduring their humiliation and pain and transforming oppressed slaves into liberated servants."[22]

Reflect and Discuss

What is your response to these theological images of the black Christ? Does it make a difference to image Jesus in one's own race or ethnicity? Why or why not? Does any image of the black Christ appeal to your experience of Jesus?

Hispanic/Latino Theology and Suffering

Context

Hispanic/Latino theologies address the suffering that arises from the marginalization of Hispanic persons in the United States. As a demographic group, Hispanics in the United States comprise the youngest and fastest growing segment of the population. Projections indicate that the Hispanic population will reach 128.8 million by 2060, which will constitute 31 percent of the US population. Yet, despite this growing population, xenophobia, along with its social, political, and economic disenfranchisement, affects the lives of millions of Hispanics in the United States.

> Wearing the wrong clothes, speaking with the wrong accent or having the wrong skin color could land you in hot water in Arizona. The state's "show me your papers" provision . . . is the second such measure to receive a green light from federal courts. The first was from Alabama, where a similar policy was implemented about a year ago.[23]
>
> Sara . . . whose daughter is an American citizen . . . was on a bus in Rochester with her daughter when three border patrol agents

---

21. Douglas, *The Black Christ*, 58.

22. Cone, *God of the Oppressed*, 125–26.

23. "Arizona's Bad Immigration Law Takes Effect," *Washington Post*, September 20, 2012, available at *www.washingtonpost.com/opinions/arizonas-bad-immigration-law-takes-effect/2012/09/20 /3516da52-02a6-11e2-91e7-2962c74e7738_story.html*.

asked her for identification. She could produce only her Ecuadorean passport, and was arrested. . . . [Her] six-year-old daughter has suffered from nightmares, had trouble sleeping and eating and expressed fear that the "police" will come again and take away her mother . . . for good.[24]

In addition to these personal examples of discrimination and abuse, the following statistics garnered in 2010–11 chronicle the daily experiences of suffering and fear that many Hispanics in the United States undergo:

- 25.9 percent of Hispanic persons lived below the poverty level (US Census Bureau).
- 30.1 percent of Hispanic persons lacked health insurance (US Census Bureau).
- 36.8 percent of Hispanic persons had not completed a high school education.[25]
- 52 percent of Latinos worried that they, a family member, or friend could be deported.[26]

As these figures indicate, suffering and marginalization of persons of Hispanic origin exist in all quarters and at all levels of American society. The American Hispanic/Latino theologians in this chapter take up the challenge of finding God in the midst of these experiences.

The Galilean Journey of the Mestizo Jesus

Methodist pastor and theologian Juan Feliciano, a native of Puerto Rico, contends that in the midst of suffering and oppression, "the theological predicament becomes . . . how to announce God . . . to an 'in-human' world . . . [and] how to tell those suffering . . . that they too are sons and daughters of God."[27] In his writings, theologian Virgilio Elizondo, a native-born American citizen of Mexican parents, engages this theological predicament in his book *Galilean*

---

24. Hirokazu Yoshikawa and Carola Suárez-Orozco, "Deporting Parents Hurts Kids," *New York Times*, April 20, 2012, available at *www.nytimes.com/2012/04/21/opinion/deporting-parents-ruins -kids.html?_r=0*.

25. US Census Bureau, "Hispanic Americans by the Numbers," *Infoplease.com*, available at *http://www.infoplease.com/spot/hhmcensus1.html*. Data is also available at the Pew Research Hispanic Trends Project, "Statistical Portrait of Hispanics in the United States, 2011," Pew Research Center, February 15, 2013, available at *www.pewhispanic.org/2013/02/15 /statistical-portrait-of-hispanics-in-the-united-states-2011/*.

26. Mark Hugo Lopez, Rich Morin, and Paul Taylor, "Illegal Immigration Backlash Worries, Divides Latinos," *PewResearch Hispanic Trends Project*, October 28, 2010, available at *www .pewhispanic.org/2010/10/28/illegal-immigration-backlash-worries-divides-latinos/*.

27. Juan Feliciano, "Suffering: A Hispanic Epistemology," *Journal of Hispanic/Latino Theology* 2, no. 1 (1994): 43.

Journey, in which he interprets the action of God within the struggle for life, identity, dignity, and liberty of many Hispanic people in America. "Does the gospel have something to offer at the crossroads between the death and life of a people?" he asks. "Does the gospel really bring life or is it more of a death mask?"[28]

Reflect and Discuss

How might you answer Elizondo's questions? Does the gospel make any difference in the life of those who suffer? If so, what difference does it make?

Writing from the Mexican American context, Elizondo asserts that their plight stems from two conquests in their history. The Spanish conquest of the indigenous peoples inhabiting the Americas gave birth to the *Mexican* people; the Anglo-American conquest of the Mexican peoples gave birth to *Mexican Americans*.[29] The word that Elizondo uses to refer to the "origination of a new people from two ethnically disparate parent peoples" is *mestizaje*. This word derives from the Spanish word *mestizo*, which means mixed or hybrid.[30] For the mestizo peoples emerging from these two conquests, the consequences were appalling: masses were slaughtered and "a mentality justifying the inhumane treatment was built up, justifying the outrages and social despoliation of entire peoples."[31] In the midst of such struggles, suffering, and even death, the presence of God was revealed to the mestizo peoples through the mestizo Jesus.[32]

According to Elizondo, for mestizos in the midst of injustice—whether Mexican American, Cuban American, or Puerto Rican American—a profound meaning exists in the life, death, and resurrection of Jesus because Jesus himself was a mestizo. As a Galilean Jew, Jesus was a member of a mixed race of people situated at the crossroads of international commerce and multiple invasions. Because of the *mestizaje* of the region, "to be a Galilean Jew was . . . to be one

---

28. Virgilio Elizondo, *Galilean Journey: The Mexican-American Promise* (Maryknoll, NY: Orbis, 2009), 1.

29. Ibid., 7–16.

30. Ibid., 5.

31. Ibid., 7.

32. Elizondo discusses the tremendous impact of *la Virgen de Guadalupe* on the Mexican people after the Spanish conquest of 1531. The Virgin Mary appeared to Juan Diego, "a poor Indian," near Tepeyac, "to listen to their lamentations and remedy their miseries, pain, and suffering." In *la Virgen*, the mestizo peoples of Mexico "came to life again. . . . They who had been silenced were now speaking again through the voice of the Lady." See Elizondo, *Galilean Journey*, 29–33. Our Lady is also significant for Cuban American persons who have great devotion to *Nuestra Señora* (or *la Virgen*) *de la Caridad del Cobre*, Our Lady of Charity, a symbol of emancipation and safety to the Cuban people since the seventeenth century.

of the ignorant, insignificant, and despised of the world."[33] For Jesus, it meant growing up as part of a rejected, marginalized, and oppressed group of people.

That Jesus was a mestizo in his own historical context holds tremendous significance for Hispanics in the United States. It means God entered human history as one of those who were despised and lowly in the world: "Without ceasing to be God, [Jesus] entered the world of the voiceless, the sick, the hungry, the oppressed, the public sinners, the marginated, the suffering."[34] Shaped by the *mestizaje* of Galilee and the dominant culture that surrounded his Galilean life, Jesus learned firsthand what it meant to be disfavored and disenfranchised. He who was marginalized and oppressed in his life was sent to those like himself to proclaim their dignity and liberation. Jesus made this clear when he identified the contours of his mission with persons who are poor and oppressed (Luke 4:18–19).

Reflect and Discuss

How do you respond to the notion of Jesus as a mestizo in his own time? What difference do you think it made to his mission and ministry? Is there any other way in which Jesus could be understood as mestizo?

Informed by his own marginalization and empowered by his absolute and intimate dependence on God, Jesus related to others beyond such categories as righteous and sinful, insider and outsider. However, Cuban American theologian Roberto Goizueta points out that relating with those the wider society judged as outcasts and undesirables had deadly consequences for him. Goizueta notes the cost of transgressing the boundaries between "us" and "them":

> In Jesus' world, everyone had his or her proper place. . . . Consequently, by walking with the poor, by accompanying the outcasts, Jesus put himself in the "wrong" place, and he was crucified as a result. . . . To walk with Jesus is thus to walk with the wrong persons in the wrong place.[35]

Understanding this radical action of God through the mestizo Jesus enables US Hispanics to interpret the struggle of their lives through the good news

---

33. Elizondo, *Galilean Journey*, 53.

34. Ibid., 92.

35. Roberto Goizueta, *Caminemos Con Jesús: Toward a Hispanic/Latino Theology of Accompaniment* (Maryknoll, NY: Orbis Books, 2005), 203.

of Jesus' life, death, and resurrection. To clarify this interpretation, Elizondo offers three principles: the Galilee Principle, the Jerusalem Principle, and the Resurrection Principle.

Reflect and Discuss

Have you ever walked with those whom others thought were the "wrong people"? What effect did it have on the way people treated you or those whom you companioned?

The Galilee Principle states, "*What human beings reject, God chooses as his very own.*"[36] In the Incarnation, God became one with the voiceless and the oppressed, revealing to the lowly and despised their true worth and dignity. While the marginality of the Galilean Jesus is the starting point for those who look to him in their suffering, the cross is its fulfillment. However, "[Jesus] did not gather unto himself the suffering of the world to canonize and legitimate suffering, but to transform it into the creative force for a new creation."[37] The event of the cross transforms and emboldens the sufferer to act on his or her own behalf and on behalf of others in similar situations of oppression. Thus liberation from suffering is always linked to action to alleviate the suffering of others as a communal obligation.

This leads Elizondo to the Jerusalem Principle: "*God chooses an oppressed people, not to bring them comfort in the oppression, but to enable them to confront, transcend and transform whatever diminishes and destroys the fundamental dignity of human nature.*"[38] During his life, Jesus did not flee the various oppressions of his day, but confronted unjust structures that excluded and exploited others. In his proclamation of the reign of God, he challenged people to enter into solidarity with those deprived of social standing, to risk living in ways that affirmed the dignity of all persons, and to do so even to the cross. For Hispanic Christians, the cross represents the suffering and injustice endured by Hispanic persons as they live in exile from their ancestral home and often on the borders of society. Yet these borders are places of divine solidarity for those who crossed boundaries of country and safety, who transgressed barriers of language and culture because "Our *mestizaje* and exile are symbols of our identification with a Jesus who also transgressed boundaries."[39] Hence, while exiles understand suffering and hardship, those who do so in the company of the Galilean Jesus also know "the

---

36. Elizondo, *Galilean Journey*, 91, emphasis in the original.

37. Ibid., 92.

38. Ibid., 103, emphasis added.

39. Goizueta, *Caminemos Con Jesús*, 204.

liberating power of *acompañamiento* (accompaniment)"[40] and find new hope in their suffering. The gospel of the Galilean Jesus demonstrates that God brings new life out of death, redemption out of rejection. For Elizondo, this is the Resurrection Principle: "*Only love can triumph over evil.*"[41]

When it seemed to the disciples of Jesus that their hopes had been dashed and that God had abandoned Jesus, God's creative and salvific love raised Jesus from the dead to a new existence. Transformed by the encounter with the Risen Lord and the outpouring of his Spirit, the community of disciples overcame fear, faced their opposition, and spoke the truth of their own dignity and that of all persons (cf. Acts 2:1–47). In like manner, Elizondo declares, in their encounter with the mestizo Christ, "Those who before had simply accepted their state of exclusion and exploitation are now coming out of their tombs. . . . Those who had been dead are now coming back to life."[42] In the power of Christ's resurrection, US Hispanic persons, once voiceless and powerless, rise to confront injustice and marginalization in memory of Jesus whose "purpose was not solely to save individuals from their sins, but also . . . to save communities from the sins of its social structures."[43]

> ### Reflect and Discuss
>
> What are your thoughts on Elizondo's principles? Do you agree with his interpretation of God in these principles? Why or why not?

Gay and Lesbian Liberation Theology and Suffering

Context

In his essay "Heterosexism in Contemporary World Religion," theologian Daniel C. Maguire makes the following claim: "Homophobia has . . . been called 'the last respectable prejudice' but, of course, no prejudice merits respect. . . . Unlike its cousins anti-Semitism, sexism, and racism, heterosexism has enjoyed undue immunity from critique."[44] The heterosexism that Maguire speaks about has a

---

40. Ibid.

41. Elizondo, *Galilean Journey*, 115, emphasis added.

42. Ibid., 118–19.

43. Miguel A. De La Torre, "Evangelism: A Hispanic Perspective," *Church and Society* 92 (January/February 2002): 17.

44. Daniel C. Maguire, "Heterosexism in Contemporary World Religion," *The Religious Consultation on Population, Reproductive Health and Ethics*, available at *www.religiousconsultation.org/hetero sexism_in_world_religions.htm.*

dual reference. First, it refers to the presumption that all humans are by nature heterosexual, that is, sexually oriented toward a person of the opposite sex. It implies that any orientation other than heterosexual is abnormal or disordered. Second, heterosexism refers to systemic expressions of prejudice and discrimination at the institutional level. As an institutionalized prejudice, heterosexism reveals itself through social, educational, and ecclesial decisions that favor heterosexual people and discriminate against homosexual persons.

Such prejudice and discrimination also manifests itself at the level of individuals and groups. At this interpersonal level, it is called homophobia. It shows itself as fear, intolerance, or maltreatment of gay and lesbian persons. The interplay between homophobia and heterosexism forms the context that foments and perpetuates the suffering and oppression of gay and lesbian persons in the United States.

> A Mississippi school district is being sued to challenge pervasive anti-LGBT harassment perpetuated by students, teachers and administrators. . . . The federal lawsuit . . . is the latest development in the case of [a] 17-year-old . . . who has said she experienced regular harassment from students and school officials because of her sexual orientation and her gender presentation. . . . [She] . . . alleges that after seeking support from her principal she was told, "I don't want a dyke in this school."[45]
>
> A review of academic research and surveys by gay and lesbian organizations . . . found that one-quarter to two-thirds of lesbian, gay, and bisexual people have lost jobs or been denied promotions because of their sexual orientation. . . . Unequal treatment based on sexual orientation can take many forms . . . such as promotions that mysteriously go to less-qualified employees or a constant barrage of insults and antigay jokes that create a hostile, threatening atmosphere.[46]

Reflect and Discuss

Are heterosexism and homophobia the "last acceptable prejudices"? If so, what makes them "acceptable" when other prejudices are criticized?

---

45. Katie McDonough, "Mississippi School District Sued for Pervasive Anti-LGBT Harassment among Students and Administrators," *Salon.com*, December 18, 2013, available at *www.salon.com/2013/12/18/mississippi_school_district_sued_for_pervasive_anti_lgbt_harassment_among_students_and_administrators/*.

46. Bruce Mirken, "Workplace Discrimination: Sexual Orientation," *Healthday.com*, available at *http://consumer.healthday.com/encyclopedia/work-and-health-41/occupational-health-news-507/work place-discrimination-sexual-orientation-646404.html*.

The United Nations Office of the High Commission for Human Rights draws attention to the worldwide extent of discrimination based on sexual orientation and gender identity:

> Deeply-embedded homophobic and transphobic attitudes . . . expose many lesbian, gay, bisexual and transgender (LGBT) people . . . to egregious violations of their human rights. They are discriminated against in the labour market, in schools and in hospitals, mistreated and disowned by their own families. They are singled out for physical attack—beaten, sexually assaulted, tortured and killed.[47]

Statistics gathered from a nationwide survey of lesbian, gay, bisexual, and transgender (LGBT) youth in American schools indicate that 92 percent report frequent homophobic slurs, 84 percent describe threats because of their sexual orientation, 64 percent feel unsafe at school, and 29 percent have missed one or more days because they felt unsafe.[48] A 2013 survey conducted by the Pew Research Center among 1,197 self-identified LGBT adults[49] widens the perspective:

- 39 percent have been rejected by a family member or friend because of their orientation.
- 30 percent have been physically attacked or threatened.
- 29 percent have been made to feel unwelcome in a place of worship.
- 21 percent have been treated unfairly by an employer.
- 58 percent have been the target of slurs or jokes.
- 48 percent say they have no religious affiliation.

Many LGBT people "internalize the negative messages about being different. These messages become beliefs that can fester and develop into two struggles: shame about who they are and what they feel, and guilt about what they do."[50] The difficulty of engaging such struggles is substantial. A 2012 US Surgeon General's report indicated that 12 to 19 percent of LGB adults have attempted suicide, compared to 5 percent of other US adults, and that at least

47. United Nations Office of the High Commission for Human Rights, "Combating Discrimination Based on Sexual Orientation and Gender Identity," *Ohchr.org*, available at *www.ohchr .org/EN/Issues/Discrimination/Pages/LGBT.aspx*.

48. "How the Homophobic Climate in the United States Affects GLBTQ Youth," *Advocates for Youth*, available at *www.advocatesforyouth.org/publications/604-how-the-homophobic-climate-in-the -united-states-affects-glbtq-youth*.

49. Pew Research Center, "A Survey of LGBT Americans: Attitudes, Experiences and Values in Changing Times," *Pewsocialtrends.org*, available at *www.pewsocialtrends.org/2013 /06/13/a-survey-of-lgbt-americans/*.

50. Al Zwiers, "LGBT People and Mental Health: Healing the Wounds of Prejudice," *Heretohelp.org*, available at *www.heretohelp.bc.ca/visions/lgbt-vol6/lgbt-people-and-mental-health*.

30 percent of LGB adolescents have attempted suicide, compared with 8 to 10 percent of other adolescents.[51]

For gay men, these personal, psychological, and social sufferings were exacerbated by "one of the most politicised, feared and controversial diseases in the history of modern medicine," HIV/AIDS.[52] In addition to the physical affliction of AIDS, persons with AIDS suffered stigma and discrimination because of the disease. Persons with HIV/AIDS were frequently demonized, condemned, feared, and distanced by their families, communities, and government at a time when access to support, health care, information, and prevention was most needed.

Reflect and Discuss

Do AIDS stigma and discrimination still exist today? Explain why you believe this is or isn't so.

Christian religious denominations have been a major voice in the criticism of the lives of LGBT persons. The Bible is the primary source of Christian teaching on homosexuality. By most accounts, seven scripture passages make specific reference to sexual relations between persons of the same sex. The Christian Epistles warn that "the wrath of God is revealed from heaven against all ungodliness" (Rom. 1:18): "Their women exchanged natural intercourse for unnatural. . . . Men committed shameless acts with men" (Rom. 1:26–27). As a consequence "none of these will inherit the kingdom of God" (1 Cor. 6: 10). In the Hebrew Scriptures, passages from Leviticus (18:22 and 20:13) issue unambiguous judgments on a man who lies "with a male as with a woman"—namely, "both of them have committed an abomination; they shall be put to death; their blood is upon them."

The most referenced passage used to exemplify God's condemnation of homosexual relations is the story of Sodom and Gomorrah, which tells of the visit of two angels in human form who visited Lot in the city of Sodom (Gen. 19:1–15). The men of Sodom surrounded Lot's house and demanded that Lot bring out his visitors "so that we may know them" (Gen. 19:5), which connotes sexual relation. Rather than turn the men under his hospitality over to the crowd, Lot offers his virgin daughters to "do to them as you please" (19:8). A similar story is found in the book of Judges 19:22–30. An old man offers a

---

51. US Surgeon General and National Council for Suicide Prevention, "2012 National Strategy for Suicide Prevention," available at *www.ncbi.nlm.nih.gov/books/NBK109917/.* Transgender persons were not included in this portion of the survey.

52. AVERTing HIV and AIDS, "History of HIV and AIDS in the US," *AVERT.org*, available at *www.avert.org/history-hiv-aids-usa.htm.*

traveler hospitality overnight in his house. Like the turn of events in the city of Sodom, "the men of the city, a perverse lot," insisted that the visitor be brought out "so that we may have intercourse with him" (19:22). Rather than turning the guest over to them, the old man offered his daughter and his guest's concubine to them to "Ravish them and do whatever you want to them" (19:24).

While the latter two passages seem clearly to prohibit homosexual behavior, biblical scholars disagree over whether the sin in these passages is homosexuality or a violation of hospitality. The New Testament Epistles that cite these stories connect them to homosexuality (Rom. 1:26–27; 1 Cor. 6:9; 1 Tim 1:10; 2 Pet. 2:6; and Jude 1:7); however, in the two references that Jesus makes to Sodom and Gomorrah, his point is hospitality (Matt. 10:14–16; Luke 10:11–13). In addition, there is the question of the heinous disregard for the dignity and welfare of women demonstrated in both passages. While most commentators would argue that the androcentric biases of the biblical culture influenced the narratives, the scandalous and wanton attitude toward women in them raises serious questions about the moral authority of these passages concerning sexuality.

Reflect and Discuss

What is your response to the biblical tradition on homosexuality? Does it continue to exert a good deal of influence on attitudes of people today? What was Jesus' position on homosexuality?

The most influential theologian in the formation of the Christian tradition concerning homosexuality is Thomas Aquinas. His philosophical foundation was natural law, which contends that God meant all creatures to fulfill a particular purpose in the divine plan for the universe. Furthermore, God created each one's nature in such a way as to be able to achieve this purpose. When human actions conform to the nature and purpose that God intended, they are morally good; actions not conforming to human nature as God intended are deemed morally wrong. According to Aquinas, as the feet are intended for walking and the eyes are intended for seeing, sexual acts are intended for procreation and preservation of the human race. Since homosexual activity is not ordered to procreation, it is considered "unnatural" and "disordered," that is, not ordered to the nature and end that God intended.[53] Although contemporary psychological, biological, cultural, and theological research has contested the traditional teaching on homosexuality based on scripture and natural law, the Christian religious tradition has remained largely unchanged.

---

53. Aquinas, *ST* 2–2.153.2.

The teaching of the Roman Catholic Church has consistently maintained that homosexual relations are "a serious depravity"[54] and "an objective disorder."[55] While affirming that homosexual persons must be treated with respect, compassion, and sensitivity and asserting that unjust discrimination should be avoided, the Church counsels LGBT persons to practice chastity and to unite their difficulties to the sacrifice of the cross.[56] Other Christian churches have set forth similar teachings. The Missouri Synod of the Lutheran Church states that "homosexuality is but one of many sinful situations human beings encounter in this life" and offers homosexual persons "the promise of forgiveness and eternal life through the person and the work of Jesus Christ."[57] The United Methodist Church acknowledges that "all persons are of sacred worth," yet forbids ordaining homosexuals as ministers.[58] The Southern Baptist Convention states that the Bible condemns homosexuality as sin, but not "an unforgiveable sin." Homosexual persons "may become new creations in Christ."[59]

Reflect and Discuss

Do these Christian teachings on homosexuality reflect your own thinking on the subject? If so, to what extent? Does this teaching continue to influence society? If so, in what way?

Coming Out of Slavery

By most accounts, the movement for LGBT liberation in the United States began with the Stonewall Riots in 1969,[60] which motivated LGBT persons to unify in support of gay rights. Envisioning this event as a liberation story

---

54. Congregation for the Doctrine of the Faith, *Persona Humana* (*Declaration on Certain Questions Concerning Sexual Ethics*), December 29, 1975, available at *www.vatican.va/roman_curia /congregations/cfaith/documents/rc_con_cfaith_doc_19751229_persona-humana_en.html.*

55. Congregation for the Doctrine of the Faith, *Homosexualitatis problema* (*Letter to the Bishops of the Catholic Church on the Pastoral Care of Homosexual Persons*), October 1, 1986, available at *www .ewtn.com/library/curia/cdfhomop.htm.*

56. Catechism of the Catholic Church, 2nd ed., nos. 2358, 2359, promulgated by Pope John Paul II on September 8, 1997, available at *www.scborromeo.org/ccc/p3s2c2a6.htm#II.*

57. A. L. Barry, "What about Homosexuality?," Lutheran Church—Missouri Synod, available at *http://lcms.org/Document.fdoc?src=lcm&id=1100.*

58. United Methodist Church, "Homosexuality: Full Book of Discipline Statements," *UMC.org*, available at *www.umc.org/what-we-believe/homosexuality-full-book-of-discipline-statements.*

59. Southern Baptist Convention, "Sexuality," in *Position Statements*, available at *www.sbc.net/ aboutus/positionstatements.asp.*

60. Leadership Conference, "Stonewall Riots: The Beginning of the LGBT Movement," *Civilrights.org*, June 22, 2009, available at *www.civilrights.org/archives/2009/06/449-stonewall.html.*

like the Exodus, Richard Cleaver, a priest of the Orthodox-Catholic Church of America, rereads the Exodus event in dialogue with the experience of "coming out" and points to the liberating presence of God in this critical process of self-disclosure.[61]

When a new Pharaoh came to power in Egypt, he set out against the Israelite people to "stop their increase"; he enslaved the Israelites and ordered that all males born to Hebrew women be killed at birth. Cleaver parallels Pharaoh's fear of the Israelites with homophobia in contemporary society. As Pharaoh's fear led to the enslavement and murder of the Israelites, homophobia brings discrimination and violence to LGBT persons today. Despite Pharaoh's command to exterminate all the Israelite males, a Hebrew woman gave birth to a son whom she hid for several months. When she could hide him no longer, she placed him in a basket among the reeds of the Nile. When Pharaoh's daughter came to bathe in the Nile, she found the child and pitied him. She adopted the child as her son and named him Moses (Exod. 2:1–10).

Cleaver points out that, into his early adulthood, Moses "passed" as an Egyptian. His deception was undermined one day when he saw an Egyptian beating one of Moses' Hebrew kinsfolk. Looking around and seeing no one, Moses killed the Egyptian and buried him in the sand. Cleaver notes the furtiveness of Moses' action; his desire to continue to "pass" as an Egyptian meant Moses had to keep this kinship secret, lest he suffer the harsh consequences of revealing his true identity. Moses feared being found out.

One day, Moses came upon two Hebrews fighting and intervened. The Hebrews asked him, "Who made you a ruler and judge over us? Do you mean to kill me as you killed the Egyptian?" (Exod. 2:14). Moses' action in defense of his kinman was revealed! Moses fled to Midian where he continued to pass as Egyptian. Back in Egypt, however, the misery of the Hebrew slaves rose to God: "God heard their groaning. . . . and God took notice of them" (Exod. 2:24–25).

One day, while Moses was tending the flock of his father-in-law, he saw a flame of fire spring out of a bush; "the bush was blazing, yet it was not consumed" (Exod. 3:2).

> God called to him out of the bush, "Moses, Moses!" And he said, "Here I am." Then [God] said, "Come no closer! Remove the sandals from your feet, for the place on which you are standing is holy ground." [God] said further, "I am the God of your father, the God of Abraham, the God of Isaac, and the God of Jacob." And Moses hid his face, for he was afraid to look at God. (Exod. 3:4–6)

God called Moses by his name and proclaimed Moses' true identity as a Hebrew, a descendant of Abraham, Isaac, and Jacob. Moses could not "pass" in the

---

61. Richard Cleaver, *Know My Name: A Gay Liberation Theology* (Louisville: Westminster John Knox, 1995).

presence of God. It is no wonder that Moses hid his face in fear! The encounter with God "called into question what Moses had tried to make of himself, the shifts and stratagems he had used to avoid facing who he was."[62]

Yet God did not deride, condemn, or banish Moses; God not only accepted Moses for who he was but also offered Moses the means to end both his suffering and the suffering of his Hebrew kinsfolk. "The God who appeared to Moses in this fire is revealed as a God concerned for . . . the suffering of the people as a whole and Moses' suffering."[63] For Moses, as for LGBT persons, liberation is found not in isolation; it is found in relation to a community of people with whom there is shared history and memory.[64] Surely it is easier to "pass" as someone else, rather than undertake the dangerous task of building a different future with a community of kin. Nonetheless, though it entailed risk, God promised to be with Moses and sealed that promise by revealing the divine name to him—a name that was both an eternal promise to the Hebrew people and a message to Moses himself: "God said to Moses, 'I am who I am. . . . This is my name forever and my title for all generations'" (Exod. 3:14–15). "I am who I am," Moses heard—and Moses assented.

Because of the risk of such self-acceptance, there is a great temptation to preserve the status quo, choosing the security of the closet instead of the uncertainty of self-disclosure. However, Cleaver encourages his LGBT brothers and sisters to hear the words that Moses spoke to his Hebrew brothers and sisters in their exodus from being nonpersons toward becoming a people peculiarly God's own:

> Do not be afraid, stand firm, and see the deliverance that the Lord will accomplish for you today; for the Egyptians whom you see today you shall never see again. The Lord will fight for you, and you have only to keep still. (Exod. 14:13–14, adapted)

Reflect and Discuss

What do you think of Cleaver's rereading of Moses and the burning bush? Does it influence your thinking on God's response to LGBT persons? How? Have you ever needed to claim "I am who I am"? How did it feel to do so?

---

62. Ibid.

63. Ibid., 33.

64. Ibid., 39–40.

Exiles in the World

While many LGBT persons have taken the journey out of slavery in the company of God, religious criticism of their sexual orientation has led others to abandon their relationship with God along with their religious affiliation. In his book *Taking a Chance on God*, theologian and psychotherapist John McNeill acknowledges the pain and despair that many gay and lesbian persons have experienced in their spiritual lives because they felt that belief in God and their sexual orientation presented "an unresolvable dilemma."[65] Nonetheless, he contends that LGBT persons must risk intimate relationship with God as they attempt to live as "exiles in the world" or else hazard spiritually bankrupt lives.[66] To find such divine intimacy, McNeill claims that LGBT persons must surmount three forms of suffering in their lives: anger, fear, and guilt.

Anger for LGBT persons often stems from alienation from family, society, church, and ultimately God. Experiencing their sexual orientation "as a given, an objective fact that is part of God's creation,"[67] LGBT persons suffer when that nature is attacked in the name of God as sinful, disordered, and intrinsically evil. If God both creates and condemns their orientation, some conclude that God is a sadist.

> Only a sadistic God would create millions of humans as gay with no choice in the matter and no hope of changing and then deny them the right to express their gayness in a loving relationship for the rest of their lives under the threat of eternal damnation.[68]

Despite this intensely painful experience, McNeill contends that LGBT persons must risk believing that "God is not homophobic."[69] Only by trusting God to hear and hold one's anger with love and compassion can LGBT persons grow in intimacy with God and acceptance of self.

The alienation that incites anger also provokes fear—fear of abandonment, loneliness, abuse, and rejection by humans and the Divine. This fear leads to "fleeing from the presence of God."[70] Nevertheless, McNeill points out that liberation from fear is the central message of the gospel and the essence of salvation. The good news that Jesus proclaimed was "do not be afraid" (Matt. 2:20, 10:19, 14:22–33, 17:8; Luke 1:30, 12:33; John 14:27). It is good news, McNeill

---

65. John McNeill, *Taking a Chance on God: Liberating Theology for Gays, Lesbians, and Their Lovers, Families and Friends* (Boston: Beacon Press, 1988), 13. McNeill is also an ordained priest and a former Jesuit. In 1986 he was dismissed from the Jesuits by the Vatican for his teaching on homosexuality and his ministry with gay and lesbian persons.

66. Ibid., 38.

67. Ibid.

68. Ibid.

69. Ibid.

70. Ibid., 44.

holds, because fear cripples one's response to self, others, and God. The gospel encourages LGBT persons to bring their fear into prayer with God and "place ourselves in the arms of a God who loves us."[71]

Reflect and Discuss

Were you surprised at the frequency with which Jesus encouraged his followers "do not be afraid"? Why do you think that was so important in his ministry?

Finally, McNeill addresses the suffering of guilt, shame, and self-hatred that "has . . . accompanied every step of gay and lesbian human development."[72] Such guilt and shame stem from what McNeill maintains are false assumptions: that all humans are by nature heterosexual and that sexual orientation is a choice. When an LGBT person assimilates these assumptions, God can sometimes become a "transcendent superego before whom we are totally exposed and, consequently, in whose presence we feel guilt and shame."[73] Nonetheless, it is critical for LGBT persons to engage the process of lifting the burden of guilt and shame and developing a sense of fearless belonging to God's family: "the good news of God's self-revelation in Jesus Christ is that no matter how badly wounded our human capacity for trust and love, we can start over. . . . Trustworthiness is the very nature of God."[74]

Reflect and Discuss

Guilt and shame are associated with many human experiences. Have you ever experienced the kind of unhealthy guilt and shame McNeill talks about? What was your experience, if any, of God at that time?

However, theologian J. Michael Clark warns that, while trustworthy, the God LGBT persons encounter in their exile in the world is not a deus ex machina, ready to plunge in and change their suffering and oppression. Writing from his experience of the AIDS epidemic, Clark rejects the concept of an all-powerful God who rescues people from the suffering they endure or punishes them through it. According to Clark, while God is "present in pain, seeking

---

71. Ibid., 53.

72. Ibid., 54.

73. Ibid., 64.

74. Ibid., 78.

good,"[75] God cannot intervene to thwart the natural or human causes of pain and suffering without compromising authentic freedom.[76] Nonetheless, confronted with the apparent silence and impotence of God, the sufferer can yet find hope in the cross and resurrection of Jesus Christ.

Reflect and Discuss

The concept of the suffering of God comes up again as it did in previous chapters. Are most people satisfied with this image of God in suffering? Why or why not?

Clark asserts that "on the cross, Jesus experienced the impotence of God and the absence of divine rescue."[77] In his misery, Jesus plumbed the depths of his religious tradition to cry out in the words of Psalm 22, "My God, my God, why have you forsaken me?" (v. 1). Like Jesus, persons with AIDS can identify with the words of that psalm; they often feel forsaken by God, "scorned by others, and despised by the people" (22:6–7). Nonetheless, Clark contends, God is present to AIDS victims and their loved ones as God was present in the apparent forsakenness of Jesus. Through the cross, persons with AIDS, their families, and their friends realize that God bears their weakness and infirmity. Moreover, in the resurrection they discover that the love of God is "the energy for transforming and transcending tragedy"[78] that enables human beings to act responsibly to alleviate the agony of AIDS and of all forms of misery, exclusion, and marginalization. Once one has relinquished the notion of God as either source or savior of human suffering, Clark maintains, "we discover in our experience of god-forsakenness God's real compassion and empowerment on behalf of the victims of oppression and tragedy."[79]

Reflect and Discuss

Have you ever felt forsaken by God? When? Were you able to reconnect with God? Who took the initiative—you or God?

---

75. J. Michael Clark, "AIDS, Death, and God: Gay Liberational Theology and the Problem of Suffering," original manuscript, Emory University, 1985, 7. This essay was later published in the *Journal of Pastoral Counseling* 21, no. 1 (1986): 40–54.

76. Ibid., 8.

77. Ibid., 13.

78. Ibid., 20.

79. Ibid.

Case in Point: "America's Exodus," Child Martyrs of Migration

This "Case in Point" focuses on "the surge" of unaccompanied minors who have fled to the United States in record numbers since 2011. These children flee from different countries in Latin America seeking refuge from violence and oppression in their home countries. Many factors provoked this exodus of children to the United States but studies show that most children cite violence, deprivation, and abuse as the predominant causes for their migration.

The United Nations High Commissioner for Refugees (UNHCR) in Washington, DC, reported the following statistics from their interviews with unaccompanied minors:

- 66 percent of 104 refugees from El Salvador reported violence by organized crime as a primary motivation for leaving, with 21 percent reporting abuse in the home.
- 29 percent of 100 refugees from Guatemala cited deprivation as their reason for leaving, with 23 percent citing abuse in the home and 20 percent violence in society.
- 44 percent of the 98 displaced children from Honduras reported threat or experiences of violence by organized crime, 24 percent cited abuse in their homes, and 21 percent pointed out incidences of deprivation as the cause of their flight.
- 32 percent of the 102 Mexican children interviewed told of violence in society, 17 percent of violence in the home, and 7 percent of deprivation. Thirty-eight percent were recruited into human smuggling precisely because they were children.[80]

Response to this "American Exodus" has been mixed.[81] The UNHCR contends that 38–72 percent of these children require "international protection" under the status of refugees: "Since, by definition, the Governments of their home countries no longer protect the

---

80. United Nations High Commissioner for Refugees, "Children on the Run: Executive Summary," *UNHRCWashington.org, available at www.yumpu.com/en/document/view/31472885/1-uac-children-on-the-run-executive-summary.*

81. Gabriela Romeri, "American Exodus," *America: The National Catholic Review*, September 15, 2014, available at *http://americamagazine.org/issue/american-exodus.*

> **Case in Point: "America's Exodus,"** (continued)
>
> basic rights of these individuals, the international community must step in to ensure that those basic rights . . . are respected."[82] The Committee on Migration of the US Conference of Catholic Bishops has encouraged the US government to protect the children crossing the border and to address the poverty and violence that provoked their flight from their home countries. The committee writes, "Young lives are at stake."[83] The Presiding Bishop of the Episcopal Church reminded Christians that "we are our brothers' and sisters' keepers" and that the response to this tragedy must be "grounded in justice and the fundamental dignity of every human being."[84] With other church and humanitarian organizations, the United Church of Christ Immigration Task Force has encouraged Christians to become foster parents to children awaiting immigration hearings.[85] While the US government and its agencies have provided funds for food, beds, clothing, and medical care to address the expanding emergency, soon "funding will dry up," even as these refugee children continue to face "unthinkable conditions."[86]
>
> Despite broad recognition of the dire needs of these children, a rising tide of xenophobia threatens to stymie efforts to meet this humanitarian crisis. Characterizing these children as "illegal immigrants," anti-immigration activists have encouraged immediate deportation of the children to their home countries. Protesters in a California city chanted pro-American slogans as they blocked and turned away three busloads of Central American refugees headed to a holding facility in their town. The citizens of one Arizona town

---

82. UN High Commissioner for Refugees, "Children on the Run: Executive Summary," 8.

83. US Conference of Catholic Bishops, "Reacting to Surge in Unaccompanied Children Crossing Border, USCCB Chair Calls on Administration, Congress to Offer Protection, Address Root Causes," *USCCB.org*, June 4, 2014, available at *www.usccb.org/news/2014/14-097.cfm*.

84. Episcopal Church Office of Public Affairs, "Presiding Bishop Addresses Crisis of Unaccompanied Children at the U.S. Border," *Episcopalchurch.org*, July 10, 2014, available at *www.episcopalchurch.org/notice/presiding-bishop-addresses-crisis-unaccompanied-children-us-border*.

85. United Church of Christ Immigration Task Force, "UCC Response to Crisis of Unaccompanied Minors from Central America," *Ucc.org*, June 17, 2014, available at *www.ucc.org/justice/immigration/ucc-response-to-crisis-of.html*.

86. Lisa Mascaro and Brian Bennett, "Budgets Raided to Address Border Crisis Amid Congress' Inaction," *Los Angeles Times*, July 30, 2014, available at *www.latimes.com/nation/la-na-border-budget-tradeoffs-20140731-story.html*.

Case in Point: "America's Exodus," *(continued)*

protested the "invasion of the United States by people of foreign countries": the sheriff of the town contended that "These children should be returned to their home country—not to . . . Arizona paid for by American taxpayers."[87] A National Day of Protesting against Immigration Reform, Amnesty and Border Surge prompted more than three hundred protest rallies in cities across the United States with a goal "to unify Americans of all races, political parties and walks of life against the . . . illegal immigrant invasion."[88] In Florida, one woman explained, "I'm against giving them free medical care. They'll end up on welfare anyway. I feel sorry for the little kids coming over, but enough is enough."[89] However, in the face of such protests, one immigrant advocate stated,

> To me, the downright racist and xenophobic reactions of some Americans (and politicians) towards the Central American children . . . signify the real fear and anxiety we have towards our growing Latino population. I understand . . . that a civilized country needs to determine and protect its borders . . . . But . . . what exactly are we protecting ourselves from? Who exactly are we fearing? What exactly is at stake?[90]

This story of forced migration, according to one writer, is a "story of desperation and survival as old as the written word . . . [and] central to the earliest biblical accounts of the people of God."[91] For some, these children are like the Israelites in their Exodus who

---

87. Michael Martinez, Holly Yan, and Catherine E. Shoichet, "Growing Protests over Where to Shelter Immigrant Children Hits Arizona," *CNN US*, July 16, 2014, available at *www.cnn .com/2014/07/15/us/arizona-immigrant-children/*.

88. Leo Hohmann, "Hundreds of Cities Fight Back against 'Invasion,'" *Wnd.com*, July 15, 2014, available at *www.wnd.com/2014/07/hundreds-of-cities-fight-back-against-invasion/*.

89. Ashley A. Smith, "Residents Protest Illegal Immigration of Children," *News-press.com*, July 19, 2014, available at *www.news-press.com/story/news/local/fort-myers/2014/07/19/immigration-protest -in-southwest-florida/12882307/*.

90. Alice Speri, "'America Is Immigrants': Jose Antonio Vargas Discusses the Border Crisis Following His Detention in Texas," *Vice.com*, July 23, 2014, available at *https://news.vice.com/article /america-is-immigrants-jose-antonio-vargas-discusses-the-border-crisis-following-his-detention-in-texas*.

91. Romeri, "American Exodus."

Case in Point: "America's Exodus," (continued)

escaped from enslavement and tyranny to wander in the wilderness in the hope of finding their promised land. To others, they are like Jesus, who fled his homeland because of the death sentence pronounced on innocent children by Herod (Matt. 2:16–18). Such biblical accounts issue a challenge to Christians to stretch beyond prejudice and discrimination; to welcome those estranged by poverty, homelessness, violence, and fear; and to minister with and to Christ in these child refugees. The words of Pope Francis on World Refugee Day 2013 clearly frames this challenge:

> We cannot be insensitive . . . towards our refugee brothers and sisters. We are called to help them, opening ourselves to understanding and hospitality. May there be no lack of persons and institutions around the world to assist them. In their faces is etched the face of Christ![92]

Reflect and Discuss

Where are you on the question of unaccompanied minors fleeing to the United States from Central America and Mexico? Do people have a moral responsibility to welcome the stranger and care for his or her needs? What would Jesus say?

For Further Reading

Cone, James. *God of the Oppressed.* Maryknoll, NY: Orbis, 1997.

Douglas, Kelly Brown. *The Black Christ.* Maryknoll, NY: Orbis, 2005.

Elizondo, Virgilio. *Galilean Journey: The Mexican-American Promise.* Maryknoll, NY: Orbis, 2009.

Goizueta, Roberto. *Caminemos Con Jesús: Toward a Hispanic/Latino Theology of Accompaniment.* Maryknoll, NY: Orbis Books, 2005.

---

92. Vatican Radio, "Pope: We See the Face of Christ in Refugees," 2013, available at *http://en .radiovaticana.va/storico/2013/06/19/pope_we_see_the_face_of_christ_in_refugees/en1-702870.*

United Nations Office of the High Commission for Human Rights, "Combatting Discrimination Based on Sexual Orientation and Gender Identity." *Ohchr.org*. Available at *www.ohchr.org/EN/Issues/Discrimination/Pages /LGBT.aspx*.

Internet Resources

Christian Community Development Association. "Dr. Virgilio Elizondo Sermon: Saturday Evening Plenary." *Youtube.com*. Available at *www.youtube .com/watch?v=lotnqErkl28*.

La Bestia. A documentary about the tragedy of Central American migrants in the passage through Mexico to the United States. Directed by Pedro Ultreras. Information about the documentary in Spanish at *www.thebeast doc.com/documentary/Home.html*.

CHAPTER 8

God in the Experience of Disability

The most astounding fact is . . . that Christians do not have an able-bodied God as their primal image. Rather, the Disabled God promising grace through a broken body is at the center of piety, prayer, practice, and mission.

—Nancy L. Eiesland, *The Disabled God: Toward a Liberatory Theology of Disability*

Introduction

In his research on theologies of disability, theologian John Swinton asserted that "doing theology is always an embodied and interpretative enterprise; we inevitably use our bodies and our minds (and our implicit and explicit assumptions about both) to make sense of the world."[1] While this assertion applies to all of the contextual theologies of suffering presented in this book, theologians writing from the context of disabilities have been acutely attuned to the impact of mind and body on the theological enterprise. They point out that the constructs of theology and the practices they engender have "assumed an able-bodied hermeneutic . . . for deciphering human experience and developing an image of God."[2] Disability theologians contend that the absence of the voices and experiences of persons with disabilities has resulted in marginalization and misrepresentation of their lives not only in theological discourse but also in church and society. Theological reflection by persons with disabilities and on the experience of disability, they claim, has the capacity to be "a way of cracking open false assumptions and revealing the true nature of God and human beings."[3]

---

1. John Swinton, "Who Is the God We Worship? Theologies of Disability: Challenges and New Possibilities," *International Journal of Practical Theology* 14, no. 2 (2011): 276.

2. Ibid., 276–77.

3. Ibid., 277.

Reflect and Discuss

As you enter into this chapter, what difference do you think doing theology from the experience of people with disabilities might make in a vision of God, of Christ, or of Church?

Disability has been variously defined throughout history. The World Health Organization (WHO) offers the following multifaceted definition:

> *Disabilities* is an umbrella term, covering *impairments, activity limitations,* and *participation restrictions.* An *impairment* is a problem in body function or structure; an *activity limitation* is a difficulty encountered by an individual in executing a task or action; while a *participation restriction* is a problem experienced by an individual in involvement in life situations.[4]

This definition covers not only the personal or individual aspect of disability, that is, the impairment, but also the functional and societal aspects of disability in terms of limited activity and social restriction. In the context of the United States, the Americans with Disabilities Act (ADA) offers the following threefold legal definition:

> An individual with a disability is defined by the ADA as [1] a person who has a physical or mental *impairment* that substantially *limits* one or more major life activities, [2] a person who has a history or record of such an impairment, or [3] a person who is *perceived by others* as having such an impairment.[5]

Like the WHO, the ADA definition subsumes impairment as well as the limitation associated with it. However, in its third category, it also calls attention to the influence that perception has in circumscribing the experience of disability. Theologies of disability emerged against the backdrop of these definitions. They have also been influenced by a variety of models for interpreting disability as well as by twentieth-century movements in disability rights and disability studies.

Reflect and Discuss

Do you know any person with a disability? What challenges has that person encountered? What attitudes and perceptions has that person experienced?

---

4. World Health Organization, "Disabilities," *WHO.org*, available at *www.who.int/topics/disabilities /en/*, emphasis added.

5. US Department of Justice, "A Guide to Disability Rights Law," *Ada.gov*, available at *www.ada .gov/cguide.htm#anchor62335*, emphasis added.

Scholars have identified four different models for interpreting disability: moral, medical, limits, and social.[6] The *moral* model interprets a disability or a person with a disability as good or bad. It lends particular attention to biblical interpretations of disability as a consequence of sin, as evidence of God-forsakenness, or as a divine test of faith. The *medical* model typifies disability as a defect in the mind or body of the individual. It engages disability as a "personal tragedy" that requires medical intervention to correct the defect and "to enable the person to live a life as close to the accepted norm as possible."[7] The *limits* model questions basic assumptions about what it means to be "normal" or "disabled." It considers impairment to be "an unsurprising aspect of the human condition . . . that we all experience at some point in our lives."[8] It invites people to consider how limits are normal and fluid in everyone's life, rather than seeing them as experiences to be avoided. Finally, the *social* model views persons with disabilities as oppressed members of a minority group who are subjected to prejudice, exclusion, and discrimination in numerous aspects of life. It contends that the disability is not created by a person's impairment but by discriminatory attitudes and inaccessible physical structures in society. This model represents the perspectives of the disability rights movement.

Reflect and Discuss

How have you thought about the experience of disability? Which model reflects your way of thinking?

The disability rights movement in the United States developed in the 1960s in tandem with the struggles of women and of African American persons denied equality, autonomy, and access in society. While the return of World War I and World War II veterans with disabilities spurred growth in technology, vocational training, and government assistance for persons with disabilities, the prevailing mind-set in the mid-twentieth century generally saw disability as "an abnormal, shameful condition, [which] should be medically cured or fixed."[9] Persons with disabilities frequently lacked access to public buildings, transportation, and facilities, which limited their self-determination and stymied their employment. This situation was exacerbated by widespread

---

6. Deborah Creamer, "Disability Theology," *Religion Compass* 6 (July 2012): 340–41, available at *http://onlinelibrary.wiley.com/doi/10.1111/j.1749-8171.2012.00366.x/full*.

7. Swinton, "Who Is the God We Worship," 278.

8. Creamer, "Disability Theology," 341.

9. Anti-Defamation League, "A Brief History of the Disability Rights Movement," *Adl.org*, available at *http://archive.adl.org/education/curriculum_connections/fall_2005/fall_2005_lesson5_history.html*.

prejudice and discrimination that labeled persons with disabilities as "less intelligent, less capable of making the 'right' decision, less 'realistic,' less logical, and less self-directed than non-disabled persons."[10]

Like those who fought for the civil rights of women and of African Americans, disability rights advocates demanded equal opportunity, access, and treatment for persons with disabilities as well. The disability movement aimed to confront negative attitudes and stereotypes, to advocate for political and institutional change, and to lobby for independence and self-determination. The movement led to national initiatives and legislative actions that addressed physical and social barriers facing the disability community and that mandated strict and immediate action in the public sector to ensure equality for people with disabilities.[11] Nonetheless, "deep-rooted assumptions and stereotypical biases were not instantly transformed with the stroke of a pen."[12]

In concert with the disability rights movement, the field of disability studies emerged as "an interdisciplinary approach to the study of disability which focuses on the particular ways in which people with disabilities are portrayed and treated within society."[13] This field of study envisioned disability as a social construct, that is, a perception of an individual or group that is created by a society or culture, rather than as a biological or psychological impairment. Like constructs based on race, sexual orientation, and ethnicity, disability as a social construct subsumes negative beliefs, values, assumptions, policies, and practices toward persons with physical, mental, or psychological impairments. The social construct of disability, moreover, tends to conflate all persons with impairments under the one umbrella concept of "disabled." This tendency makes the social construct of disability all the more detrimental since there is no single, self-evident definition of "people with disabilities." As theologian and sociologist Nancy Eiesland states, "The differences among persons with disabilities are often so profound that few areas of commonality exist."

> Different conditions produce different types of functional impairment. . . . Further, people with the same disability may differ significantly in the extent of their impairment. . . . Finally, disabilities can be either static, congenital, or acquired. . . . These dissimilarities make a broad definition of people with disabilities difficult, if not impossible.[14]

---

10. Nancy L. Eiesland, *The Disabled God: Toward a Liberatory Theology of Disability* (Nashville: Abingdon, 1994), 25.

11. These initiatives included the Rehabilitation Act of 1973, the Education for All Handicapped Children Act of 1975, the Individuals with Disabilities Education Act of 1990, and the Americans with Disabilities Act of 1990. They sought to provide help through educational opportunities, employment accommodations, architectural modifications, and adaptive services.

12. Anti-Defamation League, "A Brief History of the Disability Rights Movement."

13. Swinton, "Who Is the God We Worship," 278.

14. Eiesland, *The Disabled God*, 23–24.

> ## Reflect and Discuss
>
> Who or what comes to your mind when you think of the phrase "person with disabilities"?

Despite these profound differences, the originators of disability studies, noticed something that persons with disabilities did have in common: the social experience of exclusion, injustice, and differential treatment. They asserted that "disability" does not stem from a person's impairments, but from society's response to such impairments. In this line of thought, a disability is not something that a person *has*, but rather something *inflicted upon* a person because of social and cultural conditions that prevent a person with impairment from meaningful and unfettered participation in society. According to the Union of the Physically Impaired against Segregation,

> In our view, it is society which disables physically impaired people. Disability is something imposed on top of our impairments by the way we are unnecessarily isolated and excluded from full participation in society. Disabled people are therefore an oppressed group in society.[15]

While there is no doubt that physical, psychological, or intellectual impairments present pain, weakness, and challenge for people with disabilities on a daily basis, advocates contend that suffering stems less from their impairments than from malignant social attitudes and practices.

Context

In its history of the disability rights movement, the Anti-Defamation League points out that "People with disabilities have had to battle against centuries of biased assumptions, harmful stereotypes, and irrational fears . . . [that] left people with disabilities in a severe state of impoverishment for centuries."

> [People] with disabilities were considered meager, tragic, pitiful individuals unfit and unable to contribute to society, except to serve as ridiculed objects of entertainment in circuses and exhibitions. They were assumed to be abnormal and feeble-minded, and numerous persons were forced to undergo sterilization. People with disabilities were also forced to enter institutions and asylums, where many spent their entire lives. The "purification" and segregation of persons with disability were

---

15. Union of the Physically Impaired against Segregation, *Fundamental Principles of Disability*, in Swinton, "Who Is the God We Worship," 279.

considered merciful actions, but ultimately served to keep people with disabilities invisible and hidden from a fearful and biased society.[16]

Some actions, however, were not so "merciful." People with disabilities were among the first led to the gas chambers in Nazi Germany; they have been targeted for involuntary euthanasia, "warehoused" because of their mental retardation, and abused by their attendants and even their families. Disability advocate Jennie Weiss Block calls experiences such as these "disability's dangerous memories," that is, remembrances of past oppression that catalyze actions for liberation and transformation in the present. Such memories are not recounted for the purpose of arousing sympathy for people with disabilities, "but rather to point out that all these memories have one thing in common: they play out society's deep prejudice against people with disabilities."[17]

Disability advocates have labeled these oppressive attitudes and actions *ableism*. They contend that like racism, sexism, and heterosexism, ableism is a form of xenophobia. It is an unreasonable fear, distrust, or hatred of those perceived as different because of their impairments. Ableism has multiple manifestations: pejorative naming and expressions, denial of access, and rejection for education and employment based on real or imagined impairment. It is also reflected in dominating-behavior toward people with disabilities, such as decision-making or "doing what is best" for persons with disabilities without involving them in the process since they are perceived as incapable of reasonable or prudential judgment. The effects of ableism produce "devastating and debilitating" suffering: isolation, despair, shame, meaninglessness, resentment, humiliation, self-hatred, powerlessness, and fear of rejection and abandonment.[18]

Reflect and Discuss

Have you ever thought about the type of discrimination termed *ableism* in this section? How have you seen its behaviors manifested? What kinds of attitudes, concepts, or structures might be examples of this type of discrimination?

Census data in 2010 indicated that approximately 56.7 million people living in the United States—almost 19 percent of the population—reported some type of disability. This makes persons with disabilities the largest minority group

---

16. ADL, "A Brief History of the Disability Rights Movement."

17. Jennie Weiss Block, *Copious Hosting: A Theology of Access for People with Disabilities* (New York: Continuum, 2002), 42.

18. Ibid., 42–49.

in the United States. In 2012, the employment rate for eighteen- to sixty-four-year-old persons with disabilities was 33 percent in contrast to the overall employment rate of 74 percent. This resulted in a poverty rate among persons eighteen to sixty-four years old with disabilities of 29 percent, in contrast with a 13.6 percent poverty rate for all persons eighteen to sixty-four years old. Beyond these economic statistics, the Bureau of Justice Statistics reported that approximately 1.3 million nonfatal violent crimes—sexual assault, robbery, and aggravated assault—occurred against persons with disabilities in 2012; this is nearly three times higher than the rate of such crimes against persons without disabilities.[19] Compounding these realities are the countless experiences of indignity, degradation, and marginalization suffered by persons with disabilities every day.

> A little girl looks at photographs of children spread out in front of her and divides them into three piles: "They're girls, they're boys and they're handicaps." A disability rights activist dressed in a business suit sits in a wheelchair at the airport awaiting her flight, while another businesswoman walks up and drops a quarter in her coffee cup. . . . A 66-year old double amputee, perched atop a baggage cart "like a sack of potatoes," is wheeled onto a plane and left there for 45 minutes by airline personnel while other passengers stare at him; an airline representative then tells his daughter, "If he's that sick, he shouldn't be on a plane; he should be in a hospital."[20]

This array of prejudicial and discriminatory attitudes and behaviors delimits people with disabilities as an oppressed minority group. As a result, people with disabilities demand liberative action to eradicate their suffering and oppression through social and political change. This understanding provides the groundwork for the development of liberative theologies of disability.

Reflect and Discuss

Reflect for a moment about how you typically think of persons with disabilities. Has your reading thus far given you any different perspective?

---

19. Erika Harrell, "Crime against Persons with Disabilities, 2009–2012—Statistical Tables," *Bureau of Justice Statistics*, available at *www.bjs.gov/index.cfm?ty=pbdetail&iid=4884*.

20. "The Long and Sorry History of Discrimination against People with Disabilities in the United States—and Its Causes," *Ragged Edge Online*, available at *www.raggededgemagazine.com /garrett/causes.htm*.

Liberative Theologies of Disability

Rather than contradicting the effects of adverse social and cultural constructs on the lives of persons with disabilities, the Christian biblical tradition has in fact contributed to these negative perceptions. Despite advances in knowledge concerning the causes of illness or impairment, many Christians have not severed the connections between disability and divine disfavor, between sickness and sin, or between impairment and imperfection. This thinking not only fuels the moral interpretation of disability as a consequence of sin, as evidence of God-forsakenness, or as a divine test of faith, but also questions whether people with disabilities are made in the image of a "perfect" God. This has led one disability advocate to ask,

> Do the Scriptures have an "ableist" bias that ultimately oppresses people with disabilities? . . . Does the notion that there is a connection between sin, illness, and disability and the concept that there is something wrong with being disabled contribute to the marginalization of people with disabilities?[21]

In the Scriptures, physical impairment was often interpreted as the consequence of sin or as a sign of desecration. In Leviticus, God instructs Moses to tell his brother Aaron, "No one of your offspring throughout their generations who has a blemish may approach to offer the food of his God":

> One who is blind or lame, or one who has a mutilated face or a limb too long, or one who has a broken foot or a broken hand, or a hunchback, or a dwarf, or a man with a blemish in his eyes or an itching disease or scabs . . . shall not come near the curtain or approach the altar, because he has a blemish, that he may not profane my sanctuaries; for I am the Lord. (21:17–23)

Deuteronomy 28 describes some mental and physical impairment as God's punishment for disobedience: "The Lord will afflict you with madness, blindness, and confusion of mind; you shall grope about at noon as blind people grope in darkness, but you shall be unable to find your way" (vv. 28–29). Such impairments not only signaled separation from God but also called for exclusion from the community. Thus people not only bore their physical illness or impairment but also suffered guilt and shame because they were taught that their disabilities were signs of an unrighteous life, divine punishment and forsakenness, or a consequence of the unfathomable will of God. After all, when Moses complains that he is "slow of speech and slow of tongue," does God not proclaim to him, "Who gives speech to mortals? Who makes them mute or deaf, seeing or blind? Is it not I, the Lord?" (Exod. 4:10–11).

---

21. Block, *Copious Hosting*, 101–2.

The Christian Gospels offer little respite from this oppressive conflation of impairment and iniquity. In several passages, Jesus himself linked forgiveness of sin with physical healing, with the clear indication that "disability is a sign of moral imperfection or divine retribution for sin."[22] In Luke 5, a person with paralysis is brought by his friends to Jesus for healing. When Jesus saw the man, he said to him, "Friend, your sins are forgiven you" (5:20). When the scribes and Pharisees disputed Jesus' ability to forgive sins, Jesus answered,

> Which is easier, to say, "Your sins are forgiven you," or to say, "Stand up and walk"? But so that you may know that the Son of Man has authority on earth to forgive sins—he said to the one who was paralyzed—"I say to you, stand up and take your bed and go to your home." Immediately he stood up before them, took what he had been lying on, and went to his home, glorifying God. (Luke 5:22–25; cf. Matt. 9:1–8, Mark 2:1–12)

A similar incident from the Gospel of John tells of Jesus' encounter with a man by the pool of Bethesda who was unable to walk. Jesus healed him with the words, "Stand up, take your mat and walk" (John 5:8). However, when Jesus later came upon the man he had cured in the temple, Jesus said to him, "See, you have been made well! Do not sin anymore, so that nothing worse happens to you" (5:14). In only one passage does Jesus disavow the connection between sin and impairment and that is in the story of the man born blind in John 9.

> As he walked along, [Jesus] saw a man blind from birth. His disciples asked him, "Rabbi, who sinned, this man or his parents, that he was born blind?" Jesus answered, "Neither this man nor his parents sinned; he was born blind so that God's works might be revealed in him." (John 9:1–3)

Reflect and Discuss

Various biblical passages connect disability and sin, and people with disabilities experienced ostracism in biblical times. Do you think such biblical passages and attitudes still influence us today? Cite evidence to support your answer.

Passages such as these are sometimes referred to as "texts of terror" by people with disabilities because they portray people with disabilities as marginalized figures who are often impoverished, sinful, and contemptible (cf. Luke 14:21).[23] Moreover, several narratives foster a distorted and dangerous relationship

---

22. Eiesland, *The Disabled God*, 71.

23. Block, *Copious Hosting*, 102.

between faith and physical health. In one version of these narratives, when a person regained physical health, Jesus pronounces a variation of the phrase, "Your faith has made you well" (cf. Matt. 9:22; Mark 5:34, 10:52; Luke 8:48, 17:19). In another version, when his disciples could not heal an epileptic child, Jesus ascribed their failure to the disciples' lack of faith (Matt. 17:14–20). Such unmitigated belief in the connection between one's level of faith and experience of physical healing (or impairment) can be devastating. One father whose child was born with multiple developmental disabilities shared his story.

> I experienced anger, grief and depression over his condition and felt that my prayers fell silent at heaven's doors. My God seemed impotent as my world crumbled. My biblical theology . . . emphasized [that] . . . sickness, disability or ailment all resulted from a lack of faith. . . . [My] support group . . . prayed for my faith to be increased . . . for [my son] to be healed! And when he was not healed, it was a clear indication that God's favor no longer rested on me. . . . I was in a dangerous, downward spiral and needed a new, God-centered perspective.[24]

The scriptures also use the language of disability metaphorically. Labeling such usage "disabling theology," sociologist and theologian Nancy Eiesland points out that the language of disability appears frequently in the Bible to symbolize disobedience to God, spiritual ignorance, and hardness of heart (Rom. 11:7, 25; 2 Cor. 4:4; Eph. 4:18; 2 Pet. 1:9; 1 John 2:11; Rev. 3:17).[25] The prophet Isaiah, for example, railed against those who had turned to worship idols, asking, "Who is blind but my servant, or deaf like my messenger whom I send?" (Isa. 42:19). When Pharisees and scribes do not listen to his preaching, Jesus indicts them as "blind guides of the blind" and "blind fools" (Matt. 15:14, 23:17). Those who will not endure the trials of discipleship are called lame, with "drooping hands" and "weak knees" (Heb. 12:12). In these passages and others, disability "functions rhetorically to call attention to . . . sin, evil spirits, spiritual degeneration, and moral reprobation."[26]

Reflect and Discuss

Is this metaphorical use of disabilities such as blindness, deafness, and lameness just reserved to religious language or does a similar usage happen in common conversation? Can you think of any examples?

---

24. Steve Bundy, "God, Why Won't You Heal?" *Charisma Magazine*, January 1, 2013, available at *www.charismamag.com/spirit/supernatural/16303-god-why-won-t-you-heal*.

25. Eiesland, *The Disabled God*, 70–75.

26. Amos Yong, *Theology and Down Syndrome: Reimagining Disability in Late Modernity* (Waco, TX: Baylor University Press, 2007), 27.

This biblical tradition clearly prompts Christians to ask the question, what exactly is God's relationship to experiences of physical, psychological, and mental disability? Can theology offer new perspectives to persons with disabilities, their families, and the Christian community? This chapter offers three possibilities: the Accessible God of Jennie Weiss Block, the Disabled God of Nancy Eiesland, and the Interdependent God of Kathy Black.

Jesus: The Accessible God

Disability advocate Jennie Weiss Block calls herself a "secondary consumer," an expression in the field denoting a person whose family member has a disability. She asserts that she does not speak *for* people with disabilities because they are "quite capable of speaking for themselves."[27] In her studies, she explored the relationship between disability and theology in the context of the vision of disability emerging in the United States at the end of the twentieth century. Four guiding principles shaped her theological exploration:

> First, people with disabilities share fully in human nature and are not in any way inferior to people who are not disabled. Second, to reflect on disability is to reflect on the mystery of God's love and the great paradoxes of the Christian message. Third, people with disabilities are oppressed, and the Christian community has the obligation to respond to this injustice by challenging structures and perceptions, including their own, that are oppressive, and by making changes that lead to full access and inclusion for people with disabilities. And finally, I hold that the mandate for access and inclusion is biblically based, central to our baptismal promise and commitment and rooted in the Triune God.[28]

Based on these principles, Block proposes a theology of access for people with disabilities with the aim of "inclusion of people with disabilities in the Body of Christ."[29] So the critical question for Block becomes, "what was Jesus up to" in his healing ministry?[30]

Block emphasizes that having a disability is not a sickness to be cured, which leads her to a distinction between curing and healing. To *cure* denotes a medical treatment that restores one to health, whereas to *heal* includes a restoration of spiritual wholeness. Jesus offered the gift of this spiritual wholeness to every person he encountered, so he clearly healed far more people than he cured during his ministry. According to Block, Jesus was drawn to persons with

---

27. Block, *Copious Hosting*, 12.

28. Ibid., 22.

29. Ibid., 120.

30. Ibid., 105.

disabilities as he was to all people whom society marginalized. However, in his engagement with persons marginalized by disability or by illness, "Extraordinary things happened that were never meant to become ordinary events."[31] Block contends that Jesus' purpose in these extraordinary acts was to demonstrate that he was God "so he could fulfill his salvific mission."[32] Some of these encounters led to the association of disability with sinfulness; nevertheless, those restored in health or wholeness also gained restored access to the community (Luke 5:14, 17:14). Thus, for Block, "the Gospel of Jesus Christ is a Gospel of access."[33]

Reflect and Discuss

Do you agree with Block's interpretation of the healings that Jesus performed? Were they principally to prove that he was God or could they have had another message to convey?

Her metaphor for a theology of access is "copious hosting," based on theologian Edward Schillebeeckx's description of "Jesus as host: a copious gift of God,"[34] who conveyed "the news of God's invitation to all—including and especially those officially regarded as outcasts."[35] According to Block, Jesus' life and ministry inaugurated a new world order in which "outsiders become insiders."[36] By virtue of baptism, all Christians are called to proclaim and effect this world order by becoming cohosts with Christ, creating "the quintessential inclusive community," open to all who are deemed outsiders. The church develops this inclusivity through what Block terms a "relational Christology."[37]

To exemplify this kind of relationality, Block points to Jesus' interaction with Bartimaeus, "the blind beggar" in the Gospel of Mark.

> Bartimaeus . . . a blind beggar, was sitting by the roadside. When he heard that it was Jesus of Nazareth, he began to shout out and say, "Jesus, Son of David, have mercy on me!" Many sternly ordered him to be quiet, but he cried out even more loudly, "Son of David, have mercy on me!" Jesus stood still and said, "Call him here." . . . So throwing

---

31. Ibid.

32. Ibid.

33. Ibid., 120.

34. Edward Schillebeeckx, *Jesus: An Experiment in Christology*, trans. Hubert Hoskins (New York: Seabury, 1979), 213.

35. Ibid., 218.

36. Block, *Copious Hosting*, 132.

37. Ibid.

off his cloak, he sprang up and came to Jesus. Then Jesus said to him, "What do you want me to do for you?" The blind man said to him, "My teacher, let me see again." Jesus said to him, "Go; your faith has made you well." Immediately he regained his sight and followed him on the way. (Mark 10:46–52)

Block notes that the actions of Jesus and Bartimaeus demonstrate the relationality vital to a theology of access. Undeterred by those who seek to silence him, Bartimaeus honestly and humbly seeks to express his need to Jesus, who attends to his voice, asks what Bartimaeus desires, and responds graciously to his request. This interaction demonstrates Jesus' copious hosting, which Christians are called to imitate. Like Jesus with Bartimaeus, Christians "must be willing to stop what they are doing, be still, and listen carefully . . . [—to] respond by giving, graciously and generously, not expecting anything in return."[38]

Reflect and Discuss

If Jesus preached a Gospel of access as Block claims, do you see or experience Christianity as a Church or community of access for people with disabilities? Why or why not?

Block concludes her theological proposals with a number of practical suggestions for church communities. Since "the Body of Christ presumes a place for everyone [the] church fails in its mission if it is not an accessible, hospitable community."[39] According to Block, such accessibility requires reflection and action done in concert with persons with disabilities to ensure that "nothing [is done] about us without us."[40] However, while architectural, liturgical, linguistic, and homiletic transformations are vital, Block maintains that access must ultimately extend beyond these practical considerations to include a personal commitment to mutual friendship and vulnerability among the members of Christ's Body.

Friendship moves us . . . beyond ourselves, toward community, giving us the courage and the freedom to seek the lonely other. Friendship encourages openness, generosity, graciousness, and hospitality, and ultimately leads to vulnerability. . . . The great paradox of the Paschal Mystery is that human vulnerability is the source of communion in

---

38. Ibid., 137–38.

39. Ibid., 141–42.

40. This phrase comes from the book by James I. Charlton, *Nothing about Us without Us* (Berkeley: University of California Press, 1998).

the Kingdom. Our route to union with God and with each other is through the sharing of our joys, our tears, our pain, our limitations, and our hopes.[41]

The Disabled God

Theologian and sociologist Nancy Eiesland frankly acknowledged, "Much of my life I waited for a mighty revelation of God."[42] As a woman who had lived her life with a congenital bone condition, spinal scoliosis, and lung cancer, which finally took her life at the age of forty-four, Eiesland found it difficult to accept the ways her religious tradition interpreted disability.

> I was assured that God gave me a disability to develop my character. But by age six or seven, I was convinced that I had enough character to last a lifetime. My family frequented faith healers with me in tow. I was never healed. People asked about my hidden sins, but they must have been so well hidden that even I misplaced them. The theology that I heard was inadequate to my experience.[43]

Eiesland felt convinced that these theologies of disability were in fact "disabling" theologies because they perpetrated exclusion and injustice for many of God's people and fostered a "prejudice, hostility, and suspicion toward people with disabilities [that] cannot be dismissed simply as relics of an unenlightened past."[44] According to Eiesland, full inclusion in the Christian community requires a liberatory theology of disability with "new symbols, practices, and beliefs" that emerge from the "voices, stories, and embodied experiences" of people with disabilities themselves.[45]

Eiesland contends that the first step toward such a liberatory theology of disability consists of recognizing and challenging the disabling theology that stigmatizes and oppresses persons with disabilities. As discussed earlier in this chapter, the root of such disabling theology is Scripture itself, which brands people with disabilities as impure, unclean, and sinful—"a distortion of the divine image and an inherent desecration of all things holy."[46] In addition to finding the association of disability with impurity and iniquity damaging, Eiesland was also troubled by the biblical theme of virtuous suffering as applied to persons with disabilities. Exemplified by biblical persons like Job, Paul (2 Cor. 12:7–10),

---

41. Block, *Copious Hosting*, 163.

42. Nancy Eiesland, "Encountering the Disabled God," *The Other Side* 38, no. 5 (2002): 12.

43. Ibid., 13.

44. Ibid., 10.

45. Ibid.

46. Ibid., 11.

and Lazarus (Luke 16:19–31), the notion of virtuous suffering characterizes physical impairments as a mark of divine election through which the individual is purified and perfected. It suggests that people with impairments endure temporary infirmity in this world to secure a lasting reward in heaven.

Eiesland points out that neither perspective offers a theology that rightly represents or wholly emancipates persons with disabilities. To devise a theology that is truly liberatory for persons with disabilities, Christianity must reject the visions of disability as symptom of sin or as occasion for virtue. Rather, Christianity must embrace the reality of disability as an opportunity to engage its deepest values and traditions and to find liberating meaning and power for all persons, abled and disabled alike.

Reflect and Discuss

Have you heard or read any of the interpretations of disabilities that Eiesland discusses? Are there other ways in which the Christian tradition might interpret disabilities that are not demeaning or demoralizing?

Eiesland's experience of disabling theology led her to a spiritual estrangement from God. It was at this point, however, that Eiesland received the "mighty revelation of God" that she had been seeking—one that "bore little resemblance to the God I was expecting or the God of my dreams."[47] Eiesland indicates that her "return to intimacy with God" began when she was leading a Bible study with several residents at a rehabilitation hospital for spinal cord injuries.

> One afternoon after a long and frustrating day, I shared with the group my doubts about God's care for me. I asked them how they would know if God was with them and understood their experience. After a long silence, a young African-American man said, "If God was in a sip-puff, maybe He would understand."[48]

This image of God in a sip-puff wheelchair overwhelmed Eiesland. For her, it was an image of God in which God was neither omnipotent and self-sufficient nor pitiable and suffering: "This was an image of God as a survivor, one of those whom society would label 'not feasible,' 'unemployable,' with 'questionable quality of life.'"[49] As Eiesland continued to reflect on this image, she prayed one day

---

47. Ibid., 12.

48. Ibid., 13. A "sip-puff" is a type of wheelchair used by quadriplegics. The design enables them to maneuver the chair by sucking and blowing on a strawlike device.

49. Ibid.

with a post-Resurrection passage in Luke's Gospel. In it, Jesus said to his disciples, "Why are you frightened, and why do doubts arise in your hearts? Look at my hands and my feet; see that it is I myself. Touch me and see" (Luke 24:38–39). At that moment, she recognized the resurrected Christ of the Gospel as the God "whose hands, feet, and sides bear the marks of profound physical impairment."[50] Here was the Risen Lord, "embodied . . . disabled and divine."[51] Here was the Disabled God, the symbol and source of a liberatory theology of disability.

Reflect and Discuss

What is your reaction to the image of the Disabled God? Can you imagine God in a sip-puff wheelchair? Is the resurrected Christ a Disabled God? Why or why not?

Eiesland understands her theology of the Disabled God as a contextualized Christology that "emerges in the particular situation in which people with disabilities . . . live ordinary lives of worth and dignity."[52] As Eiesland explains it,

> Jesus Christ, as a living symbol of the Disabled God, shares in the human condition; he experiences in his embodiment all our vulnerability and flaws. In emptying himself of divinity, Jesus enters into the arena of human limitation, even helplessness. Jesus' own body is wounded and scarred, disfigured and distorted.[53]

As a living symbol of the Disabled God, Jesus lived his life and ministry in solidarity with persons who were disabled, stigmatized, ostracized, and denied their human dignity. In so doing, he undermines the association between disability and sin and affirms that persons with disabilities are the image of God "not in spite of our impairments and contingencies but *through* them."[54] The Disabled God embodied in the Risen Christ also revises the meaning of perfection and wholeness. Rather than rooted in a notion of perfection that assumes able-bodiedness, wholeness in the Disabled God is understood as unself-pitying survival in which limitation is real and tangible, but not devastating. Thus Jesus, the Disabled God, symbolizes the ability to bear the challenging complexities of life and bodiliness without falling into despair.

---

50. Ibid., 14.

51. Ibid.

52. Eiesland, *The Disabled God*, 98.

53. Eiesland, "Encountering the Disabled God," 14.

54. Ibid., 14, emphasis in the original.

According to Eiesland, the revelation of the Disabled God discloses a God who both "celebrates joy and experiences pain," and thus renews hope for "a justice that removes the barriers which constrain our bodies, keep us excluded, and intend to humiliate us."[55] Eiesland believes that the symbol of the Disabled God has the capacity to inspire new Christian symbols, practices, beliefs, and rituals accessible to people with disabilities. She admits that those who adhere to belief in the radical transcendence of God may find this symbol disconcerting, while those who cling to belief in an all-powerful God may find it painful. However, for Eiesland, the Disabled God is Emmanuel, God-for-us, who "enables both a struggle for justice among people with disabilities and an end to estrangement from our own bodies."[56]

Reflect and Discuss

What difference might it make theologically if Christians imaged God in Christ as a Disabled God? What might change in the way we interpret God and suffering?

The Interdependent God

As a professor of homiletics and a United Methodist minister, Kathy Black realizes the power that ministers have to liberate or to oppress, to promote justice or to reinforce prejudice through the language, images, and insights they use in their preaching. This power has a particular impact on the lives of persons with disabilities when ministers preach the healing narratives in the Scriptures. Black indicates that ministers often conflate biblical persons with their disabilities in their preaching by referring to the "paralytic," the "leper," the "cripple," the "blind," and the "lame," rather than recognizing such persons as having personal dignity and agency. She also points out the tendency of preachers to use these terms metaphorically to indicate a lack of obedience or responsiveness toward God and is keenly aware that many persons have difficulty viewing people with disabilities as made in the image of God. Black is all the more attuned to these issues because she herself has a disability that causes episodes of severe muscle weakness and paralysis. She therefore strives to communicate through her preaching and teaching that people with disabilities are "holy people with the same gifts and graces God gives to all for the ministry of the church in the world."[57]

---

55. Eiesland, *The Disabled God*, 103.

56. Ibid., 105.

57. Kathy Black, "A Perspective of the Disabled: Transforming Images of God, Interdependence, and Healing," in *Preaching Justice: Ethnic and Cultural Perspectives*, ed. Christine M. Smith (Cleveland: United Church Press, 1998), 9.

While Black focuses primarily on preaching, she is also concerned that ministers confront questions about God in the midst of suffering on a daily basis.

> A person has been in a car accident and wakes up in the hospital without the ability to walk. The long-awaited birth of a baby arrives, but joy turns to unknown fear as the expectant parents wait in silence while doctors rush the newborn off to ascertain her physical condition. What do clergy have to offer to those who experience such suffering . . . and [to] the questions . . . raised about why this happened to them? Where is God in the midst of their pain?[58]

Acknowledging responses like those discussed throughout this text, Black admits that all such responses attempt to make sense of a senseless situation while preserving faith in God. Nonetheless, she asks, "do these doctrines affirm belief in a God who is loving and wills the well-being of all of creation or in a God who is distant, erratic, and manipulative?"[59]

Reflect and Discuss

Have you found yourself in the position of trying to console someone in situations like those described above? What did you say?

For her own part, Black rejects the belief that disabilities are God's will or that God causes such experiences. While Black acknowledges that experiences such as these often do test faith, build character, and teach life lessons, she questions,

> Did God cause the disability . . . or does God resurrect the various situations in our lives, fill us with grace, and help us make meaning out of our disability without God's causing or allowing it? . . . Can we find meaning in the midst of suffering without believing that it is somehow part of God's divine plan?[60]

Reflect and Discuss

How would you answer Black's questions?

---

58. Kathy Black, *A Healing Homiletic: Preaching and Disability* (Nashville: Abingdon, 1996), 19.

59. Ibid., 33.

60. Black, "A Perspective of the Disabled," 19.

As a first step toward answering these questions, Black contends that one must redefine the notion of an omnipotent God. She points out that people commonly believe that to be all-powerful, God must be in control of every moment and each event in the world. According to this view, God is "the great puppeteer" who decides what happens at each instant or at least deliberately opts not to prevent things from happening. However, Black states that this viewpoint runs the risk of making God's power more essential than God's compassion and love. If, therefore, disabilities are not caused by God or are not part of God's plan, how can Christians conceive of the relationship between God and disability, as well as suffering in general?

Black submits that the choices people make cause many of the situations of suffering in which they find themselves and that these choices impact the lives and well-being of others. This happens because "we are all interconnected and interdependent upon one another . . . and the earth itself."[61] According to Black, this fact applies not only to people's decisions and their outcomes, but to the very nature of matter itself.

> A person's DNA is directly related to his or her parents' genes and their parents' genes, and sometimes combinations create the condition where disability will be the result. Sometimes matter is affected by other matter and mutations occur. Cancer and HIV are living organisms that are vying for control in the context of other living organisms. Everything in the universe is interconnected. All of life is interdependent.[62]

Because of the interconnectedness of the universe and human experience, it need not be the case that God wills or causes suffering, frustrations, or disabilities. Moreover, she asserts that God is part of the interdependence of the universe.

Reflect and Discuss

What is your response to Black's assertion of an interconnected universe? Does her proposal effectively address the presence of suffering in the world? Where is her claim valid? What are its limitations?

In making this claim, Black first points out the Christian belief that God wills what is good for all of creation. For her, the resurrection best demonstrates this divine will: out of the suffering and death of the cross, God brought about new life and salvation. In a similar way, Black sees God transforming experiences of disability or difficulty toward fullness of life and well-being. Black is quick to

---

61. Black, *A Healing Homiletic*, 34.

62. Ibid.

emphasize the limitation of this image of transformation, as many people with disabilities do not associate the suffering and death of the cross with disability. Nonetheless,

> whether one is dealing with prejudice and ignorance from the surrounding society or dealing with total dependence on machines and attendant care for survival, there is a word of hope and grace. God works to transform our lives at every moment, in all our various circumstances, through the power of love. God wills the well-being that is possible for each one of us.[63]

Black adds that God does not bring about such transformation by divine intervention from outside the universe, but as part of the interdependence that constitutes the universe itself. For Black, a comforting touch, an invitation to fellowship, or an act of acceptance is an experience of God's presence in human life. Furthermore, when the Christian community uses images like the communion of saints or the Body of Christ, it identifies Christians "as agents of God . . . [who] work interdependently with God to achieve well-being for ourselves and others."[64]

Reflect and Discuss

Are the actions Black describes the presence of God in an interdependent world? Why or why not?

As Black indicates, American culture does not highly value interdependence. It esteems and promotes independence, which can lead to intolerance, avoidance, and alienation of persons with disabilities because "dependency is frowned on by society."[65] Nonetheless, in an interdependent view of life, no one is actually independent; each person relies on other people and on the created world itself for survival. According to Black, a theology of interdependence honors the reality of the interconnectedness of all of life. It "acknowledges not only our dependence on God . . . but also God's dependence on us to be agents of God's healing compassion in the world."[66] While millions of persons experience disability, God neither wills nor causes it. God is, however, present in the midst of persons' lives, bringing healing and compassion through the community of faith.

---

63. Ibid., 36.

64. Ibid., 38.

65. Ibid., 40.

66. Ibid., 42.

Reflect and Discuss

Is Black's theology of interdependence an adequate theology of disability? Would it be fruitful for discussions of God's relationship to other types of suffering in the world? Why or why not?

Case in Point: Joni Eareckson Tada—*Something Greater than Healing*

This "Case in Point" focuses on Joni Eareckson Tada, an internationally known speaker and author and the founder of Joni and Friends, an organization dedicated to Christian ministry in the disability community. Although a renowned disability activist, Tada readily admits that she is no theologian.

> I've never read Calvin's Institutes all the way through, nor do I know Greek or Hebrew. But years ago, when I snapped my neck under the weight of a dive into shallow water, permanent and total paralysis smashed me up against the study of God.[67]

As a result of that diving accident, Tada has been quadriplegic since the age of seventeen. She writes and speaks candidly about her own struggles and acknowledges that understanding God's relationship to suffering is difficult: "Sometimes you wake up in the middle of the night with chronic pain, and you think to yourself, *Who is this God?*"[68]

> I mean, does He say, "Into each life a little rain must fall," and then aim a hose at the earth to see who gets the wettest?. . . . Perhaps He was off somewhere listening to the prayers of more obedient saints. I didn't know where God was. . . . I figured God had been caught off guard while Satan threw a monkey wrench into God's plans for my life.[69]

---

67. Joni Eareckson Tada, "Turning Evil on Its Head," *Ligonier.org*, available at *www.ligonier.org/learn/articles/turning-evil-its-head/*.

68. Joni Eareckson Tada, "Finding God in Our Suffering," *Veritas* 9 (July 2009): 2, available at *www.dts.edu/download/publications/veritas/veritas-2009-july.pdf*, italics in the original.

69. Ibid., 2–3.

Case in Point: Joni Eareckson Tada *(continued)*

While Tada concluded that thinking of God as "caught off guard" in the midst of misfortune makes God as helpless and hostage to her disability as she was, she continued to wrestle mightily with the question of whether her accident was the will of God. In the process of coming to grips with a response that she could accept, she challenged others with the same gut-wrenching questions she herself confronted: "Think of the times when suffering has ripped into your sanity, leaving you numb and bleeding. Can this be God's will for you?"[70]

An early insight into that question came for her through a young man with whom she was studying the Bible after her accident. In response to her uncertainty about the will of God in the event of her injury, the man said to Tada, "Joni, think of Jesus Christ."

> He is the best man who ever lived, and if we can find answers for His life, they should be able to work for your life. Do you think it was God's will for Jesus to suffer as He did? Well, I want you to look at all the awful things that happened to Jesus on that cross. . . . How can any of that be God's will? Injustice? Murder?[71]

At first, Tada was convinced that it *was* God's will that Jesus go to the cross. However, after further prayer and study, "God has showed me that . . . [when] babies die, when whole populations starve, when young girls break their necks, God weeps for His world."[72] However, while God deems such events tragic, Tada contends that God transforms and uses such events as a means to divine ends. This reality is what Tada calls the sovereignty of God.

> Whether hardship is brought on by our own negligence or through the direct assault of the hand of a wicked person, or our own ignorance and misinformed decisions, or our lack of awareness or misdoings, or some catastrophe of nature . . . God's sovereignty extends over all these things. God permits all sorts of things that he doesn't approve

---

70. Ibid., 4.

71. Ibid.

72. Tada, "Turning Evil on Its Head."

of . . . but in his sovereign decree he has allowed them. I don't care if you use *permit*, *allow*, or *ordained*; it's all the same thing. Ultimately it goes back to God being in charge.[73]

Therefore, although God did not compel those who crucified Jesus to inflict suffering and death upon him, God permitted the crucifixion to accomplish God's own purpose—the salvation of the world. In the words of the young man with whom Tada studied the Scriptures, "God permits what He hates to accomplish what He loves."[74] In so doing, claims Tada, God redeems suffering.

Tada takes comfort in the Bible verse that God "accomplishes all things according to his counsel and will" (Eph. 1:11), while conceding that "His will, purpose, and sovereign design may be a bit more obscure and enigmatic on this side of eternity."[75] According to Tada, "God's joy is real, but He shares it on His terms, and those terms call for us to suffer as His precious Son suffered."[76] However, the salvation achieved by the suffering and death of Jesus transforms the cross from a symbol of torture to a symbol of hope. For Tada, the same kind of transformation can take place as persons with disabilities bear their cross in the midst of the Christian community. As Tada states, persons with disabilities remind the community that "the greatest good that suffering can work for a believer is to increase his or her capacity for God."[77]

Reflect and Discuss

Black and Tada both contend that, in the context of disability, God transforms or redeems suffering. Can one say that their image of the relationship between God and disability—as well as suffering—is therefore the same? Defend your position.

---

73. Joni Eareckson Tada, "Something Greater than Healing," *Christianity Today* 54 (October 2010): 30.

74. Tada, "Turning Evil on Its Head."

75. Tada, "Something Greater than Healing."

76. Tada, "Finding God in Our Suffering."

77. Ibid., 6–7.

For Further Reading

Black, Kathy. "A Perspective of the Disabled: Transforming Images of God, Interdependence, and Healing," 6–25. In *Preaching Justice: Ethnic and Cultural Perspectives*. Edited by Christine Marie Smith. Cleveland: United Church Press, 1998.

Block, Jennie Weiss. *Copious Hosting: A Theology of Access for People with Disabilities*. New York: Continuum, 2002.

Eiesland, Nancy L. *The Disabled God: Toward a Liberatory Theology of Disability*. Nashville: Abingdon, 1994.

Tada, Joni Eareckson. "Finding God in Our Suffering." *Veritas* 9 (July 2009): 1–9.

Internet Resources

Guth, Christine. "From Cure to Community: Biblical Interpretation that Challenges the Stigma of Disability." Widening the Welcome, United Church of Christ National Disabilities Conference, Columbus, Ohio, September 2011. Available at *www.youtube.com/watch?v=FqqgJe103Kk*.

Tada, Joni Eareckson. "Centennial Chapel Series." *Biola University*, September 19, 2007. Available at *www.youtube.com/watch?v=mvZurt4ls2M*.

"The Disability Rights Movement." *National Museum of American History of the Smithsonian Institution*. Available at *http://americanhistory.si.edu/disability rights/exhibit.html*.

CHAPTER 9

God in the Travail of the Cosmos

> The whole epic of evolution in its biological phase has seemed to many sensitive scientists, beginning with Darwin himself, to involve too much pain and suffering, culminating in death, for it to be the creative work of any Being who could be called benevolent.
>
> —Arthur Peacocke, *Paths from Science towards God: The End of All Our Exploring*

Introduction

According to science, the evolution of the universe began thirteen to fourteen billion years ago. No more than a fraction of a second old, the universe was a compressed fireball, a "primeval, unimaginably condensed mass of fundamental particles and energy," consisting of the most basic subatomic elements of matter-energy-space-time.[1] Suddenly this fireball erupted in what scientists call the "the big bang," but which others have termed "the primordial flaring forth"[2] of life. From an original unity came all the diversity that has existed in the cosmos. From a primeval darkness came life-giving light. From the most elemental particles and energies came the conditions through which the evolution of life began on planet Earth.

Evolutionary understandings of the cosmos have frequently been perceived as threatening to a Christian cosmology based on the Genesis narrative of the Bible. However, most scholars now suggest that evolutionary theory is so well-established that Christian theology can no longer operate solely within a biblical understanding of the origin of the universe. In an address in 2014, Pope

---

1. Arthur Peacocke, "Theology and Science Today," in *Cosmos and Creation: Science and Theology in Consonance*, ed. Ted Peters (Nashville: Abingdon, 1989), 30.

2. Brian Swimme and Thomas Berry, *The Universe Story: From the Primordial Flaring Forth to the Ecozoic Era—A Celebration of the Unfolding of the Cosmos* (San Francisco: Harper San Francisco, 1994), 7.

Francis declared that "The evolution of nature does not contrast with the notion of creation, as evolution presupposes the creation of beings that evolve."

> [God] created beings and allowed them to develop according to the internal laws that he gave to each one, so that they were able to develop and to arrive at their fullness of being. . . . And so creation continued . . . precisely because God is . . . the creator who gives being to all things. . . . The Big Bang . . . does not contradict the divine act of creating, but rather requires it.[3]

Reflect and Discuss

Do these statements by religious leaders surprise you? Why or why not?

The theory of evolution traces its origin to the work of British naturalist Charles Darwin, who published his findings and insights in his book *On the Origin of Species by Means of Natural Selection, or the Preservation of Favoured Races in the Struggle for Life*.[4] While most naturalists in his time believed that each species had been specifically created, a few like Darwin believed that "species undergo modification, and that existing forms of life are the descendants . . . of pre-existing forms."[5] Darwin was convinced that the most important process by which this modification of species took place was natural selection.[6] According to Darwin, the process of selection follows from "the struggle for life"[7] through which beneficial variations in a species are preserved. Offspring then inherit these variations, giving them a better chance of survival as well. While Darwin described the phenomenon of selection, he did not identify the specific mechanisms of evolution that resulted in this survival of the fittest.[8]

The specific mechanisms of evolution, however, provide the context for the discussion of God and suffering in an evolving cosmos. If, as Pope Francis

---

3. Pope Francis, "Francis Inaugurates Bust of Benedict, Emphasizes Unity of Faith, Science," October 27, 2014, *Catholic News Agency*, available at *www.catholicnewsagency.com/news /francis-inaugurates-bust-of-benedict-emphasizes-stewardship-43494/*.

4. Charles Darwin, *On the Origin of Species by Means of Natural Selection, or the Preservation of Favoured Races in the Struggle for Life* (London: John Murray, 1872), available at *www.talkorigins .org/faqs/origin.html*.

5. Ibid., *www.literature.org/authors/darwin-charles/the-origin-of-species-6th-edition/preface.html*.

6. Ibid., *www.literature.org/authors/darwin-charles/the-origin-of-species-6th-edition/introduction.html*.

7. Ibid., *www.literature.org/authors/darwin-charles/the-origin-of-species-6th-edition/chapter-03.html*.

8. A key aspect of this mechanism would be explicated by biologist Gregor Mendel, who described the laws of heredity and the science of genetics.

proposed, God created beings with an internal law to guide their fulfillment, then such a law exists both in human beings and in nonhuman beings as well. This internal law within all created beings provides for human free will and for what physicist and theologian John Polkinghorne calls free process, the potential of the cosmos to act in accordance with its own nature. According to Polkinghorne, God allows the world and its inhabitants to exist "in that independence which is Love's gift of freedom to the one beloved . . . which makes it capable of fruitful evolution."[9] Because all manner of creatures are beloved by God, not only do human beings have a freedom proper to their nature, but nonhuman creatures and processes do as well. Nonetheless, the very God-given freedom that enables created beings to fulfill their potential also creates the possibility of conflict, chaos, and catastrophe among them. These possibilities often give rise to suffering, which suggests that suffering is an inherent part of the process of evolution itself.

Many say that the free process of creation and the free will of humans result in too much suffering and death to be the intent of a loving and provident God. Nevertheless, the theologians discussed in this chapter contend that the very fact that the Creator fashioned the creatures and the processes of the cosmos with the freedom to evolve according to their nature reveals divine love and providence. Moreover, the Creator continues to be intimately involved as these creatures and processes evolve, even to the extent of suffering "in, with, and under the creative processes of the world with their costly unfolding in time."[10]

Reflect and Discuss

Have you ever thought of the natural processes of the world having a type of freedom? What might this mean for the question of God's relation to natural evil?

Context

The concept and consequences of human free will have appeared throughout this text, and the suffering sometimes involved in its use is abundantly clear. However, it has said little about the suffering that arises from the free processes of evolutionary creativity. Like human free will, these free processes produce abundant life and energy for the continued development of creation and

---

9. John Polkinghorne, *Science and Providence: God's Interaction with the World* (Philadelphia: Templeton Foundation, Press, 2005), 77–78.

10. Arthur Peacocke, "The Cost of New Life," in *The Work of Love: Creation as Kenosis*, ed. John Polkinghorne (Grand Rapids: Eerdmans, 2001), 37.

its creatures. However, these processes also create situations of "natural evil" that provoke difficult questions about God in an evolving universe. Therefore, in sketching the context for an evolutionary theology of suffering, this chapter focuses on those free processes associated with such natural evil, namely, the suffering caused by experiences and events resulting from the cosmos acting in accord with its nature—experiences like disease and death, events like volcanic eruptions, floods, hurricanes, or earthquakes. To do so, this chapter examines the operation of chance within natural law and the function of pain, suffering, and death in an evolving cosmos.

Reflect and Discuss

Are natural events such as hurricanes, earthquakes, eruptions, and the like properly called evil? Are they evil in and of themselves? If so, what makes them evil?

The Operation of Chance within Law

According to scientist-theologian Arthur Peacocke, the evolution of life involves "a continuous, almost kaleidoscopic, recombination of the component units of the universe into an increasing diversity of forms."[11] This "recombination" occurs as the result of two interrelated characteristics of the cosmos: natural law and random chance. On the one hand, the universe reveals a remarkable continuity and regularity in the development of life-forms. Scientists have charted this regularity in the taxonomy of living things, which classifies living things according to the commonalities they share with other organisms. The evolutionary process responsible for this continuity among life-forms is *natural law*. Its presence does not imply a rigid determinism in nature. Rather, natural law represents patterns of relationships within forms of life that guide their ongoing development. As the universe continued to evolve, however, unanticipated variations within species occurred, yielding a splendid diversity of forms in different environments. It seemed that natural processes produced organisms that manifested not only commonality but also increasing uniqueness. These unpredictable outcomes led scientists to conjecture that evolution unfolded not only through the guidance of natural laws but also through the impact of random chance.

Scientists define the phenomenon of chance in different ways. On one hand, chance may describe a situation in which scientists are unable to detect or measure the variables that caused a particular outcome. In this case, the term

---

11. Arthur Peacocke, "God as the Creator of the World of Science," in *Interpreting the Universe as Creation*, ed. V. Brummer (Kampen, Netherlands: Kok Pharos, 1991), 103.

chance denotes a lack of knowledge or tools that would enable scientists to identify what caused the novel outcome. On the other hand, chance may describe the interaction of two unrelated causes that produce a new outcome. These causes could be environmental, physical, or genetic. However, there is no connection between the causes until they intersect and, thus, nothing would have enabled scientists to predict the outcome of such a random event.[12] The mutation of the genetic material DNA provides one example of this latter kind of chance. As evolutionary biologist Julian Huxley explains it, mutation of genetic material "is a random affair, and takes place in all directions."

> Some of these alterations are truly chance rearrangements, as uncaused or at least as unpredictable as the jumping of an electron from one orbit to another inside an atom; others are the result of the impact of some external agency, like X-rays, or ultra-violet radiations, or mustard gas. But in all cases they are random in relation to evolution. . . . They occur without reference to their possible consequences or biological uses.[13]

The point is that whatever the causes might be, the effect in an organism is novelty that cannot be attributed to natural law alone.

Reflect and Discuss

Can you think of any examples of environmental causes that produced changes in species? What were the changes produced? What effect did this have for the continuation or extinction of that species?

Jesuit paleontologist and geologist Pierre Teilhard de Chardin termed this process of stimulating novelty through chance *tâtonnement* or "groping." Envisioning the process through the lens of Christianity, Teilhard described *tâtonnement* not as mere chance, but as "directed chance," directed by God immanent and active within the cosmos itself.[14] The notion brings to mind Albert Einstein's famous statement against quantum theory and randomness in nature: "God does not play dice with the universe."[15] One response to this statement

---

12. Arthur Peacocke, *Creation and the World of Science*, The Bampton Lectures 1978 (Oxford: Clarendon, 1979), 90–93.

13. Julian Huxley, *Evolution in Action* (Middlesex, UK: Penguin, 1963), 43–44.

14. Pierre Teilhard de Chardin, *The Phenomenon of Man* (New York: Harper & Row, 1959), 294.

15. See Stephen Hawking, "Does God Play Dice?" *Stephen Hawking: The Official Website*, available at *www.hawking.org.uk/does-god-play-dice.html*. An exhibit by the American Institute of Physics Center for History of Physics reports that "Einstein liked inventing phrases such as 'God does not play dice,' 'The Lord is subtle but not malicious.' On one occasion [physicist Neils] Bohr answered, 'Einstein, stop telling God what to do.'" See *www.aip.org/history/exhibits/einstein/ae63.htm*.

came from chaos theorist Joseph Ford. According to Ford, "God plays dice with the universe. But they're loaded dice. And the main objective of physics now is to find out by what rules were they loaded and how can we use them for our own ends."[16] Arthur Peacocke amplifies Ford's reply by suggesting that the dice are "loaded" in favor of the emergence of new life. However, while God may have "loaded the dice" in favor of life and cosmic potential, creation through randomness and chance "is no picnic but an adventure, a risk, a battle, to which [God] commits himself unreservedly."[17] Moreover, according to Teilhard, God too enters into it gropingly, "step by step by dint of billionfold trial and error."[18]

Reflect and Discuss

How does Teilhard's description of the creative process as "groping" influence your thinking about God as Creator? Does it correlate with the orderliness described in Genesis 1 and 2?

The operation of chance within law offers one example of the inherent creativity of the cosmos. It modifies the physical structure and appearance of many species so that they can better adapt, survive, and reproduce under changing conditions of climate and habitat. However, it may also mutate bacteria or intensify weather patterns, causing events destructive to the environment and its inhabitants. In humans, chance within law can foster genetic diversity, improve health, or have no discernible effect whatsoever. Nonetheless, the operation of randomness also accounts for genetic variations that cause disorders including cystic fibrosis, sickle-cell anemia, Tay-Sachs disease, and Huntington's disease.

In his book *When Bad Things Happen to Good People*, Rabbi Harold Kushner asks, "Can you accept the idea that some things happen for no reason, that there is randomness in the universe?"[19] That question is not only about randomness at the micro-level of genes but also at the macro-level of human events. According to Kushner, the response to that question proves critical since physicists suggest that the world is evolving in the direction of more randomness, rather than less. As a result, Kushner warns, "chaos, chance and mischance, things happening for no reason, will continue to be with us."[20] How humans respond to this reality impacts not only their fundamental trust in existence but also their faith in God.

---

16. James Gleick, *Chaos: Making a New Science* (New York: Penguin Books, 1987), 314.

17. Pierre Teilhard de Chardin, *Christianity and Evolution* (New York: Harcourt Brace Jovanovich, 1971), 85.

18. Teilhard de Chardin, *The Phenomenon of Man*, 302.

19. Harold Kushner, *When Bad Things Happen to Good People* (New York: Avon, 1981), 46.

20. Ibid., 55.

The Function of Pain, Suffering, and Death in the Cosmos

When Teilhard spoke of evolution as a risky and embattled process, he was describing the presence of what he called the shadow side of the creative process, which produces cataclysmic environmental events. While these events have occurred throughout the formation of the planet, increased population, habitation, and development over eons have intensified the impact of these environmental occurrences, making them into environmental disasters that result in pain, suffering, and death in the cosmos and its creatures. Science suggests, however, that such environmental events, as well as pain and death, are often necessary conditions for the survival and transition of life in the universe.

The *environmental events* referred to here occur naturally and are frequently destructive. They include earthquakes, hurricanes, floods, landslides, tornados, and volcanic eruptions, to name but a few. Their causes have roots in the natural processes and structures of Earth—the movement of tectonic plates in Earth's crust, the effect of the moon on tides, the changes in oceanic currents, the interaction of atmospheric systems, the pressure from volcanic gasses and magma—and thus remain beyond human control. As part of the free processes of the cosmos, these events play a role in the evolution and transformation of the planet as a whole, yet they tend to be assessed according to their impact on human life and well-being. Thus, while floods can increase the fertility of soil, add nutrients to rivers, and balance the aquatic population, they also result in the destruction of lives, vegetation, and infrastructures. Although volcanoes enrich the surrounding soil and release chemicals that enhance the water cycle, they threaten lives and landscape, produce massive dust clouds, and trigger earthquakes, tsunamis, and floods. And granting that hurricane winds can redistribute topsoil, lower temperatures, and build up the coastal areas of islands, the ecological and human damage from such events are far-reaching and incalculable.

In sentient creatures, *pain* ordinarily functions as a warning signal for danger and disease. The physical ability to feel pain developed and increased with the evolution of sense organs and nervous systems in organisms. These structures increase an organism's sensitivity to both positive and negative stimuli in the environment, and this sensitivity intensified as consciousness developed. Biologically, the experience of pain is advantageous; when recognized and responded to, it enhances the possibilities of survival for creatures faced with threats to their existence. It constitutes one type of "natural evil" with obvious purpose.

Scientists also insist that *death* comprises a necessary and purposeful part of the evolutionary process. The death of certain organisms in the cosmos provides for the ongoing existence and emergence of other forms of life. Myriad plants and animals give their lives for the feeding and nourishment of other organisms. Adverse environmental changes continually affect flora and fauna; as a result, existing creatures often die and make way for those that have adapted. Thus, Peacocke observes,

> There is a kind of *structural* logic about the inevitability of living organisms dying and of preying on each other, for we cannot conceive . . . of any way whereby [the] immense variety of developing, biological, structural complexity might appear, except by utilizing structures already existing, either by way of modification (as in biological evolution) or of incorporation (as in feeding).[21]

Reflect and Discuss

Scientists describe death as an inherent part of an evolving cosmos and yet religious traditions suggest that death is a result of sin. Where do you stand? Can these positions be reconciled?

From Teilhard's perspective, the presence of death in an evolving universe is not just logical, but *statistically necessary*. To understand what Teilhard means, one must grasp his understanding of what it means "to create." For Teilhard, primordial matter at the origin of the universe—the Big Bang—was manifold and unorganized. Through evolutionary processes, the numerous elements of matter became unified and organized. Just as human creativity produces words, sentences, and paragraphs by combining some letters and eliminating others, so the evolution of matter combined some elements and cast off others over great expanses of time. However, if creativity takes place through the union of some elements and the casting off of others, then evolution, according to Teilhard, cannot take place without death "appearing as a shadow," that is, as a byproduct of this creative process.[22] Because of free process in the cosmos, evolutionary creativity "cannot progress toward unity without giving rise to . . . some evil here

---

21. Arthur R. Peacocke, "The Challenge and Stimulus of the Epic of Evolution to Theology," in *Many Worlds*, ed. Stephen Dick (Philadelphia: Templeton Foundation, 2000), 106, emphasis in the original.

22. Teilhard de Chardin, *Christianity and Evolution*, 134.

or there and that *by statistical necessity.*"[23] Hence, Teilhard suggests, so long as disorder, disunity, and disorganization endure within the creative movement of evolution, so too will pain and death endure as inescapable elements of the process. To concretize these claims, Teilhard invites one to consider human experience:

> We have seen the world proceeding by means of groping and chance. . . . [Even] up to the human level on which chance is most controlled—how many failures have there been for one success, how many days of misery for one hour's joy, how many sins for a solitary saint? . . . Statistically, at every degree of evolution we find evil always and everywhere, forming and reforming implacably around us.[24]

While environmental events, pain, and death may be statistically or structurally necessary, they frequently produce in humans the psychological experience of *suffering*. Unlike the physical nature of environmental events, pain, and death, the experience of suffering results in the disruption of inner harmony and well-being, in a sense of anxiety and tragedy that has no parallel in other creatures. Those who have survived hurricanes and floods, tornados and tsunamis, earthquakes and mudslides, forest fires and drought commonly experience shock and denial, nightmares and panic attacks, post-traumatic stress disorders and depression. Although people may acknowledge that environmental events and experiences of pain and death can have a necessary and potentially positive effect, "Nothing . . . can diminish our sense of loss and tragedy as we experience or witness particular natural evils, especially in individuals known to us."[25] The sense of meaninglessness and powerlessness in the face of such events is profound and enduring.

Reflect and Discuss

Does the distinction between pain and suffering make sense? It is suggested that pain can be advantageous. Can suffering also have advantages?

God and Suffering in an Evolving Universe

In view of the perplexing mixture of processes and events in an evolving universe, with their positive and negative impacts on human and nonhuman

---

23. Pierre Teilhard de Chardin, quoted in Georges Crespy, *From Science to Theology: An Essay on Teilhard de Chardin* (New York: Abingdon Press, 1968), 99, emphasis in the original.

24. Teilhard de Chardin, *The Phenomenon of Man*, 311–12.

25. Arthur Peacocke, *Theology for a Scientific Age: Being and Becoming: Natural, Divine and Human* (Minneapolis: Augsburg Fortress, 1993), 126.

creatures, how might one speak of God in the midst of this? What kind of God fashions and participates in a creative process so characterized by pain, suffering, and death and yet so abundant with new life? Physicist and theologian John Polkinghorne speaks of a kenotic God, Arthur Peacocke of a vulnerable God, and Gloria Schaab of the creative suffering of the Triune God.

The Kenotic Creator

John Polkinghorne is an Anglican priest and mathematical physicist who has made significant contributions to discourse concerning God's interaction with the world. His insights have focused in great measure on the question of how God acts providentially in a cosmos "made to make itself." Like others in the theology-science dialogue, Polkinghorne maintains that God created the cosmos with the potential to evolve and prosper through its own self-creative interplay of natural law and random chance, which he considers natural endowments of the world God created. This understanding does not suggest that God creates and then abandons creation or the creative process. For Polkinghorne, God shares thoroughly in the evolutionary course of creation in concert "with creatures who have their divinely allowed, but not divinely dictated, roles to play in its fruitful becoming."[26]

Polkinghorne points out that while human activities may exacerbate some natural disasters, humans tend to place responsibility for these events squarely on the Creator, who is presumed to decide, direct, and control such cosmic occurrences. Nonetheless, according to the notion of a universe endowed with free process, Polkinghorne claims that God intends the cosmos to exercise its innate freedom and to act in accordance with its own nature. As a result,

> No longer can God be held to be totally and directly responsible for all that happens. An evolutionary world is inevitably one in which there are raggednesses and blind alleys. Death is the necessary cost of new life; environmental change can lead to extinctions; genetic mutations sometimes produce new forms of life, oftentimes malignancies. There is an unavoidable cost attached to a world allowed to make itself.[27]

The unavoidable cost attached to creating a self-creative world demonstrates what Polkinghorne calls the kenotic nature of God. The term "kenotic" comes directly from the Greek *kenōsis*, which means "to empty." In Christianity, *kenōsis* is most often translated as "self-emptying" and is primarily associated with the Incarnation in which Christ "emptied [*ekenōsen*] himself, taking the form

---

26. John Polkinghorne, "Kenotic Creation and Divine Action," in *The Work of Love: Creation as Kenosis*, ed. John Polkinghorne (Grand Rapids: Eerdmans, 2001), 94.

27. Ibid., 95.

of a slave, being born in human likeness" (Phil. 2:7). Applied to Christ in the incarnation, kenosis refers to his voluntary relinquishment of divine attributes in order to become human. In Christ's "act of divine self-limitation . . . the invisible God took our flesh and became a visible actor on the stage of creation."[28] In his evolutionary theology, however, Polkinghorne also applies the movement of kenosis to God. In the Creator, kenosis refers to God's voluntary limitation of divine attributes in order to allow creation and its creatures the true freedom to be and to act according to their God-given natures. This God does with absolute freedom out of infinite love for finite creatures. According to Polkinghorne, such divine self-limitation does not make God impotent or preclude God's creative interaction with the world. It does, however, emphasize the freedom of natural processes and thus provokes perplexing questions about the interplay between divine love and divine power in responding to suffering in the cosmos.

Reflect and Discuss

What is your initial response to the concept of God's self-limitation of divine power and control?

Polkinghorne examines four aspects of divine kenosis revealed in God's loving relationship with creation: (1) the kenosis of omnipotence, (2) the kenosis of simple eternity, (3) the kenosis of omniscience, and (4) the kenosis of causal status. Polkinghorne notes that scholars widely acknowledge the *kenosis of omnipotence* and they cite it as the basis for the evolutionary concept of a creation made to make itself.[29] This aspect of divine kenosis implies that God deliberately limits divine power and control to give authentic autonomy and agency to both the creatures and the creative processes in an evolving cosmos. Like caring parents who choose to ease their absolute authority over their children to promote their maturity and self-reliance, this concept holds that God's loving letting-go of control in creation allows everything that occurs in the cosmos; nonetheless, while God allows all that occurs, not all of what occurs accords with God's providential will.

Furthermore, creating and acting in a cosmos in which time is a reality suggests that time has a real significance for God. Because of this, God also chooses a *kenosis of simple eternity*, which implies that time influences not only creation, but the Creator as well. "While God has not set aside the timeless and eternal nature of divine Being," Polkinghorne explains, "there has been 'added' to

---

28. Ibid., 104.

29. This position has been recognized and developed by a variety of Christian theologians such as Arthur Peacocke, Jürgen Moltmann, Denis Edwards, Keith Ward, and Gloria Schaab, among others.

that (so to speak) a temporal pole of divinity that corresponds to the Creator's true engagement with created time."[30] Although God must remain free from anything that diminishes the fullness of divine mercy, love, and faithfulness, God must relate somehow to the varying circumstances of creation to effectively respond to the changing lives and needs of each creature. Like self-limited omnipotence, God's embrace of the experience of time is wholly free and stems from love. Polkinghorne acknowledges, however, that this form of kenotic self-limitation does not enjoy the same level of acceptance by scholars as that of omnipotence. Many insist on a divine transcendence that prevents God's entanglement in the vicissitudes of time. However, he suggests that the incarnation symbolizes just such a radical involvement of God with created time and space. This viewpoint can offer an insight not only into the nature of Christ, but into the nature of God, because "the Incarnation was the historical enactment of what is eternally true of the nature of God."[31]

A third kind of self-limitation undertaken by the Creator of an evolving cosmos is the *kenosis of omniscience*. A temporal, self-creative world subject to law and chance leaves the future radically open. While God knows all that can possibly be known, free process, free will, and God's freely chosen relationship to time implies that God does not know the future, for the future in principle remains unknown and unknowable. Yet to say that God does not know the future does not leave God floundering and unprepared for it. Although God does not see the unformed future in all its details, God clearly sees the movements of history, the processes of evolution, and the hearts of people and thus can prompt creation and its creatures toward fullness of life. Nonetheless, God "is not the puppeteer of either men or matter"[32] and therefore the future remains ineffable.

The final type of restraint God self-imposes is the *kenosis of causal status*. Polkinghorne proposes that "the Creator's kenotic love includes allowing divine . . . providence to act as a cause among causes."[33] Classical theology has always maintained a distinction between divine causality and creaturely causality. It considers divine or "primary causality" unique and transcendent and, thus, essentially of a different order and nature than creaturely causation. According to classical theology, divine causality supersedes all natural causes; it is not simply one cause among other causes in the cosmos. To affect the cosmos, primary causality works through creaturely or "secondary causality."

While it remains impossible to demonstrate how these two ontologically different forms of causality relate to one another within creation, a more critical issue for Polkinghorne is that the absolute link between divine and creaturely

30. Polkinghorne, "Kenotic Creation and Divine Action," 103.

31. Ibid.

32. Polkinghorne, *Science and Providence*, 78.

33. Polkinghorne, "Kenotic Creation and Divine Action," 104.

causality militates against the free process and free will that he considers to be key components of evolutionary creativity. If all creaturely activity is traceable to the initiative of God, then one must conclude that God is undeniably responsible for evil and suffering in the world. This constitutes an untenable position for Polkinghorne, who contends that God allows creatures to exercise *genuine* freedom and participation in evolution. Once again, Polkinghorne points to the "kenotic paradox" of the incarnation in which "God submitted in the most drastic way to becoming a cause among causes."[34] In so doing, God demonstrated the extent of divine willingness to give creatures a genuinely free stake in the unfolding of the universe. When one conceives of natural processes, human agency, and divine providence as interacting within the evolving cosmos, then each contributes to the interplay of flourishing and floundering that characterizes the life and death, the triumph and tragedy of an evolving cosmos.

> ### Reflect and Discuss
>
> What are the ramifications of humans' having a genuine stake in the unfolding of creation? Does this imply a responsibility for creation and its creatures?

The Vulnerable God

In his exploration of the influence of evolutionary science on Christian theology, Anglican theologian and biochemist Arthur Peacocke divided his insights concerning creation into cosmic "being" or "what there is" in the cosmos and cosmic "becoming" or "what is going on" in the cosmos. According to Peacocke, this distinction between the being and becoming in an evolving cosmos impels theologians to rethink how God relates to such a continually changing world and whether this implies a God who can be changed or affected through this relation. To test this possibility, Peacocke applied the distinction between cosmic being and becoming to distinctions in the attributes of God, proposing that one consider God not solely in terms of Divine *Being*—who God is in Godself—but also in terms of Divine *Becoming*—how God acts in the world.

Peacocke first examined the Divine Being of God through the lens of evolutionary science. Based on scientific observations of the cosmos as contingent, that is, dependent on a cause beyond itself for its existence,[35] Peacocke inferred that God must be the transcendent Source of all the entities and processes in the universe. Because these aspects of the universe display both a remarkable unity

---

34. Ibid.

35. Science would point to the initial singularity as the cause through which the space-time-matter-energy universe had its beginning about fourteen billion years ago. Theists point to God as Creator.

and a kaleidoscopic diversity, he further contended that its Source must exist in unity and diversity as well. Since further observation disclosed that the universe exhibits an internal order and regularity, Peacocke claimed that its Source must be supremely rational. Moreover, the persistence of order in a universe that evolves over time implied to Peacocke that God acts not only as the creative Source of the cosmos but also as its Sustainer and Preserver throughout the passage of time. Nonetheless, because scientists have observed a remarkable dynamism within this order, Peacocke proposed that God must not only be conceived as the creative Source of the cosmos but also as its Continuous Creator. Moreover, from such continuous creativity in the cosmos has emerged the human person. Because of this, Peacocke inferred that God, the Source of such a personal being, must be personal in nature as well and must have divine purposes that are expressed through God's creative activity in the universe.

Shifting his focus to "what is going on" in the cosmos, Peacocke discussed the Divine Becoming of God. As noted earlier in this chapter, a kaleidoscopic variety of forms in the cosmos results not only from the lawful order of the cosmos but also from the operation of random or chance occurrences within such lawful order. Since Peacocke had already argued that God continually creates, he inferred that God is the Source not only of natural law but also of randomness and chance in the cosmos. However, since science insists that the operation of chance within law is both unpredictable and uncontrollable, Peacocke, like Polkinghorne, concluded that God must choose to freely limit the power and control that God exercises in the universe.

Reflect and Discuss

How would you evaluate the validity of the inferences Peacocke makes from his observations of the universe? What principle from classical theology could validate such assertions?

As a result of the operation of chance within law, Peacocke envisioned the universe as an "arena of improvisation," a creation divinely intended to realize its potential through evolution in autonomy and freedom. He recognized, however, that this divinely intended freedom comes at a cost, since, for God and for the cosmos, both good and evil are possible in a freely evolving universe. In such a universe, God acts, but does not control; God guides, but respects creation's freedom. As "evolution unavoidably makes 'mistakes,' enters blind alleys, and produces much suffering,"[36] according to Peacocke, granting the universe freedom of

---

36. Ron Highfield, "Divine Self-Limitation in the Theology of Jürgen Moltmann: A Critical Appraisal," *Christian Scholar's Review* 32, no. 1 (2002): 63.

creativity demonstrates that God "has allowed his inherent omnipotence . . . to be modified, restricted, and curtailed by the very open-endedness . . . bestowed upon creation."[37] God's loving self-limitation serves as the precondition for free process and free will.

While God's self-limitation allows for the free creativity of the cosmos, it also runs the risk of permitting outcomes harmful to the life and well-being of creation. Nonetheless, the divine choice of self-limitation "arises from the logic of love, which requires the freedom of the beloved."[38] For Peacocke, in fact, divine self-limitation is the definitive demonstration of why Christians describe God as love (1 John 4:8). According to Peacocke,

> [Christians] have affirmed that God has to be described as 'love' because, in creation, he deliberately limits himself, by allowing a cosmos to remain in being which is other than himself, which is given its own autonomy and so limits his freedom . . . ; they have affirmed that God was revealed as self-offering love in the self-limitation which was his incarnation in Jesus Christ and in the self-offering of Jesus's human life for men.[39]

Nonetheless, this divine choice has immense implications; it places God's purposes for the cosmos at risk and involves the threat of continuing pain, suffering, and death in creation. The cosmos and its creatures certainly bear these costs and risks; however these are also borne by God "in the act of self-limitation . . . [which is] a self-inflicted vulnerability to the very processes God had himself created."[40]

Therefore, the act of creation must be regarded as an act of self-emptying by God, a letting-go of power and of control. Peacocke pointed out that this self-emptying is revealed not only in God's gifts of free process and free will to creation but also in God's participation in the evolutionary processes themselves. According to Peacocke, as continuous Creator in an evolutionary cosmos, God must be immanently active in the processes that bring about the evolution of the cosmos. If that is the case, then the pain, suffering, and death that affect the cosmos in these processes must also affect God. As Peacocke explained:

> [The] processes of creation are immensely costly to God in a way dimly shadowed by and reflected in the ordinary experience of the costliness of creativity in multiple aspects of human creativity—whether it be in giving birth, in artistic creation, or in creating and maintaining human social structures. . . . Now, as we reflect on the processes of

---

37. Peacocke, *Theology in a Scientific Age*, 121.

38. John Polkinghorne, *Science and Christian Belief: Reflections of a Bottom-up Thinker* (London: SPCK, 1994), 81.

39. Arthur Peacocke, *Science and the Christian Experiment* (London: Oxford, 1971), 137.

40. Peacocke, *Theology in a Scientific Age*, 124.

creation through biological evolution, we can begin to understand that this . . . involved God's costly, suffering involvement in them on behalf of their ultimate fruition.[41]

Here Peacocke drew a parallel between the cost of human creativity and divine creativity. In each experience of human creativity, Peacocke suggested, a person can control only a limited number of things. The characteristics of a child, the flow of paint, the curve of clay, the endurance of social or cultural mores—each of these lie beyond the power of any individual to fully regulate. Each has a life of its own to unfold freely, with the distinct possibility of diverging from the intention of the one who brought it into being. And so it is with God. According to Peacocke, "there is a creative self-emptying and self-offering (a *kenosis*) *of God*, a sharing in the suffering of God's creatures, in the very creative, evolutionary processes of the world."[42]

For Peacocke, this sharing in the suffering of creation is a manifestation of the suffering love preeminently communicated in and through the life, suffering, death, and resurrection of Jesus Christ. Peacocke contended that those who believe in Jesus Christ as the Word-made-flesh, the self-expression of God in a human person, find in him the God who is vulnerable, self-emptying, and self-giving suffering love. Furthermore, if God was in Christ, "reconciling the world to himself" (2 Cor. 5:19) as the Scriptures and the incarnation proclaim, then this confirmed for Peacocke his evolutionary theology of divine suffering, for "the suffering of God, which we could infer only tentatively in the processes of creation, is in Jesus the Christ concentrated into a point of intensity and transparency that reveals it as expressive of the perennial relation of God to the creation."[43]

However, Peacocke emphasized that Christ's suffering is not the only manifestation of divine love. The Christ event dramatically revealed that God not only undergoes suffering and death on the cross but also overcomes suffering and death through the resurrection. For Peacocke, creation reflects this dynamic of death and resurrection brought about by God. While God does not prevent the pain, suffering, and death that accompany evolutionary creativity, neither does God intend that such pain, suffering, and death endure or triumph. Dimly reflecting the divine love and creativity that raised Jesus from the death, the evolutionary process demonstrates the potential for new life that proceeds from the demise of life-forms that have existed in the cosmos. Hence both the resurrection of Jesus and the evolutionary process reveal that suffering and death are not final, but lead to new life within the embrace of the creative love of God. For Peacocke,

---

41. Arthur Peacocke, *Paths from Science towards God: The End of All Our Exploring* (Oxford: Oneworld, 2001), 86–87.

42. Peacocke, "The Cost of New Life," 38, emphasis in the original.

43. Ibid., 42, italics in the original. The reference to the "crucified God" is, of course, that of Jürgen Moltmann in *The Crucified God*.

what were "hints and faint echoes of the divine in nature" became in Jesus Christ "a resonating word to humanity from God's own self"[44]—a word of self-offering, self-emptying, and creative love, capable of bringing newness of life from suffering and death for the transformation of the natural and human world.

Reflect and Discuss

Peacocke and Polkinghorne arrive at similar theological conclusions. Do you discern any differences between them? If so, what are they? What difference do they make in terms of God's relation to suffering?

The Creative Suffering of the Triune God

The insights of Arthur Peacocke ground the work of Catholic theologian Gloria Schaab. Like Peacocke, her discussion of God and suffering in her book *The Creative Suffering of the Triune God* is rooted in God's intimate and enduring relationships with the cosmos that God has created, relationships that she conceives as wholly Trinitarian. As the "Maker of heaven and earth, of all things visible and invisible," the First Person of the Trinity has a *transcendent* relationship with creation. As the One who became flesh in Jesus Christ, the Second Person of the Trinity has an *incarnate* relationship with creation. As the Spirit of God who "has filled the world, and . . . holds all things together" (Wisd. of Sol. 1:7), the Third Person of the Trinity has an *immanent* relationship to creation.[45] For Schaab, these relationships between the Persons of the Trinity and creation suggest a model of God-world relation called panentheism. Panentheism is the belief that the Being of God, as incarnate and immanent, indwells and permeates the whole universe, but that the Being of God, as transcendent, exceeds and is not identified with the universe.

Reflect and Discuss

What difference does a Trinitarian perspective make when reflecting on God's relation to suffering? Does it provide any advantages over a strictly monotheistic conception of God?

---

44. Peacocke, *Theology in a Scientific Age*, 300.

45. These relations between God and creation are reflected in the Nicene Creed, available at *http://www.usccb.org/beliefs-and-teachings/what-we-believe/*. For a fuller discussion of these relations from an evolutionary viewpoint, see Gloria L. Schaab, *The Creative Suffering of the Triune God: An Evolutionary Theology* (New York: Oxford University, 2007).

This model of God-world relationship offers intriguing possibilities for the question of God in the midst of a suffering cosmos. Whereas many conceptions of God's relation to creation imply that God exists "spatially" separate from the world, panentheism denotes no such detachment. In this conception, the cosmos with its delight and pain, joy and suffering, life and death are internal to the being of God—and God to it—in a real and intimate way. The word "real" in this sense, however, does not mean "literal." In using this model, Schaab attempts to express the deep and profound relationship between God and creation through certain symbols or models, knowing that every expression falls short of the mystery of God. With this proviso, Schaab, with Peacocke and others, proposes the image of a mother pregnant with child as the most appropriate one for a panentheistic model of God-world relationships.

Traditional models of God's creative relationships with the cosmos stress an interventionist model, in which God creates from outside the universe. A female model of procreation, however, focuses on how God also fosters life from within the universe, based on the way women nurture new life within themselves. Elaborating on this model, theologian Elizabeth Johnson writes,

> To be so structured that you have room inside yourself for another to dwell is quintessentially a female experience. To have another actually living and moving and having being in yourself is likewise the province of women. . . . This reality is the paradigm without equal for the panentheistic notion . . . of God and the world.[46]

This model evokes a key insight for Schaab into the way God relates to suffering in creation. If God creates and nurtures the world within the divine being—transcendently, incarnately, and immanently—then God must be conceived of as experiencing the world's suffering *within* Godself, rather than outside Godself. Pregnant with an evolving yet suffering cosmos, God can heal and transform suffering through the love and creativity that characterize the Trinity. Thus divine suffering is not passive, but active with creative purpose, "for suffering is widely recognised as having creative power when imbued with love."[47]

Reflect and Discuss

Do you agree or disagree with this last statement? How can love make suffering creative?

---

46. Elizabeth Johnson, *She Who Is: The Mystery of God in Feminist Theological Discourse* (New York: Crossroads, 1993), 234–35.

47. Peacocke, *Paths from Science towards God*, 88.

Schaab identifies three female images of God drawn from the Jewish and Christian traditions through which to develop her Trinitarian theology of divine suffering: the theological image *She Who Is*, the mystical image *Shekhinah*, and the biblical image *Sophia*. Each corresponds to one of the Trinitarian relations of transcendence, Incarnation, and immanence, and each one pulses with a specific form of creative suffering with and for creation and its creatures. To describe these types of suffering, Schaab uses the terms *sympathy*, *empathy*, and *protopathy*.

The Transcendent God: She Who Is

In her influential text *She Who Is: The Mystery of God in Feminist Theological Discourse*, Elizabeth Johnson develops the name *She Who Is* to refer to the mystery of God. For Johnson, the image of God as She Who Is signifies in female terms the God who is "pure aliveness in relation, the . . . fullness of life in which the whole universe participates."[48] Johnson grounds this image in both the Jewish and Christian traditions: the Hebrew name of God as YHWH, translated "I Am Who Am," and Thomas Aquinas's assertion that the most appropriate name for God is, in Latin, *qui est*, translatable as "who is." Since "who" is an inclusive pronoun that can refer to males or females, Johnson translates it as "She" to emphasize that women too are created in the image and likeness of God.

In Schaab's theology, She Who Is, as the fullness of life in which the universe participates, represents God in transcendence. As the Creator who mothers all creation, "all is created through her; all is created for her. In her everything continues in being" (Col. 1:16–17, adapted). She envelops in her womb all created beings—stars and planets, earth and sky, land and sea creatures, humans of all races—and supports all its processes—natural selection and evolutionary emergence, regularities of law and randomness of chance. As this chapter demonstrates, these entities and processes are fraught with pain, suffering, and death, which She Who Is endures together with the creatures of the world. Nevertheless, according to Schaab, She Who Is has a suffering distinctively her own, a creative suffering unlike any other. As Divine Mother, heavy with the life of the cosmos, She Who Is bears the weight of creation laden with pain and death; she is sickened morning and evening by the violence, oppression, and exploitation that ravages the developing life within her. Furthermore, this labor abides for all created time, for the birth of the cosmos in its fullness reaches completion only in the new creation in which all weeping and suffering and death will be no more (Rev. 21:1–4). Until that time, the transcendent Mother suffers *with* the cosmos and its processes, suffering and laboring, stretching and straining, pushing and burning with passion for the life of the world.

---

48. Johnson, *She Who Is*, 240.

Schaab terms the suffering of the Divine Mother *sympathy*, the quality of being "affected by the suffering or sorrow of another; a feeling of compassion or commiseration."[49] Like a mother who does not forget the child of her womb or a father attentive to the needs of his offspring, God in transcendence responds sympathetically when creation and its creatures are afflicted with physical pain, emotional suffering, or natural disaster. This sympathetic suffering provides solace, support, and strength to persons who yearn for the knowledge that God companions them in their suffering. Like a child with his or her mother or father, they find God available to them in their time of need, soothing, attending, and encouraging them on their passage to healing and growth.

The Incarnate God: Shekhinah

Shekhinah, a Hebrew concept that has accompanied the Jewish people for some two thousand years,[50] derives from the Hebrew *shakan*, meaning "act of dwelling," and is female in gender. Despite differing interpretations of Shekhinah, each identifies Shekhinah with God's own self. The people of Israel experienced Shekhinah not only as presence but also as intimacy. She is understood as the first of all creation, who develops into a mediator between humanity and God, heaven and earth. Through her, God enters the world and human beings encounter God. Shekhinah shares the joys and the affliction of the Jewish people and community. According to the tradition, "When a human being suffers, what does the Shekhinah say? 'My head is too heavy for me; my arm is too heavy for me.'"[51] Shekhinah accompanied the Israelites in their Exodus through the desert, as a cloud by day and a pillar of fire by night (Exod. 13:21–22). The Tractate Megillah states, "Come and see how beloved are the Israelites before God; for whenever they went into exile, the Shekhinah followed them."[52] She not only weeps for the suffering of her people but also suffers their persecutions with them. Shekhinah draws close to the sick and the dying to comfort them. Like Jesus, Shekhinah embraces the fate of the afflicted, experiencing their suffering, and groaning with their anguish.

Schaab proposes that the tradition of Shekhinah provides a means by which to envision God Incarnate in a suffering cosmos. Coupled with the tradition of Jesus Christ, Shekhinah reveals herself as intimately involved with the afflicted

---

49. "Sympathy," *Oxford English Dictionary Online*, available at *www.oed.com/ search?searchType =dictionary&q=sympathy&_searchBtn=Search*.

50. For a fuller discussion of *Shekhinah*, see Gloria L. Schaab, "The Power of Divine Presence: Toward a Shekhinah Christology," in *Christology: Memory, Inquiry, Practice*, ed. Anne M. Clifford and Anthony J. Godzieba (Maryknoll, NY: Orbis, 2003), 92–115.

51. Abraham Heschel, *God in Search of Man: A Philosophy of Judaism* (New York: Harper&Row, 1955), 21.

52. Tractate *Megillah* 29a, in J. Abelson, *The Immanence of God in Rabbinic Literature* (New York: Hermon, 1969), 12.

of the world. However, both traditions testify to the liberating action of Jesus and of Shekhinah on behalf of the suffering and the oppressed. The intercession of Shekhinah and the resurrection of Jesus symbolize that suffering and death can be overcome and transformed through the presence and power of the God whose life and love bring renewal. While God may not prevent the evil that afflicts creation and its creatures, such evil does not overcome Shekhinah. Rather, she moves through suffering and death toward new forms of life.

God Incarnate in Shekhinah offers hope for those who garner strength and consolation from the sure knowledge that someone has experienced suffering and pain like their own. Schaab terms this description of suffering *empathy*, an implicit awareness and sensitivity to the feelings and experience of another. It is rooted in and shaped by one's personal experience of suffering so as to facilitate an "identification with and understanding of another's situation, feelings, and motives."[53] According to Schaab, empathy is an experience uniquely attributable to God incarnate in Shekhinah, because, as God's presence with those wandering, homeless, and oppressed, she bore Israel's sorrows and shared in their grief firsthand. Shekhinah has known the rejection they have known; she has suffered their losses and yearned like them for well-being. Because of her intimate knowledge of human suffering, Shekhinah, like Jesus, is able to move with those who suffer through their trials and tragedies to restoration and new life.

Reflect and Discuss

Can you see the parallels between Shekhinah and Jesus? Might these parallels have influenced the ways in which the Jews interpreted the meaning and person of Jesus?

The Immanent God: Sophia

Schaab points out that the Christian tradition has always associated the immanence of God in creation with the Holy Spirit. This tradition enables Christians to envision God as creatively active in the cosmos and thus has consonance with the creative processes that drive evolution. In Schaab's model, the energies of the Holy Spirit permeate the life incarnate in the womb of the transcendent Mother. Envisioned in this way, the Holy Spirit resonates with the female image of God known as *Sophia*. The name Sophia is Greek for "wisdom," female in gender not only in Greek but also in Hebrew (*hokmah*) and Latin (*sapientia*). While her name literally means "wisdom," the purview of

---

53. "Empathy," *American Heritage Dictionary of the English Language*, available at *https://ahdictionary .com/word/search.html?q=empathy.*

Sophia is creativity. At the moment of creation, Sophia was present, delighting in the work of creation and in the creatures of earth (Prov. 8:27–31); as immanent within the evolving cosmos, Sophia "can do all things" and "renews all things" (Wisd. of Sol. 7:27).

Nonetheless, because of free process and free will, Sophia's creativity sometimes gets diverted, resisted, and rebuffed. As Schaab points out, the Scriptures witness to her passionate response. She groans within creation, rails against those who squander life, and rages against those who reject transformation. Her heart breaks over those who rebuff her invitation to flourish, and she mourns over those whose self-will leads to death (Prov. 1:24–25, 28, 33, 30, 32). Nevertheless, in her righteous passion and suffering, Sophia stands "as a permanent sign of protest . . . a permanent witness against" suffering because "over Sophia evil can never triumph" (Wisd. of Sol. 7:30).[54] Sophia enters into creation and its creatures "and makes them friends of God, and prophets" (Wisd. of Sol. 7:27) who rise up against suffering and death within the cosmos. By continuously inspiring humanity and exercising creativity in the cosmos, Sophia delivers a message of life that endures in the face of suffering and that wells up in its midst through the dynamism of Holy Spirit Sophia.

In Schaab's theology of suffering, Sophia accompanies those who suffer because of their dynamic resistance to injustice, exploitation, violence, and destruction in themselves or in others. The suffering of Sophia is, therefore, a primal suffering that wells up within those who strive for fullness of life when such life is threatened by devastation or death. It is called *protopathy*[55] because it is a suffering "first felt" in the movements that hinder the life-giving potential of creation—movements of pollution, deforestation, strip-mining, and fracking, as well as those of poverty, oppression, sexism, and xenophobia. While Sophia resists all that frustrates fullness of life and that spawns senseless suffering, her efforts are sometimes obstructed. Nonetheless, by the protopathy of Sophia, those who suffer with her for the sake of creation and its creatures find inspiration and support that no suffering can thwart. In the words of Elizabeth Johnson, Sophia

> keeps vigil through endless hours of pain while her grief awakens protest. The power of this divine symbol works not just to console those who are suffering, but to strengthen those bowed by sorrow to hope and resist. If God grieves with them in the midst of disaster, then there may yet be a way forward.[56]

---

54. Susan Cole, Marion Ronan, and Hal Taussig, *Wisdom's Feast* (Kansas City, MO: Sheed and Ward, 1996), 198. The translation of Wisdom 7:30 is drawn from this text.

55. From the Greek *protopathos*, "affected first," and *protopathein*, "to feel first." See "Protopathy," *The Free Dictionary*, available at *http://www.thefreedictionary.com/protopathy*.

56. Johnson, *She Who Is*, 260–61.

Reflect and Discuss

What is your assessment of Schaab's Trinitarian model of suffering? Do the various modes of suffering make sense? Have you ever had these different experiences of suffering?

Case in Point: The Haitian Earthquake

The 7.0 magnitude earthquake that struck the country of Haiti on January 12, 2010, caused the deaths of nearly 316,000 people, left more than 300,000 injured, and displaced 1.5 million others. More than 33 aftershocks followed, ranging in magnitude from 4.2 to 5.9, which rendered many structures unsafe for use or habitation. However, it was only the most recent catastrophic event in a country that had already withstood wave after wave of natural disasters, devastation, and death. In 2008, four separate hurricanes within 30 days killed nearly 800 people, destroyed 60 percent of the country's harvest, and desolated entire cities. In the period from 1935–2004, hurricanes killed more than 13,500 people, caused flooding and landslides, and destroyed countless natural resources. These events, combined with the political problems that have plagued Haiti over decades, have left Haiti the poorest country in its hemisphere, with 80 percent of the population below the poverty line and 54 percent in abject poverty.[57]

There has been no dearth of questions raised about God in the wake of these events. Headlines like "Why Did God Allow This?" "Where Was God?" "Did God Cause the Earthquake in Haiti?" and even "Does God Hate Haiti?" result from a simple Internet search. This final "Case in Point" examines some of the responses to such questions—both theistic and atheistic—prompted by the natural disaster that decimated Haiti and its people. Many of these responses

---

57. This data was gleaned from several sources including "Haiti Disaster: The Essential Facts," *The Week*, available at *http://theweek.com/article/index/105201/haiti-disaster-the-essential-facts*, and "FAST FACTS: Haiti Earthquake," Fox News, available at *http://www.foxnews.com/world/2010/01/13/fast-facts-haiti-earthquake/*.

Case in Point: The Haitian Earthquake (continued)

will sound familiar, having already been examined elsewhere in this text. Nevertheless, at the end of this book as in the beginning, the question continues to be less *why,* and more *who:* "When you send up your prayers for the victims, who is listening? . . . To what kind of God can one pray in such circumstances?"[58]

Like a number of theologians in this chapter, many religious leaders invoked the paschal mystery of Christ when addressing the tragedy in Haiti. In his remarks, England's Archbishop of York acknowledged, "I have nothing to say that makes sense of this horror. . . . [All] I know is that the message of the death and resurrection of Jesus is that he is with us."[59] Other clergy interpreted the events as a message from God—a sign of God's judgment or a call to conversion. As one Haitian pastor claimed, "When God speaks we must listen. The earthquake is God's voice and He will do other things. The stars will crash down onto the earth."[60] A few commentators proposed that "believers can find blessings in the calamity, for in heaven the dead will finally find tranquility and repose,"[61] and others that the tragedy provided an opportunity to extend charity to the victims: "Haiti calls into question the role of people of faith. . . . The age-old question found in Genesis, "Am I my brother's keeper?" must be answered with a resounding, 'Yes!'"[62] Many more people invoked the mysterious will or purposes of God. However, as one writer remarked, "Saying 'there is a reason for everything' may be true, but that is a cruel and heartless response at the point of great suffering."[63]

---

58. Cathy Lynn Grossman, "Haiti Earthquake Blame Game: God or the Devil?" *USA TODAY,* January 17, 2010, available at *http://content.usatoday.com/communities/Religion/post/2010/01/haiti-earthquake-blame-game-god-or-the-devil/1#.VGTJMPnF9yx.*

59. Samuel C. Baxter, "The Haiti Earthquake—Why Did God Allow This?" *Realtruth.org,* available at *http://realtruth.org/articles/100210-001-analysis.html.*

60. Ibid.

61. Lisa Miller, "Haiti and the Theology of Suffering," *Newsweek.com,* January 14, 2010, available at *www.newsweek.com/miller-haiti-and-theology-suffering-71231.*

62. Bill Schuler, "Is God Punishing Haiti?" *Foxnews.com,* January 15, 2010, available at *www.foxnews.com/opinion/2010/01/15/shuler-haiti-earthquake-god.html.*

63. Fleming Rutledge, "Where Was God in the Earthquake?" *Christianity Today,* available at *www.christianitytoday.com/women/2010/january/where-was-god-in-earthquake.html.*

Case in Point: The Haitian Earthquake (continued)

Atheistic responses also abounded. They contended that the calamity in Haiti clearly indicated that an all-loving and all-powerful God was nonexistent. In an editorial called "Haiti's Angry God," one commentator expressed her incredulity that Haitians continued to pray "to a God who seems to be absent at best and vindictive at worst."[64] It even caused some formerly devout Christians to turn away. As one lifelong Christian and Bible scholar explained, "I just got to a point where I couldn't explain how something like this could happen, if there's a powerful and loving God in charge of the world. . . . [There] are a lot of answers, but I don't think any of them work."[65]

Reflect and Discuss

Do you agree or disagree with any one of these particular theistic or atheistic responses? Do any reflect your thinking? Why or why not?

The theologians presented in this chapter would not ascribe the earthquake or its devastating aftermath to the will or the work of God. They would point to the laws of physics, the incidence of randomness and chance, the movement of continental crusts, the uneven heating of the atmosphere, and countless other processes characteristic of an evolving universe.[66] Each would acknowledge, however, that proposals claiming that God treats the processes of the world and the activities of humanity with the same respect leave many unsatisfied. Such claims seem to present a God "so evacuated of power that he becomes little more than a colluder with cosmic

---

64. Pooja Bhatia, "Haiti's Angry God," *NYTimes.com*, January 13, 2010, available at *www.nytimes.com/2010/01/14/opinion/14bhatia.html?_r=0*.

65. Miller, "Haiti and the Theology of Suffering."

66. For an intriguing discussion of such processes and the events they cause, see Rich Deem, "Where Is God When Bad Things Happen? Why Natural Evil Must Exist," *Godandscience.org*, available at *www.godandscience.org/apologetics/natural_evil_theodicity.html*.

Case in Point: The Haitian Earthquake *(continued)*

processes."[67] Nonetheless, standing in the spaces where theology and science meet, these theologians assert that both evolutionary processes and human actions originate from the self-emptying love of a Creator God and are thus endowed with the freedom that authentic love demands. One thing to them is clear:

> God hates senseless suffering. He sees a dead father and his infant son lying side-by-side a week after an earthquake, a woman with her hands raised to the sky mourning the loss of her husband who was buried under the rubble of a collapsed building, a family of five subsisting on a bottle of water and cup of rice in a tent city. He hears the cries of His . . . children and it pains Him, as it would any father. He is "not willing that any should perish" (2 Pet. 3:9) and would "have all . . . to be saved" (1 Tim. 2:4).[68]

Reflect and Discuss

Are love and freedom enough to justify the suffering in the world? Why or why not?

For Further Reading

Peacocke, Arthur. *Paths from Science towards God: The End of All Our Exploring.* Oxford: Oneworld, 2002.

Polkinghorne, John. *Science and Providence: God's Interaction with the World.* Philadelphia: Templeton Foundation Press, 2005.

Schaab, Gloria L. *The Creative Suffering of the Triune God: An Evolutionary Theology.* New York: Oxford University, 2007.

---

67. Polkinghorne, *Science and Providence*, 78–79.

68. Baxter, "The Haiti Earthquake."

Internet Resources

Cosmic Thinkers on Camera. Interviews with Robert Wright. Available at *http://meaningoflife.tv/index.php?&topic_minimum=0*. See in particular Wright's interviews of Arthur Peacocke, John Polkinghorne, and Keith Ward on the problem of evil:

Arthur Peacocke: *http://meaningoflife.tv/video.php?speaker=Peacocke&topic=evil.*

John Polkinghorne: *http://meaningoflife.tv/video.php?speaker=polkinghorne&topic=evil.*

Keith Ward: *http://meaningoflife.tv/video.php?speaker=Ward&topic=evil.*

Epilogue

urely, as T. S. Eliot wrote, words do "strain, crack and sometimes break under the burden" when one tries to speak rightly of God in the midst of suffering.[1] However, that is what the scholars surveyed throughout this book have ventured to do in the face of one of the most critical challenges theology faces. Those who have risen to this challenge throughout the centuries have not simply engaged in intellectual speculation, but have profoundly shaped how believers have viewed and related to God in their suffering. Ultimately, they have attempted to respond to the question posed in the letter to the Romans which leads to the title of this book: "What then are we to say about these things? If God is for us . . ." (Rom. 8:31).

Some who have explored the mystery of God and suffering through this text may have desired a resolution to the problem of God and suffering or at least a convincing argument for favoring one approach above the rest. Nonetheless, the aim of this book was not to offer one solution, but to invite readers to think with the authors through the various Christian perspectives—each grounded in Scripture, tradition, and human experience—and to evaluate their lines of thought through their reflection, discussion, and human experience. In the process, readers may have discovered that, in the midst of suffering, God is not a problem to be solved, but a Mystery to encounter in humility and prayer. For, despite the variety of Christian interpretations of the God who "is for us" in our suffering, one affirmation is implicit in all of the theologies of suffering in this text: "that neither death, nor life, . . . nor things present, nor things to come, . . . nor anything else in all creation, will be able to separate us from the love of God" (Rom. 8:38–39) in the midst of suffering. In that conviction, those who suffer can find hope.

---

1. T. S. Eliot, "Burnt Norton," *Artofeurope.com*; available at *www.artofeurope.com/eliot/eli5.htm*.

Index

Note: The abbreviations *s* or *n* that follow page numbers indicate sidebars or footnotes, respectively.